ALL MY SONS

Christer Kihlman

ALL MY SONS

A Novel

Translated by Joan Tate

PETER OWEN
London & Washington DC

ISBN 0 7206 0628 4

Translated from the Swedish *Alla mina söner*

PETER OWEN PUBLISHERS
73 Kenway Road, London SW5 ORE

First published in Great Britain 1984
© Christer Kihlman 1980
English translation © Joan Tate 1984

Photoset in Great Britain by
Rowland Phototypesetting Ltd, Bury St Edmunds, Suffolk
and printed by St Edmundsbury Press
Bury St Edmunds, Suffolk

No sigas
donde conducen
las huellas.
Mejor vé donde no hay
huellas
y deja un sendero.

Words of wisdom on the wall of
Juan's and Lilita's living-room
in Azcuenaga.

25.6.79.

Q phoned. He was in Bonn with a trade delegation and had a message from Juan. Lilita and Juan had both been ill, but they were better now. Juan was unemployed again, but was still planning for the future all the time. His doctor – Arturo, I presume – had urged him to go steady on tobacco. Juan smoked too much, nervously, often smoking to fill the inactivity, the emptiness, subduing his need for activity, which he was unable to satisfy in a more purposeful way.

Q had kept in fairly regular contact with Juan during the months that had passed since we had parted. I at once found myself wondering what they had been doing. But I didn't ask. Morning coffee at the Blue Horse? Lunch together at the Morsa Blanca? Sipping at a nightly Smuggler at the Establo? Without Q, I certainly would not have been able to maintain such good contact with Juan over the years. Q had been a pigeon postman between me and Juan, a telex-pigeon, a telephone-pigeon. At the same time, Q is almost the only connection I have with the Argentinian establishment.

The telephone call from Bonn was as unexpected as longed for. I hadn't heard from Juan for over three months, although I had written a letter in May to ask him to send me some sign of life. I knew he was like myself, a poor correspondent, and also that his concept of time, of the passing of time, was quite different from mine. He didn't count the days, hardly even the weeks. I counted the days, sometimes the hours, anyhow when it came to signs of life from him. And in the silence, in the absence of letters, the absence of contact, my doubts grew inexorably, suspicions, evil thoughts, gnawing imaginings that I had been wrong, that Juan didn't . . . In other words, that all was as it appeared to be.

But I had not been wrong. Deep down, I knew that. Despite everything, everything between Juan and me was as I had decided it should be. Neither more nor less.

7

Q was as verbose as usual, talking for a long time from Bonn, and I finally had to remind him that the call would be very expensive for him. Juan had told him that he had innumerable acquaintances, but only three friends, and he had named the three friends: Marcelo his father, Claudio his childhood friend. And me. That's how it should be. Because I know what friendship means in Argentina.

Most stories are about something concluded. They are written in melancholy or sorrow over a lost happiness, or over a person who is no longer there to be fond of and close to. My story is inconclusive; it has begun and it goes on, and the idea is that it will continue as long as life lasts. That's what we have decided, or rather that's what I have decided, and if it turns out differently, then there's no point in telling it.

Life isn't all losses and farewells, or rather in the end is just that, always losses and farewells, of course, but then owing to the circumstances of death, a natural conclusion, which we ourselves can do nothing about. We wanted to show, Juan and I, that life's circumstances can sometimes be edifying, subversive, that they can sometimes buttress what is enduring. We wanted to show in our tiny ripple of the great current of life, our microscopic ripple in the whole immense current of life, that occasionally you can find benediction, not necessarily always bitterness or sorrow or disappointment. We had almost everything against us, the circumstances, everything that usually precedes unhappiness. But we had decided not to give in, not to give way to circumstances. We wanted to overcome the circumstances. We felt stronger than the circumstances. We had made a pact. We had created an alliance of a very special kind. It was all our own work, and just because it was all our own work, we thought it important to tell others about it.

'What are you writing now? Is it your great work on happiness?' one of my friends asked me a few days ago.

'Yes, it's my great work on happiness.'

She shook her head.

'You're mad. You can't write about things like that.'

No, that's true. You can't write about that sort of thing, not about happiness, the cheap kind. But about happiness, the difficult kind – you can write about that. About how horribly difficult it is to keep that happiness.

I didn't know Juan the first time I went to Buenos Aires, didn't ask after him, wasn't aware of his existence. I was there for other reasons, mostly to prepare a literary work I was planning. Nothing came of it. Juan gave me something else to think about.

I had a list of addresses with me, and Q's name happened to be the first on the list. I phoned Q and mentioned the name of a mutual friend in Stockholm. Q invited me to dinner. It was November, and springtime in Buenos Aires (the avenues a brilliant blue of jacaranda trees in flower, and beneath the jacaranda blossom the tanks and soldiers, young men with stony faces and machine-guns, their barrels pointing skywards like . . . like . . . It's not at all difficult to make associations with rifle barrels in this country, where masculinity is a myth and the norm, like religion, and anyway I've written about that so many times . . .) and the nights so warm that jackets were left at home.

Q invited me to dinner at the Jockey Club, together with a couple of the leading lights of the Argentinian arts scene. There was much weighty baroque and strict checks at the entrance, a gathering place for the specially chosen. I did not feel altogether at ease. Panelling, tapestries, dark paintings of battle-scenes from the chequered history of Argentina, huge vases and ceramic jars on the floor or on pedestals in corners. And then the gentlemen, well-mannered gentlemen in white shirts, discreet ties and dark jackets.

Q was almost overwhelmingly friendly, and at this stage I still presumed this was because he didn't really know where to place me, but was playing safe with his business contact in Stockholm in mind. He is an ex-cavalry officer, very upright, thinning hair, a sharp look which never wavers, his hands making discreet sweeping gestures. The elder of his two guests was in his sixties, small, ugly and ironical. He looked like a beetle with his glossy hair brushed back and his nails polished pink. He talked about women in the way some men talk about horses, enjoyable objects. A genuine connoisseur. The younger man was about my own age and was more bohemian, heavy features, bushy untidy hair, already greying at the temples. He was wearing a crumpled blazer and in that way alone deviated from the norm in this rigidly reserved gathering. He talked about world literature, but fell silent when I brought up the subject of Marquez.

I distrusted them both. Before I had left home, I had read in *Le Monde* that all honourable artists in cultural life in Argentina were either in prison or lived in exile. They showed a polite interest in both myself as a person and my plans. They asked me how they could help me. I had no concrete suggestions. The beetle suggested we should go out together one evening with a couple of women. Anyone who didn't know Argentinian women didn't know Argentina. I was prepared to say yes thank you to everything. He telephoned me at my hotel a few days later, but the conversation was broken off before he had time to complete his errand, and then he never telephoned me again. The other man wanted me to meet Borges, but Borges was in the country and wished to be left in peace.

Late that same night, Q introduced me to Juan. He had talked about a good friend of his and I had expected a cultured gentleman in a white shirt and tie. Instead it was Juan, in his worn jeans and sports shirt. At the Union Bar. The tango bar.

Juan was a slim, shapely youth, good-looking, swift at repartee, swift in his movements, a few inches shorter than me. He smiled a lot and when he smiled his smile filled the whole of his dark Creole face. He smiled with his eyes, black almond-shaped eyes. He was almost always happy. Sometimes he complained of illness or aches in different parts of his body. Despite almost insuperable difficulties in communication, we rapidly became good friends. Juan was twenty years old at the time. I was forty-six.

We couldn't really converse. We gave each other information about ourselves with the help of a phrase-book, he leafing through the Spanish-Swedish, me the Swedish-Spanish. I hadn't bothered to learn Spanish before leaving, which was extremely stupid of me. In line with European cultural imperialism and tourism, I had allowed myself to be governed by the naive and nonchalant idea that English was a world language, usable everywhere. I was quite wrong. Juan had obvious difficulties with the phrase-book. He kept fumbling and getting words wrong. It was the first time he had been confronted with that kind of means of human co-operation.

I told him about myself, that I was a writer and that I had written novels as well as plays. He wanted to know if I was famous and I answered that I was about as famous as I could stand – 'quite famous'. I told him that I had a wife and two children. He asked me what their names were. I told him their names.

'Happy?'

'Yes, on the whole,' I replied.

Later on, I tried to explain to him what kind of a writer I was, that I had grown up in a middle-class home, but that my books contained criticism of precisely that environment and that this criticism had social, moral and political content. I also tried to explain that because of this I was controversial, argued about and sometimes hated. As a

11

writer. I did this because I thought it would bring me closer to him. A kind of ingratiation. Or because I thought it would please him. He was young, wasn't he? And all young people are 'radical', I thought. He carefully took in what I said, but didn't really know how to react. He was in fact not at all 'radical' in that way, and didn't even wish to be six or eight months after the military coup that had brought Videla to power and had had such a brutal and bloody epilogue.

On his part, he told me that his old parents lived in a small country town a few hours by train from Buenos Aires, far out on La Pampa. He had a sister who was a hairdresser and a brother who was a pilot. He had a cousin who was also a pilot, whose apartment he shared. He was a singer by profession, really, but conditions in the trade were not good at the moment. So he was unemployed. For how long? Six to eight months. So he became unemployed at the same time as the coup. I was immediately convinced there was a connection and that his unemployment had a political background. For someone like me, who had got all his information about Argentina from European newspapers, everything that had happened in the country was for political reasons. Even the food one ate was political. And the song one sang.

On the other hand, all the time I was assuming that everything he was telling me was a lie. His parents did not in fact live in a small country town. He had no brother who was a pilot. He couldn't sing. He was a liar. He was waiting for an appropriate moment to steal my money. He was false and untrustworthy. He was like all southerners. I had learnt that back home. I was a European and a northerner and bourgeois and Protestant. He was a Catholic and a southerner and ... well, a street-boy. Imperceptibly, and despite conscious resistance on my side, all the social concepts and distortions of my own upbringing had been inoculated into my blood. Juan was charming but unreliable. Be on your guard!

But it was true, everything he told me. He also had a fiancée called Lilita.

My hotel was in the centre of Buenos Aires, on the main street, Córdoba, just where it crosses the pedestrian street Florida on its route between the two main streets, Corrientes and Santa Fé. All streets in Buenos Aires are main streets, for the city is immensely large. The largest city in the world, Juan says. The best city in the world, too. Fourteen million inhabitants, over half the population of Argentina. An El Dorado for human beings, Juan says. That's what the hotel was called, too, Eldorado. My room was number 505. A wide bed, very comfortable, with a blue bedspread. An armchair with rattan framework. A standard lamp and a small sideboard. Pictures on the walls of horse-racing and English aristocrats out hunting. I also had something which other guests lacked in their rooms, a real desk. When Q heard I was a writer, to show me a little extra attention he had phoned reception and urged them to acquire a desk for me. To ease my work. I felt touched and honoured. I stayed there for five weeks.

Juan very soon started coming to see me almost daily. He came in the morning and we got along as best we could, then went out to town. Or he came in the evening to keep me company at some place, or just to be invited out to dinner. He tried to teach me Spanish, but I was too sluggish and not a good pupil. But I did gradually learn a little. One Monday, he came in his jeans and checked summer shirt and told me he had had a terrible time on Saturday because he had had no money and so had had to sit at home watching television at Lilita's parents' place all evening. Suddenly I noticed I had understood a whole sentence, word for word. That pleased me. For the first time, he had managed to convey some information to me verbally, through words. Perhaps after all we would one day be able to communicate with each other in that way!

But he mostly just talked and I presumed he meant this or that, and then I usually answered either yes or no, according to what I presumed he had been trying to say to me. Sometimes I couldn't make head or tail of anything, but I was usually right, as I was tremendously attentive, and because I had unconsciously acquired a sensitivity to everything to do with him, a sensitivity which was probably already greater than towards any other person.

But we mainly enjoyed each other's company without words, not intellectually, but outside language, and I brooded a great deal on how it was possible for two people to be so close to each other, to take such a liking to each other, without what is usually an inescapable tool of relationships, a common language.

Bit by bit, the trust between us grew. We told each other that fate had brought us together and that a friendship had developed between us – in the Argentinian sense – which nothing could break and which would last all our lives. I felt something wonderful had happened to me, something which I had been waiting for since childhood and which would at last change my life. Even Juan said sometimes:

13

'You've changed my life.' But neither of us yet knew in what way or how this had really happened.

One memorable morning, I had been to the bank to draw a largish sum of money. I was going to pay my weekly hotel bill, buy some clothes, have some cash available for a few days ahead, and so on. I had put the money in the desk drawer for the time being, about 100,000 pesos or thereabouts, lying there in thousand and five hundred peso notes.

Then Juan comes. He phones from reception and a few minutes later he is knocking on the door. We embrace each other. He is happy. He says something I don't understand. I ask him to repeat it. But he doesn't and asks me for a cigarette. I have no cigarettes that morning. He offers to go down and buy some from the kiosk round the corner. He stands there, his hand out ready for me to give him a hundred-peso note. I suddenly feel I should go myself. He is so willing to help, and he is always running errands for me. But he isn't my errand boy. We are equal. Our friendship presumes that. If we're not equal, the whole situation would be different, dubious, and our friendship would not work. I tell him I'll go myself. He accepts that immediately, without protest. He nearly always does, for that matter, falling in with all my wishes surprisingly easily, always ready to please. All right, that's what he's like, I suppose. A nice boy, flexible like all southerners. Not awkward like us northerners. I take the lift down and buy two packs of Marlboro at the kiosk, one for him and one for myself.

When I return ten minutes later, he is transformed. He is no longer smiling. His dark face is black with rage; I have never seen him like this before. His eyes sparkle like pearls of coal. He is standing quite still, staring at me. I hand him a pack of Marlboro.

'I don't want your cigarettes,' he says in a muffled voice.

Then I notice he has opened the desk drawer and is standing with the bundles of notes in his hand.

'Count them,' he says.

'Why should I count them?'

He flings them down on to the desk in front of me.

'Count them,' he repeats.

'You've no cause to go rummaging in my drawers.'

'You don't trust me.'

'Of course I trust you.'

'You're no longer my friend.'

'I don't understand.'

14

'You're just like all the others, just a stupid tourist. I was mistaken about you. We're not friends any longer.'

'I don't know what you're talking about.'

I didn't. I could make neither head nor tail of any of it. But my heart quickly filled with anguish, an inconsolable despair at the hideous prospect of suddenly losing him in this puzzling, utterly inexplicable way. He is just standing there, almost insane with rage.

'Juan, my dear,' I say. 'What's the matter?'

'You think I'm a thief. You wanted to test me. You wanted to catch me stealing.'

'No . . .'

'You'd planned it beforehand. You left the money here to tempt me, because you don't trust me. You're like all the others of your class, a bad person . . .'

I am incapable of replying, utterly helpless.

'You'd got cigarettes, too. You lied to me, so as to catch me stealing.'

Almost maliciously, he takes an opened pack of Marlboro out of the drawer and ostentatiously places them in front of him. I had forgotten them.

'Count it. Count it,' he repeats.

'Who said you could look in my drawers?'

'Count it.'

His voice is now very much more threatening, authoritative, importunate, and I feel bound to do as he says, forced to obey him, for otherwise something terrible will happen; it is not clear what, but something such as forty years ago when my mother started counting to three in a voice full of foreboding. Without wishing to do so, I picked up the bundle of notes and started counting them.

Five thousand pesos was missing.

I looked at him, hesitant, confused, essentially terribly afraid. The room was quite quiet, the only sound the car horns and the roar of traffic from the city. I was sweating, the heat billowing in through the window. He was looking straight into my eyes all the time. He was very beautiful, even in his rage. I stared and stared. Then he slowly moved his hand towards the pocket in his tight jeans and extracted five-thousand-peso notes, which he handed over to me.

'I hate being tested,' he whispered.

'I wasn't testing you. It's a misunderstanding.'

'Either there is trust, or there isn't.'

15

'I wasn't testing you,' I repeat.

At the same time, I felt I had to swallow and my eyes blurred with tears. He is looking at me, sizing me up. He wanders aimlessly around the room. A few minutes go by in silence. I want to explain, but I have no words with which to explain, only ten thousand Swedish words which stick in my throat and in these circumstances are totally useless.

'A mistake, a mistake, Juan, dear, believe me . . .'

He just goes on brooding. Then he suddenly sits down on the bed. He beckons me over to him. I go across and sit down beside him. I obey. I always obey him, have to. We sit there staring at the floor. Then he looks up, his black eyes glittering. He takes my hand.

'I believe you,' he says.

My head falls heavily against his shoulder. He presses my hand, hard.

'I am poor, but proud,' he says.

San Pedro

Argentina at this time was seething with unrest, or rather nothing short of a bloody battlefield. It was 1976 and the military junta had been in power for several months. Press censorship was strict, but in the English-language *Buenos Aires Herald* one could read every day of encounters between the guerillas and government troops, as well as massacres of the section of the population labelled 'terrorists'. I estimated that an average of fifteen to twenty undesirable citizens were thus eliminated every day. Sometimes there was shooting right in the centre of Buenos Aires, which was disturbing and challenging, but circumstances meant that this concerned me less and less each day. I went to a party and conversed with a Consul's wife, a distinguished elderly society lady, who explained that Argentina was in a situation that could be compared with civil war. I accepted that this was so, but I did not see it, naturally partly because – and fortunately – I never happened to be there, but mainly because, over less than two weeks, Argentina had been whittled down in my mind to a social microcosm, miraculously confining itself to the boundaries of Juan's physical presence. It was irresponsible of me, it was painful, it was unworthy of an adult, I resisted it, but soon noticed it was already far too late.

Q was non-political. He was a business man and his only real interest lay in a political situation in which he could do good business. He was genuinely sorry about what was happening and was far from inhuman. He flung out his hands in the Argentinian gesture of helplessness; what could he do about it? What could he do? A year earlier, when Isabella, the widow of Perón, had still been in power, there had been total chaos, quite hopeless, utterly unendurable to put it bluntly. Now, however, there were some signs of hope, for him anyway, for the affluent business man. Why then should he be so bitter? What genuine reason had he to be so bitter? Argentina was a rich country, anyhow for those who had power and the means to profit by wealth. I did not like his reasoning. Back at home in Finland, I would have despised him. Here in Argentina, circumstances had made him my friend.

It was Saturday afternoon. We were sitting drinking soft drinks on the veranda outside the hotel, the heat devastating, even in the shade of the awning. Córdoba was empty of people, basking in the sun, the calm of the weekend having suddenly fallen on the city. We were waiting for Juan, who was already twenty minutes late.

We were going out into the country. Q wanted to show me La Pampa. We were to stay the night in San Pedro and have lunch on Sunday in San Antonio de Areco. Q had invited Juan to come with us, to cheer us up with his youth, as he put it. Unfortunately, at that moment it seemed that Juan had better things to do.

'We'll go in five minutes. He has only himself to blame. I refuse to be pushed around by young pups like him,' hissed Q, half an hour after the agreed time.

I didn't reply. I didn't dare protest. I didn't want to reveal what I was feeling. Least of all could I admit that if necessary, I was in fact prepared to sit there waiting all afternoon. Three minutes later, Juan arrived. He got out of a taxi on the other side of the street and came running across to us. He was laughing. Q grumbled at him in an avuncular way, explaining that everyone sooner or later had to learn to be punctual. Juan took no notice. He had been delayed, but by what was unclear. I felt huge relief, joy. Juan had a crumpled plastic carrier-bag in one hand and in the other a small brown handbag of the kind apparently fashionable at the time among the young men of Buenos Aires.

We drove across La Pampa in Q's white Mercedes, Juan sitting alone in the back talking incessantly and Q translating selections of this torrent into English for me. He was less tense in the company of Q than when alone with me, understandably enough, as when Q was there he could use his natural means of communication. He was exhilarated now, almost liberated in some way, and clearly delighted the outing had come about. Lilita had been furious when he had left, he told us cheerfully, as she considered they should at least be together over the weekend. They had had a violent scene and he had wrenched off his engagement ring and left it on the table at her parents' place. What would happen now, I asked with pretended anxiety. No problem, laughed Juan. It'll be forgotten by Monday.

La Pampa, the plain, the pampas, eternity, it is . . . well, one can say no more than that it is hundreds and hundreds of miles, at first still plenty of vegetation, bushes, clumps of trees, eucalyptus trees, cypresses, flowering oleanders, and nearer to Buenos Aires, a whole lot of other tree-like, leafy shrubs whose names I did not know. I asked Q to tell Juan to name the plants and trees for me, and Juan willingly rattled off a whole series of Spanish names which meant nothing to me. I didn't believe him. I thought he was inventing names of his own for the trees and bushes as we passed them, convinced that Q was no botanist either.

Orange groves, agaves, lemon groves. Strauss's waltz, *Wo die Zitronen blühn*, starts singing in my head and I can't shake it off. And Goethe's poem. Again and again, I silently answer Goethe's question to myself, more and more disturbed, . . . *ja, ich kenne das Land wo die Zitronen blühn, ja, ja, ich kenne* . . . it is Juan . . .

And the car just rolls on. Dead straight, mile after mile. We have left the small farms behind us, not a human dwelling in sight, not a human being. It is flat and green and monotonous, and perhaps not so monotonous after all. Rows of cypresses in the distance, almost black against the pale green billowing waves of grass, the sun glittering on the stalks, as on the sea, the clouds passing, blue reflections, a deepening blue above the green. Juan falls asleep in the back. Q talks about Stockholm, where he's been a great many times on business.

The flat plain simply goes on and on, hour after hour. This country is a flat as a pancake. I start doubting everything I ever learnt at school as a child. Two years later, when Juan and I went on a two-hour train journey to Tucumán, I was finally convinced. What you learn in geography is all lies, that the earth is round. It is not round, cannot be so; where did they get such a mad idea from? The earth is as flat as a dish, flat as a pancake; I know, because I've seen it with my own eyes.

Then suddenly there is a tornado, nature's own drama. In the space of a few minutes we're in the centre of a thunderstorm. Later on, I find out there are always thunderstorms in Argentina on Saturdays. But this is the first time for me. A blue-black wall of cloud looms up before us, apparently from nothing, moving quickly towards us, settling over us like a roof and then off-loading itself. Lightning flashes, the thunder rumbles and crashes. A wind gets up and rushes sideways across the road, buffeting the car, huge leaves, twigs and branches swirling around in the air, a lone shoe slapping our windscreen in passing on its swift journey to some distant goal, darkness lowering. Q stops the car. We sit imprisoned in our tiny room in the great wide world, watching this mighty performance. For a change, Juan says nothing, and I am sure he is frightened but ashamed to show it. He's a man. We are three small men, abandoned to this extraordinary, overwhelming, emotional outburst of nature. Then the rain comes. Hailstones as big as thumbnails splatter or thunder against the windscreen and the body of the car. The ground turns as white as winter in Lapland and it is as dark as the Lapland winter. The car is covered with melting hailstones. Snowed up. Then suddenly it is all over as swiftly as it began. The sun comes out. We get out and sweep the hailstones off the car with our bare hands, all three of us feeling great relief, almost elation. The sun glitters on the drops of rainwater.

On the road into San Pedro, Q runs over a dog. Half-blind and almost paralysed with starvation, it comes trotting along in the dust towards the car.

'Look out!' I cry.

We feel the thud against the front wheel, nothing but a slight bump.

'You've run over a dog!' I shriek.

Q turns round casually and looks through the back window.

'Look at that, for Christ's sake, there it is,' is all he says.

Blood is pouring out of its mouth, its rib-cage is flat, its legs jerking. Juan is quite unmoved. A dog? I feel sick.

It was raining in San Pedro, dusk falling. We had installed ourselves in our hotel. I was sharing a room with Juan. Q had a room to himself. When he was booking rooms a few days earlier, he had asked me how I wanted things, whether I wanted a room of my own or would mind sharing, and I had replied I wouldn't mind sharing. We had dinner in town. Q was keen that I should also get to know Argentina from a culinary point of view and chose an Argentinian speciality for me from the menu. Naturally it was entrails, the intestines of a cow or something like it, something straggly and slippery, which I was expected to consume. Both Q and Juan looked expectantly at me as I raised my fork to my mouth. The consistency was revolting, but the taste was not too bad. I nodded with satisfaction but not entirely honestly; it's good. They congratulated me eagerly and verbosely and explained politely that I was very quickly becoming a real Argentinian.

Juan talks about himself and Q translates into English. We both think Juan is unusually mature for his age, and Q is more condescending in his attitude than I am. Juan has an aphoristic way of expressing himself, which later he almost systematizes into a kind of linguistic method which will enable me to understand his Spanish better.

About life, Juan says: 'Life is a tango you have to learn to dance.'

And about his interrupted career as a singer: 'I don't want to be famous. I want to be happy.'

He also says what I am to hear him say so many times in the future in various situations, that he is poor but proud.

After dinner, Juan asks if we can drive around the centre of San Pedro for a while. By then it is eleven o'clock or later. There are a lot of people on the streets. Argentinian night-life. Q's Mercedes is probably the only one of its kind in this little town. Q is not enthusiastic about the suggestion, but nevertheless follows the stream of cars for a few rounds of the central streets, just to please Juan. Juan is obviously delighted as he sits there in the front beside Q.

'We're attracting attention,' he repeats over and over again with delight.

'Yes, for Christ's sake,' says Q wearily.

Then Juan starts singing, and I realize that he really can. He sings tangos, for me still an unknown form of Argentinian folk-music. His repertoire is large, his voice sensitive, and it carries. The car is filled with tango, with Juan, and I am moved without really understanding why. Juan writes his name in the mist on the window. When he gets to the last letter n, he pulls the two strokes on the n down so that the letter is heart-shaped. He does this spontaneously and then points with his finger at the heart drawn on the window. Q and I realize that he suddenly wished to send us a secret message. He wanted to tell us that he likes being with us and the heart is the concrete symbol for what he feels for us at this moment, but he does not or won't express it in words.

I wake in the small hours. The rain has stopped, the sun just risen. There are pale patches of sunlight on the wall above my head, patterned by the trees outside the window. Silence. Outside, the landscape is powerfully green, a long green slope running down to the River Paranam, which is flowing along majestically. Birds are singing. Already an occasional voice can be heard in the far distance.

Juan is asleep in the bed beside mine.

His face relaxed, calm. Not slack or puffy, as in older people, but features borne by their own firmness even in sleep. His mouth is

21

closed and his dark, veined eyelids twitch slightly. He is breathing almost soundlessly through his nose.

Chin, lips, nostrils, those black eyebrows.

The black hair is untidy and makes graphic patterns on the white pillow. His forehead is perfectly smooth, golden brown, shifting between blue and milk-white. Not even a wrinkle above the ridge of his nose. His cheeks, the soft skin, a darker tone over the jaw-bone, the beginnings of a growth of beard. He is lying on his left side with his head resting on his left hand. His shoulders powerful and forearms slightly hairy. Right hand resting on the quilt, surprisingly small, almost a woman's hand, but finely wrought, slim fingers, the back of his hand veined, the nails curved but not particularly well cared for.

'My hands are the hands of an artist, not made for heavy work,' he had said a few hours earlier. If only I could help him in his artistry.

He is lying there, sleeping and breathing almost soundlessly through his nose, that boyish nose. I watch him. The minutes slip by.

I turn away. Dawn is breaking outside, morning giving respite to the night, and the birds adding their contribution. The patches of sunlight have moved. I turn back to him. He is still there. He is real. It is no dream. I try it out several times, and each time he is still there, lying there beside me, sleeping. Real. Juan.

He is with me all the time. He does not disappear. It's a miracle.

I love you, I whisper. He doesn't move.

Slowly I stretch out my hand and slowly I run my fingertips over his eyebrows, his nose, the corners of his mouth, his chin. He opens his eyes and looks at me without expression. Then he turns over in bed, turning his back to me. The valley between the ridges at the back of his neck is almost white. Black down grows down his spine between the shoulder-blades, scarcely visible, nothing but a dark shading. He at once falls asleep again. I can't sleep any more that night. There are no questions and no answers, only an overwhelming certainty that something has happened and that the future will look quite different from what it would have if I hadn't come.

Again and again, I whisper his name, Juan . . . Juan . . . Juan . . . and every beat of my pulse hammers it more deeply into my heart, the image of him more deeply than my consciousness. So that I will never be able to forget.

That morning we drove to Areco, chatting happily. We were all in a good mood, feeling great satisfaction, contentment, which touched layers of personality deep down inside me. We were inside the circle of friendship, in the atmosphere of male comradeship, and I had hardly ever experienced this before so intensely or so thoroughly. I was almost rapturous, and at the same time it was strange and incomprehensible to think of the short time we had really known each other and how different we were, how different our lives and cultural backgrounds, without even a common language in which to speak. And yet.

We had lunch at a village inn, underneath the sun-roof, out of doors. Q was host. He was in an expansive mood, almost exhilarated, which I was later to learn was not particularly common among Argentinians, who on the contrary are usually marked by reserve and a slightly weighty dignity. Q laughed loudly. Sometimes one could sit for a whole evening in a crowded inn in Buenos Aires without hearing one single spontaneous burst of laughter. We drank considerable quantities of red wine.

It was a hot day, the sun burning, the wind sweeping in from La Pampa, but bringing with it no coolness. Despite being in my shirt-sleeves, I was sweating, but that did not embarrass me. On the contrary, it was simply part of my contentment. The food tasted wonderful. *Empanadas* to start with, small pasties, sharp on the tongue. Then an enormous juicy steak, *bife de chorizo*, and a sweet dessert. No menu. We ate what the house had to offer.

We were surrounded by Argentinian families out for their Sunday lunch. Local young people entertained us with songs and dancing, two boys and a girl, all three of Juan's age or slightly younger, but equally handsome, the boys wearing traditional black gaucho costumes with red ribbons and money-belts, the girl with the guitar wearing her finest flounced pink nylon dress. Brown almond eyes, smiling lips, soft voices and folk-tunes, sometimes almost as melancholy as those back home in Scandinavia. And all the time, Juan at my side, his physical proximity, the shifts of his expression, listening, applauding, nodding appreciatively, '*son buenos, son buenos*'. He was not like us European intellectuals, fundamentally critical, but, in a way quite different from ours, disposed to hand out praise.

After that comes the village poet, emphatically declaiming his poem of homage to his native country and the wonderful Argentinian spring. He is an old man, nearer eighty than seventy, short, almost toothless, his hands deformed by hard labour and rheumatism, his face wrinkled and weatherbeaten, like a dried fig. When he hears I am a foreigner, he improvises a long poem in my honour, in honour of the foreign guest. I understand nothing of the words, but feel the warmth in his voice, in his gestures even more. Later on, we converse, Q acting as interpreter. Argentina is the best country in the world, I am told. But on the other hand, Europe, especially Sweden, is in many ways better. In Sweden everything is very well ordered. Argentina is in many ways backward. Argentina would have a lot to learn from Sweden. On the other hand, Argentina is a rich country, full of resources, natural wealth. Nothing wrong with the people. The Argentinian people are good people, perhaps the best in the world, but the government is wretched. Argentina has always had the misfortune to have bad leaders. I was to hear the same tune many times in Argentina.

It was late afternoon when we began to bid farewell to Areco. For me it was a turning-point and I told myself I had never before been so happy as I had that day. Perhaps it was a superficial or fleeting happiness, compounded as it was with transient atmospheres, external impressions and a growing feeling, the permanence and object of which I was unsure of until then. And yet I was quite certain I was right. My mind was filled with a sense of life so near to bursting point that, on my way out, I had to deviate into the lavatory to weep. But not to weep because it was all over, but because the sense of happiness persistently pouring through me was so palpable and unprecedented, so real, indeed because it was so real and overwhelming.

I felt that life had somehow reached its culmination and there would never be more than this for me. My life had reached its peak and I felt that whatever happened to me in the future in the way of unhappiness, loss or disappointment, I would be able to bear it without anguish or complaint, for a person who has experienced complete happiness has nothing more to ask of life. Not even death was threatening or frightening any longer. For even if death that afternoon was more distant than anything else, I said to myself, from this moment onwards, calmly and without resistance, I would accept it, should it suddenly appear in the form of a thunderbolt, for instance, or a road accident, or a heart attack. For after someone has once experienced perfection, he has nothing more or better to wish for and can at the most look forward to a repetition.

In its boundless generosity, life has allowed him to experience his peak, pure and unclouded happiness, and death, the natural finale, can consequently no longer seem a painful interruption, as nothing can break what is already completed. Death has been reduced to what it is in reality, a natural end, neither more nor less. I was so happy, and my happiness was so simple, based on the simplest of impressions of life, a meal, peasant-style, ancient traditions, human company, song and music, as in the Bible, young people and old people merging into an eternal landscape, the sun over the landscape, all swept by a mild wind. My happiness was as simple as that, gathered within me, still secluded, not shared, but radiating from Juan, his presence, and from the fact that he did not leave me but was there, his figure, his appearance, the wind in his black hair, his smile, his voice and the alien words, his eyes and the gaze that met mine, that look of affection, the movements of his hands, that he was, and that he was Juan.

Luján

Juan often talked about Lilita. They were engaged and were to marry as soon as an opportunity arose. At present, the outlook was not encouraging. Juan was both unemployed and homeless. He slept on the sofa in Claudio's living-room, but he had no key to Claudio's apartment, and Claudio was mostly away flying, from Buenos Aires to New York, from New York to Paris and Madrid and Zürich. Sometimes weeks could go by before he was back home in Argentina again. Lilita could type and had a badly paid job in the office of a leather factory, earning about a hundred dollars a month. Most of her earnings went towards the family household expenses. She lived at home with her parents, in two rooms and a kitchen, sharing a room with two younger siblings.

She's small, that small, Juan says, demonstrating with his hand at roughly armpit height. Very small, but very clever. He has had hundreds of women in his young life, he tells me, and still has for that matter, but Lilita is the best of them all. Far and away the best. He admires her and needs her, and the fact is, she is the only person in the whole world who really understands him. He can talk to Lilita about everything.

'I can have any woman I want, if I like,' he says.

Women are crazy about him. They fall like skittles for his manly charm, women a hundred times more beautiful than Lilita, famous women, rich women, society women with mink coats and diamonds and Mercedes of their own. He can have them all. He has already had them all. He has experience of women of all kinds. I doubt it. He is only twenty.

'I've slept with Sylvie Vartan,' he says, smiling proudly, looking at me expectantly, curious about my reaction.

I don't believe him. But nevertheless it turns out to be true. It happened when he was at the peak of his career as a singer, when he

26

was about seventeen. She had been making a guest appearance in Buenos Aires on a concert tour. He had been the great promise, the hope of the commercial record industry. Promotion had brought them together. While they slept with each other in her suite at the Sheraton, the directors of both the French and the Argentinian record companies were rubbing their hands, listening to the money pouring into the tills in rhythmical thrusts in sexual time. A meeting of pop stars.

Yet he preferred Lilita. Or perhaps for that very reason he definitely preferred Lilita.

My relationship with Juan had already reached a degree of complexity that presupposed everything, abandoned everything, and reckoned with every possibility. I asked it if were possible to meet his fiancée.

He looked at me with his dark eyes. He was very serious. Naturally it was possible, any time, whenever it suited me. Without having understood at all, I had taken our relationship into a new dimension with my request, and in terms of the future this was to turn out to be decisive.

He was my son. I was his father. And from that starting-point it was not more than natural that I should meet his fiancée.

We agreed on an evening a few days later. They were waiting for me down in the hotel vestibule at the agreed time. We strolled up to the pedestrianized Lavalle, sat down at a café and ordered coffee and soft drinks.

Lilita was indeed very small, but in proportion. A shapely woman, if pocket-sized. At first she regarded me with uninhibited suspicion, and the conversation was more than sticky. I said I was sorry we could not converse with each other and Lilita replied with the standard Argentinian expression.

'*N'importa, n'importa,*' she kept repeating. 'It doesn't matter. It's not important.'

But it was. It was painful.

Juan did his best to appear unmoved. He talked on and on and, so that I would understand what was going on, used such childish simplifications that I would have blushed with shame in any other context. He was in control of the situation. He was supreme, although for him, and most of all for him, it must have seemed ambivalent. Anyway, the strange thing was that I couldn't help noticing that I understood him very much better than I understood Lilita, just as he understood me considerably better than Lilita understood me. In less than a month we had had so much together, got to know each other so well, that we had succeeded in developing a language entirely of our own. This language was fundamentally based on intuition, emotion, acquaintance through feelings, and was expressed in gestures, looks, scattered words, and most of all in concrete actions. By carrying out concrete actions as signs of quite definite perceptions, attitudes and desires, we had swiftly got to know where we both stood. While Lilita to me, and I to Lilita, were still totally blank pages.

She was taking a course in English to enable her to qualify for better-paid jobs in the leather factory. Before we had met, Juan had talked rather verbosely about her knowledge of the English language and had put me at ease by saying that conversation would thus be no problem at all. But it soon turned out that her English was no better than my Spanish. She had only a handful of words which came reluctantly off her tongue and which she found very difficult to pronounce. Anyway, we tried out the English words for a while and I explained what 'coffee-cup' meant. She could ask me the time. She softened slightly when I admired her lovely chestnut brown hair, and I was told that 'hair' was '*pelo*' in Spanish. I would not forget that.

Then suddenly we became good friends. I had been watching them for a while and could not help noticing how alike they were in appearance. I pointed it out to them. The atmosphere was immediately transformed and at once became warm, happy and intimate. I was not the first person to say that. They were aware of it themselves and the similarity between them was like a secret sign that they were created for each other by nature. They were very much in love. By discovering and openly admitting the external similarity between them, I had not only accepted their love, but had also earned the rôle of a confidant within the same framework of love.

A moment later, without consulting Juan first, Lilita suggested that all three of us should go on an outing the coming Sunday to the lovely little town of Luján, which was out on La Pampa, a two-hour bus journey or so from Buenos Aires.

I had passed through the eye of the needle. I was approved.

Luján turned out to be a typical tourist resort, just as Mar del Plata down on the south coast, or Carlos Paz in Córdoba are. Going abroad for your holiday was an alien idea in Juan's and Lilita's small world. If you could afford holidays at all, you almost automatically chose Mar del Plata. Or Carlos Paz. People who had more money, higher education, who had seen more of the world, took a charter flight to

South Africa or Mexico or Florida for a couple of weeks. But Juan and Lilita were not such people. Their world was a world of poverty, limited by the lack of money as well as of education, and geographically limited to a few places within the borders of Argentina, which in exchange evoked a strong, almost magical attraction in their minds: Buenos Aires, Mendoza, Mar del Plata, Bariloche, Luján. But for those who lived in Buenos Aires, Luján was the only place near enough to be suitable for a Sunday outing. So Luján it was.

Everyone who did not own a holiday house but still wanted to get out of the capital at the weekend, went to Luján.

That Sunday, the sun was already burning hot in the early morning. Juan was to fetch me at the hotel at nine o'clock. He was an hour and a half late, by which time I was almost insane with worry, irritation and disappointment. Lilita telephoned and asked where we were and all I could say was that Juan had not yet appeared. She took it very calmly and simply said there was nothing to do but to wait. When he finally did arrive, he had no explanation to offer for his lateness. He pretended nothing was wrong. I was forced to swallow my annoyance, as under no circumstances could I lecture him in Spanish.

We took a taxi at my expense to La Boca, where Lilita was waiting, and then sped off to the *estacione* Once to take the bus. Plaza Miserere was full of people enjoying the weekend off. Loving couples, mothers and fathers and children, old men on crutches, in other words just like Helsinki, though in far greater numbers.

The queue was endless, but buses drove up in a steady stream, so that no one need stay behind in the city this glorious early-summer Sunday. We got seats in the back row and I sat squashed between Lilita and Juan. All through the journey to Luján, I could feel the warmth of his body from knee to shoulder, all up my left side. He pressed against me, and at regular intervals made silent signals, thigh, hip, upper arm. I felt it, I knew it. Physical proximity. A child spewed like a fountain on the seat in front of us and the sickly smell of vomit spread through the bus. Lilita felt ill and, with our combined forces, we managed to open a window.

I thought Juan had no sense of the beauties of nature. During the journey to San Pedro, he had slept in the car most of the time. But my social prejudices, my limited human experience had led me astray. I thought his lack of a sense of aesthetic values in the landscape was something to do with his simple origins, his working-class background. Or that in some ways he was a native, so he saw in the landscape nothing but what it could be used for. I was wrong. Two years later in Salta, I was to witness how he literally imbibed the red mountain range, the desolate, stony moon landscape several thousand metres above sea level, the sharp contours of the mountains soaring mile after mile up into the blue eternity of the sky. But he knew La Pampa. He knew the plain by heart. He was born there, had grown up there and there was nothing there to see he had not already seen a thousand times.

And yet he felt it his duty to be polite and attentive. The age difference between us alone demanded that. He was Argentina and I was a tourist, and Argentina was to show herself off, Argentina was to show Argentina, for every detail of this geographical composition was undeniably remarkable, and almost certainly the best and most beautiful of its kind in the world. Consequently, he makes a sweeping gesture towards the landscape rushing past.

'La Pampa!' he says, smiling proudly. At that moment, he is Argentina, and looks at me in tense expectation of my enthusiastic and admiring comments.

But he hasn't even bothered to look at what he is showing me. I look out of the bus window. We are just driving through the outskirts of a small village. Dusty bushes along the edge of the road, and behind them a grove of sickly-looking eucalyptus trees. Wooden shacks under the shade of the trees, with rusty corrugated roofs, a goat tethered on the dry trampled earth between the shacks, half a dozen hens, two thin pigs and an indefinite number of semi-naked, dark-skinned children standing immobile, staring without expression at the passing bus. Then it is gone. I nod at Juan. La Pampa, I say. We accelerate. The air rushes in through the window and ruffles Lilita's chestnut-brown hair. The bus is crammed with people.

Luján was bathed in sunlight. The road into it is handsome, a broad highway lined with sparkling white houses with low arcades, in the distance the church dominating the town, the biggest in the world according to Juan. I had been to St Peter's, Rome, Cologne Cathedral and Canterbury Cathedral, and protested that there must be some misunderstanding. The biggest in Argentina, then, says Juan, changing his mind, but guaranteed to be the most beautiful in the world. I do not contradict him. The town had its history, like all towns. Lilita scraped the barrel of her knowledge of history and told me about presidents and generals in friendly tones and brief, easily understood, staccato sentences, so that I should understand, speaking as if to a child. I didn't learn very much, but it was enough for me, as I wasn't fundamentally interested. What interested me more was being together with these two young people, not really anything else. The white buildings on the way in, with their clean lines and arcades, were from colonial days, I was told.

We wandered round for a while in the packed crowds of tourists. There were stalls in front of the church and under the arcades, long rows of stalls full of gewgaws and useless objects for sale; home-made, up to three foot long votive candles hanging on strings, pictures of saints, amulets, Catholic symbols, objects of no practical use. Both Juan and Lilita appeared totally uninterested in this rubbishy market. They quite simply lacked the desire to buy. They had both grown up in a world of extremely tight economic circumstances, in which consumerism as a human quality had never had a chance to develop. Their consumer demands were on the whole more emotionally than materially directed, and from a material point of view were exclusively directed at the basic needs that enabled people to survive, bread, wine, clothes.

The tourists did not look like tourists to me, but more like native inhabitants, and they also spoke what seemed to me to be the native language. To me, a real tourist was fair-skinned, sometimes pink or bright red in the face, with fair hair and blue eyes, often semi-drunk, obtrusive, loud, rude, chattering or laughing in a language which I could generally make out, German, Swedish, Finnish, Dutch. These tourists were more dignified and, as far as I could see, not drunk. They spoke Spanish or Portuguese. At first it was hard to identify them as tourists. I found myself thinking that I was probably the only European in this compact sea of people, who came from different parts of Latin America, but mainly from Buenos Aires, ordinary people from Buenos Aires. It was a peculiar thought. Quite alone among strangers. Out in the world. It exhilarated me.

We went into the cool of the cathedral. Juan made the sign of the cross, slightly surreptitiously, so that no one should notice. At the time, I knew nothing of his relationship to religion or the Catholic Church and my own religious indifference had meant that I hadn't even thought that he might have some active or positive connections in that direction. That stealthy gesture on our entrance into the sanctuary surprised and confused me, but at the same time immediately moved me, filling me with warmth and tenderness, as if that simple ritual movement of the hand, the fingertips finally brushing the lips, had somehow clarified or made the image of Juan human in my mind.

Not a puff of wind in the town of Luján, with a mercilessly hot sun and heat that was beginning to be truly fierce. I was bathed in sweat all over my body. We had lunch at an inn in the centre. I paid. When the bill came, Lilita explained that we were to share, equally, they were to pay for the journey, I for the lunch. We agreed. Afterwards we went on to explore Luján. Occasionally I was left out and alone. They talked together in Spanish and I understood nothing, so soon the inevitable question arose: what am I doing here, what kind of pleasure *can* they find in my company? But then Juan turned back to me, drawing me politely and affectionately back into their fellowship. I was no longer left out. Without warning, that sense of happiness poured out, filling me with its sweetness. They are my children, I thought, over and over again. They are my children. And in Juan's look, which met mine, I could read the answer. We are your children, the look said. You are our father.

The amusement park was a few minutes' walk away from the cathedral, surrounded by open-air restaurants, cafés and soft-drink stalls, a river running though it with weeping willows and green bushes hanging over the river. Juan became as excited as a child, wanting to try out everything. We rode on roundabouts, we floated in a little boat through the tunnel of ghosts among skeletons and other horrors, we sat in a little open railway wagon among larking and screaming children and allowed ourselves to be ferried from one end of the park to the other and back again. We smashed china with old tennis balls and enjoyed ourselves hugely. Juan laughed loudly, crying out with delight. Lilita was more reserved, and I, who had never before been able to let myself go at childish amusements of this kind, felt happiness like a distant roar of a waterfall inside me. I was alive.

The cable-cars ran from the amusement park right over the town. Juan took me to one side before we went up the tower, keen to explain something to me and articulating very clearly and slowly. We were standing on the gravel outside the ghostly tunnel in the glare of the sun. The cable-cars were designed for two people. Juan wanted to make it quite clear to me that he would ride with Lilita, and that I was to ride alone. I was astonished, touched. Not for one moment had it occurred to me that Lilita should sit there alone, floating between heaven and earth. She was his fiancée, wasn't she, and I was only a stranger, an ageing man, too. Why did he have to make it so clear to me – so that I would not be hurt, so that no unnecessary misunderstanding should arise? Because despite everything, he . . . ? No, it was unthinkable. And yet at that moment, for the very first time and only because he had implied with his words the actual possibility, I felt something that was not yet jealousy, but similar to jealousy, like a faint stab of the half-sister of jealousy, so faint as to be scarcely recognizable, brought out, evoked, not by the actual situation, which was obvious and self-evident, but by his consideration, his sensitivity, his delicate sensitivity. I was not to be carried through the air over Luján with Juan at my side, but alone. Like a drop of disappointment, welded into my consciousness not by my own consciousness, but by Juan.

You have to get on the wagon at speed. Juan and Lilita vanished out over the greenery of the amusement park. I fumbled with the safety arrangements and for a moment felt as one does when about to fall over the edge of a precipice. Prodigiously horrible. Then the little wagon took off, inexorably. Hanging from a string, floating above the world. Wagon is putting it rather grandly, too, for it wasn't much more than a plank to sit on and a little bar in front to hold on to. During those terrible seconds, as long as years, I bitterly regretted being lured into this. Afraid of flying? Afraid of swaying? No. Afraid of falling.

Then quite suddenly it was great fun, finding yourself where you ought not to be, in space; space neither welcoming nor exactly inhospitable, but indifferent, definitely indifferent to your fate. Castle in the air. This was what castles in the air really looked like, always, the interior and architecture a creation of human imagination. I was in my own castle in the air, floating in the castle in the air, hanging from a cable, slowly moving along a cable, of the strength of which I had no idea, borne by technology, driven on at my own risk and on my own responsibility, abandoned to the indifference of space and the benevolence of the cable and the strength and endurance of my own imagination, gliding further and further away from the dismal grey earthly place where one stood firmly on both feet.

We took a return trip on the space flight; far below us were sparkling black and red roofs, right-angled roads with toy cars on them, clusters of people as in an ant-heap. And beyond the houses, La Pampa in its blue endlessness. Closer to the starting point, the treetops made a green carpet for space to rest on, people spread out beneath the trees, lunch baskets, ball-games, all pocket-sized as in childhood games with dolls' houses and toy soldiers. The sun glared down on to this peaceful Sunday world and on the horizon, in the distance, clouds massed, majestic, mysterious, like castles of the gods in the air.

Juan and Lilita are twenty metres ahead of me, constantly the same distance, driven along at the same leisurely pace as I am. Unattainable. Juan turns round and waves. I wave back. He smiles. I see his face indistinctly in the sea of light and sense that he is smiling. I let go of the safety rod and raise my camera to take a photo of them both just as Juan turns round and smiles at me. He is the castle in the air.

Floating between heaven and earth, chasing a reality that constantly maintains the same distance between me and my dream, I build a future in the reality, as remarkable and wonderful as Castle Far-Away and Never-Seen. And my fantasy, hectic as vertigo, restless as the wind, hands over responsibility and the realization of my love, limitless and invincible, like the landscape we are being carried over.

Late that afternoon, when we returned to Buenos Aires, the thermometer was registering thirty-eight in the shade and for me the heat was close to the boundaries of what it was possible to endure without torment.

Saul and David

I realize suddenly that no one knows where I am, truly and fundamentally, I mean. Do I even know myself? Truly? I sit on the bus saying nothing, thirty or forty people sitting all round me, also saying nothing. Women and men, young people and old people, all mixed up; no one knows me, I know no one. And no one knows what I am thinking. I don't know what any of the others are thinking. And yet presumably we are all thinking about something, including the driver at the wheel. What a strange unknown quality is this conglomeration of invisible, inaudible secret thoughts. What a boundless, unresearched, unexplored world, this endless series of human thoughts, coming and going every minute, coming and going and vanishing and leaving traces in everyday reality, edifying, destructive, but nearly always impossible to trace back to their origins, the very first spark of the thought, impulse of the thought, inspiration in the mind grasped the first time at thirty-seven minutes past four in the afternoon one Wednesday in July in the year nineteen hundred and . . . or earlier, or later . . .

. . . or in the family circle, exchanging views, discussing, quarrelling, defending opposite viewpoints, but no one knowing about the opinions we really hold, which all correspond to the thoughts we think at the same moment. And what is a thought, anyway? Nothing but a sequence of words, ordered into comprehensibility, a sentence graspable by the mind? Or the other way round, not simply a sequence of words at all, but a feeling like a plinth or a base, eternally linked by experience, remembrance, joy, sorrow, disappointment, and in that combination scattered words, like pieces of Lego slotted into a Lego-base. *Cogito, ergo sum? Siento, por lo tanto soy?*

No one knows who I am, just as no one knows what I think. I don't know who I am myself, just as I don't know why I think what I think.

The feeling precedes the thought, but what precedes the feeling?

The feeling determines certain thoughts, but what determines the thoughts that are not determined by the feeling? The will? What determines the will?

Sometimes I say one thing and mean another, sometimes from conscious calculation, naturally, but sometimes without really knowing why. Self-defence? What is that image of myself like, that picture I sometimes, spontaneously and unpremeditatedly, feel I have to defend? I am not the same person within myself as I am outwardly towards other people. How do I wish to present myself outwardly to other people? Do I know myself? Partly, yes. Wholly? No. How do I wish to present myself inwardly? Do I even know? No.

There is experience of life deep down inside all of us, determining both the feeling and the thought, or steering the feeling and the thought, an unlimited quantity of life-experiences, memories, traces in the soul of people who have been there and vanished, human encounters forgotten but ineradicable, shocks, caresses, desire and revulsion, joy and despair. It is a chasm of experience the dimensions of which we cannot even imagine, veiled in mists and darkness as it is, the mists of our conscious ambitions, the darkness of our conscious life, oblivion.

Why is Juan my son?

Why did my feeling for Juan almost immediately become so strong that it overshadowed everything else important in my life, giving me the impression that I would be capable of committing a crime for his sake, if success for him should ever demand it?

And how is it that the dimensions of feeling for Juan in my mind can be expressed most clearly by my readiness to commit a crime for his sake? What is a crime to me? An illegal act? The last possible way out? The most inconceivable? But why?

Juan did not know what I was thinking. I did not know what Juan was thinking. Would our relationship have been influenced in some direction, either positive or negative, if we had known what the other was thinking? Probably not. Juan's image of me was complete from the start, and it remained uninfluenced by dimensions or explanations on my side. My image of Juan was also complete from the start, determined as it was by me, first only as inspiration, but very soon as a conscious decision. And that image could not be altered, for it already contained within it all possibilities, that I was always prepared for anything. Sometimes he could hurt me profoundly, almost beyond healing. He could fill me with happiness or despair, but he could never surprise me. For whatever he did, I had already reckoned with that as a possibility beforehand.

We were together for five weeks without being able to express in words more than the most elementary, the simplest possible things, hardly more than what a dog expresses when it barks or a cat when it miaows. We had no common language, and we knew when the five weeks were at an end that we had penetrated deeply into each other's lives, decisively and irrevocably.

What does language mean to the emotions? What do words mean to love?

We had an overall image of each other and our actions contradicted nothing of that image, on the contrary, they strengthened it. Secretly, we each expected the other to betray us, and just because of that, for each of us betrayal was out of the question. So we did not betray each other, either of us. This mutual trust very soon became an almost magical factor in our relationship, unprejudiced and impossible to violate as long as we had no words in common which would have enabled us to formulate conditions for each other. Our relationship was unconditional and therefore indissoluble. For protest against conditions is possible, but when there are no conditions, all protest is superfluous. I trust you because I want to trust you and I will not let you down because I don't want you to let me down. That is how you can bind someone to you without uttering a single word of confirmation or clarification. That is how love arises, wordlessly.

The world we lived in was immensely simple, because we were steered there by circumstances. What if we'd been able to converse together? What if our feelings and actions had been complemented by language, by words, clarifying and illustrating them? Sometimes I think that would have destroyed our fellowship long before it had had time to mature into its form of indestructibility. Or it would never have arisen, for words would only have emphasized our dissimilarities, our separateness, without being able to bring out the similarities to the same extent, the puzzling similarities we deep down and quite intuitively recognized in each other and were spontaneously attracted by.

Misunderstandings exist in words. But what is never said is ineffective. We understood each other so well because we could hardly express anything at all that might be misunderstood. So each of us was able to form an ideal image of the other, perhaps an image far from reality, or simply nothing whatsoever to do with reality, but one which would serve just as well as truth and reality, difficult or even impossible to correct, as we lacked the means to do so, language, the tool of words.

Our prerequisites for life were so different, our innate dissimilarity so great, that somehow this ceased to be of any significance. This was the actual base, the fundament, of our fellowship. We knew this was so, and that was the starting-point. Consequently, we were pleased when we discovered similarities, common perceptions, standpoints, characteristics. They became what mattered. What finally influenced us most strongly was something we both valued very highly and which at first we only intuitively felt the other possessed as fundamental to him, a leading element in his actual attitude to life: a spontaneous respect for human beings, even in their degradation and nakedness, even when they are forced by life into peculiar, unusual, usually despised forms of existence. For Juan this was primarily a result of his experience. For me it was a standpoint that to some extent I had *thought* my way through to. Juan soon noticed this difference, and the fact that he noticed it, when he noticed it, gave rise in its turn to increased mutual respect. For, in my eyes, he then became wiser. In his eyes, I then became more human.

'*Eres un ser humano.*'

'*Tu también, eres un ser humano.*'

You're a human being. That was enough. That was humanism. Hard-won in both hemispheres, as it is always hard-won. Juan's humanism. And mine.

When I went to Argentina, it was a time most Argentinians considered painful, difficult, often horrible. Sons were imprisoned, brothers and sisters murdered, friends and relations simply disappeared, never to return. Prices rose, but not salaries and wages. In every week that went by, life became more expensive to live. There were goods, but little money with which to buy them. Inflation soared at a pace people in Europe would find it hard to imagine. People in Q's position managed. People in Juan's position managed considerably less well.

Back home in Finland, I had carelessly prepared a piece of work which in Argentina proved to lack any kind of anchorage in reality. I was going in search of the past, but nowhere did I find a single trace of it. I was tired of the present, tired of man's insanity in the present, tired of politics, tired of culture, tired of lack of imagination, lack of ideals, of intellectual sloppiness and lack of honesty and courage. The future had fewer troubles to offer; it would come, and however terrible it looked like being, one would have to accept it, for that is what the future is. Its foundation lies in the present. I was part of its foundation and I was not ashamed, had no guilty conscience about my contribution. I had long done as much as I was able to. If the future depended simply on me, it would not have seemed nearly so frightening.

But the past disturbed me. I felt imprisoned in time. I felt the need to widen my perspectives in time. There existed a perspective of time that I lacked. What was it like, truly, behind the words, behind the pictures? I read books about the past, historical accounts by historians, but I did not find the past in the words of books. I looked at pictures from the past, but the pictures were lifeless, rigid, and I could see not a glimmer of life behind their rigidity. In Argentina, the past would at last come alive. I believed that. I felt it, for I had a link, a distant relative who had lived there, once, long long ago. The papers he left behind.

But in Argentina, the past was more distant than ever from anyone or anywhere in Europe. I could not find the slightest sign of it. In comparison, Europe seemed to be a huge warehouse of the flotsam of the past. Yet scarcely a year later and after endless conversations, we found, Juan and I, a perspective of a hundred years earlier, like a lone glow-worm in the evening grass, a secretive glimmering speck of the past, far up in the north, in northern Argentina, in the jungles of Misione, or the rugged mountains of Tucumán, place unknown, people unknown, but the actual event magically experienced by both of us, as the paths of our lives, long before either of us was born, met for the first time, touched each other, only to separate and meet again a hundred and fifty years later in Buenos Aires, in reality, for always. We recognized each other. We had a common origin; we had met before, in another life. It was a vertiginous discovery. But all that was later.

Tired of the present, disappointed by the refractoriness of the past, I stopped searching. By then I had already found another task, an impossible one, almost simple-minded, but equally unconditionally obligatory. That was Juan.

To write a person! To change the course of reality!

In Juan's eyes, I was at first just an ordinary foreigner, an ordinary tourist, and the fact that I occasionally mixed with ambassadors and tycoons did not in any way impress him, did not affect his attitude at all. In my own eyes, I was probably rather more than an ordinary tourist, but in the way I gradually began to spend my days, even I was finally forced to admit that the difference was but a hair's breadth: tourist, layabout, moneyed. That was me. I had stopped searching for the past. I was thinking about Juan.

That was the starting-point, and it seemed immediately to involve an urgent moral summons, which I saw very clearly and felt very strongly as a challenge.

Juan had practically approached me in the street. There was little between him and the casual acquaintances a tourist comes across in countries in which tourism is a source of income. Compared to Finland and Sweden, Argentina was an underdeveloped country. I was a tourist in any underdeveloped country; it could have been Greece, or Tunisia, or Ceylon, by which I mean Sri Lanka, of course. My family and I had travelled as tourists in a number of different parts of the world in the 'seventies and we had also gradually begun to see how profoundly ambiguous, how foolish and constantly unsatisfactory the elements of travelling in this way were. We had met a great many native inhabitants over the years, of varying colours, and we knew quite well what happened in such casual human encounters, how superficial they were, how doubtful in human terms, forced or sentimental, false or over-emotional. Because of the circumstances. Because of the situation. Because of the limited time. Because of inbuilt concealed class-differences. Because of developed and under-developed countries.

We had guilty consciences about all those letters which were never written to 'friends' in various parts of the world. We found it difficult to forget the guitar we had promised to send, but never did, to musical but poverty-stricken 'Tiger' in Tunisia. And even between ourselves we avoided talking about little Anura in Sri Lanka, son of a fisherman, with eight brothers and sisters, whom we promised to adopt and take back to Finland to a better future. In the nonchalance of our secure well-being, we had strewn promises around which we had never bothered to keep. We felt bloody wretched about it. We had every reason to do so. We had behaved like the sentimental aristocrats in Chekhov, the lachrymose swine.

Then Juan's turn came. I was a tourist in Argentina, but was not to behave like one this time. All right, Anura again, but that shame would nevertheless never be repeated.

But instead of doing what common sense usually prescribes, being discreet, not involving myself in questionable encounters with strangers, being politely dismissive to the importunate, and constantly maintaining a benevolent distance, or generally being dull and having a dull time, I did exactly the opposite. I laid it on thick with promises and prospects, blinding both Juan and myself equally, and this seemed exhilarating and overwhelming, not only because they seemed totally unrealistic the moment I gave them, but also because in an absolute sense I felt at the same time morally bound to realize them. Juan had moved into my life and aroused love; I was going to move into his life and change it, providing a platform for his future. And it was to be a better future.

We went on long excursions together in Buenos Aires, in the daytime and at night. Juan took me with him to all the tango places I would never have found on my own, for tango was his hidden language just as the romantic symphony was mine. I took him out to lunch and dinner. We wandered back and forth along Florida and Lavalle and Corrientes in the midday heat, among the people, in the never-ceasing torrent of people. I bought Argentinian long-playing records which Juan chose for me. We mostly went around in silence, exchanging occasional ordinary words, or if there was something Juan needed to say, something important, he kept on explaining and explaining. To be quite sure I understood. The backs of our hands brushed each other. His arm brushed mine and he did not withdraw it. He put his arm round my waist to pilot me past a cluster of people. He put his hand on my shoulder-blade or shoulder, so that I should watch out where I was going. And each time, I felt his touch as a caress that filled me with happiness. I put my hand on his shoulder and we walked like that for a while, among people, in the torrent of people. He looked up, his eyes meeting mine. And he smiled.

He was always with me, even when I was alone, because I thought of nothing else and quite often when I was alone it happened that a presentiment came to me. 'Juan's coming now,' I thought, and naturally it was a thought prescribed by my longing. But longing and presentiments are one and the same for anyone living in the dimension of love, so that is what happened, a few moments later he was there, as large as life, present and real, coming swiftly towards me along Florida as if in a hurry, as if on an important errand, which he almost never was. For he was unemployed. But one must keep up a good front, pride demanded that. And that little brown handbag under his arm, containing . . . what? Not money, anyhow. Wearing worn jeans, brown ankle-boots with high heels and a white sports shirt with blue flashes on the shoulders. I could pick him out among millions.

In my memory of this time, my first five weeks in Buenos Aires are almost wholly a bright time of expectation and happiness. For that is how memory works, largely loyal to our happiest daydreams, always adapted for our own consolation and solace. But the bright memory is like a soft rug recently spread over reality and easily drawn aside, and underneath something else is inexorably revealed. For what love, security and happiness wants of the past is largely what the imagination has created and seldom corresponds to what the past was really like. Neither was it really all that bright. There were already drops of anguish in the sea of happiness, patches of disappointment, bitterness, despair, like patches of oil, still small but shimmering glaringly.

We were to have gone to a football match. He was to have come to the hotel at seven o'clock. I was waiting, but he did not come. I waited in my room until eight o'clock, but heard nothing from him. There was plenty of time, of course, as the match didn't start until ten, but all the same. I took the lift down and sat on the veranda of the inn right next to the hotel. I ordered a whisky, Argentinian, a Smuggler. There was no sign of him. 'There he is,' I thought, but it wasn't him. 'Now he's come . . .' 'He'll be here in five minutes,' I thought, but he didn't come. I sat there until after ten o'clock getting rather drunk. I waited and waited, and although I had long since realized it was pointless, although I knew he wouldn't appear again that evening, I could not give up waiting. Or hoping. As if in despair. Not because of the football, but because of his treachery. It became a paralysis and a curse in my life, to be repeated a hundred times over during the years to come. That planless waiting, that hell of hopeless waiting.

Finally I took a taxi and asked the driver to take me to the football stadium; he shook his head and asked me what I wanted to go there for, as there was no match that evening. I persevered and he drove me to a deserted, ill-lit area of Buenos Aires which I did not know. He had seen I was drunk, and he fleeced me, the very first time I had ever been fleeced by an Argentinian taxi-driver. He demanded three thousand pesos instead of the three hundred the meter showed, and I paid up without protest because I reasoned, as I usually do in such situations, that under any circumstances he needed the money more than I did. Nevertheless, it was just as much of a humiliation.

Drunk and unhappy, I was now all alone in a murky street which was apparently the ideal place for murderers, robbers, thin cats and fat rats. Empty fields with piles of timber silhouetted against the darkness on my right. Decaying warehouse buildings on my left. I had no idea that the taxi-driver, despite the shameless way he had cheated me, as I saw it, had taken me almost straight to the right place, and that the stadium was less than a hundred metres away, though now in darkness. Neither had I any idea that Lilita lived slightly further than a stone's throw from where I was standing. This was not revealed to me until two years later. At the time, I was just the innocent, unsuspecting victim of a double treachery. What the hell if I was robbed. Or eaten by rats.

I started making my way through the darkness between the warehouses. I was soon back again among lighted houses, in lighted streets in an inhabited area, but different from the area from where I lived. This was a poor area, slums, decaying houses and neglected streets. I went into the first bar I saw and ordered a whisky at the bar counter. Here too, among working people, poor people, I was the only one drinking alcohol. Beside me at the bar and all around at the tables, they were drinking coffee and soft drinks. Hardly anyone drinks heavily in Argentina.

No one took any notice of me. I could feel myself swaying. A black-haired bearded man was standing beside me in a white shirt with a dirty collar and a grey jacket covered with greasy patches. He was sipping a small expresso coffee. He looked like an Indian. I felt like asking him if he were Indian, but couldn't find a single usable Spanish word through the thickening veils of whisky. Anyway, such things shouldn't be asked, highly inappropriate, almost like asking someone with a hooked nose if he is Jewish. A car stopped outside on the street. It was very hot. I was sweating.

The door was flung open just like Billy the Kid making an entrance in Tombstone. But it wasn't funny at all. The little Indian was arrested. Two soldiers with machine-guns at the ready at hip-level were guarding the exit, and a plain-clothes policeman, almost as small as his victim and wearing an almost equally greasy jacket, did the job. The Indian was frightened. He tried to explain something, but of course it was useless. Suddenly, I found myself in the Latin America of repression, and the private idyll I'd been so occupied with recently seemed misplaced and obscene, almost an impertinence. I was indignant, angry, and made a vague attempt to protest, for I had

43

the Scandinavian notion of human rights in my blood and that was what I was now demanding, although I probably realized at the same time how pointless and dangerous it was.

One single look from the plain-clothes policeman was enough to make me refrain from any further involvement. A wave of fear washed through me. No one had ever looked at me like that before, a look of supremacy, a look of evil power, icy, utterly indifferent and threatening, without mercy. I stiffened. I turned away. The whole place was totally quiet, the barman busying himself in a corner behind the bar, the other customers pretending they hadn't even noticed what was going on. But the hot air trembled with restrained fear. It was all over in less than two minutes. The Indian disappeared through the door with his dreadful escort. A car started up outside.

That look. That police look. I would never forget it. During my second visit to Buenos Aires, I was to see it again many times, recognize it, identify it, so that I knew to be on my guard, although the situation was always trivial, apparently innocent, and although nothing about the man himself, either his garb or behaviour, revealed who he was or what he was doing. That look contained no humanity, only authority and such absolute hatred that it appeared to lack any kind of rational motivation. I saw that look from a window of a car parked day after day outside where I lived. For a while I imagined that it concerned me. But if so, why? It was nothing to do with me however. It was for one of the generals who happened to live in the same block. So, indirectly, it did also concern me.

I paid for my Smuggler and left the bar. I staggered around the alien streets, unable to decide whether to hail a taxi and go home. Anyway, taxis were rather thin on the ground in this poor part of the city. Juan was afraid of the police. Nothing in Buenos Aires is dangerous, I was told, but if you see a policeman, watch out and keep out of the way. During my second visit to Argentina, the situation had changed a great deal. Largely thanks to the world football championship. The police had carried out a successful 'charm' offensive and even Juan kept praising them for their decency. But in November 1976 there was still open war between the police and the Argentinian people. One afternoon in the rush-hour in Corrientes, I asked Juan about his political standpoint and affiliations. I didn't conceal where I stood, on the left of socialism. He suddenly looked frightened and urged me to speak more carefully. I had thought he was a Perónist. He emphatically denied it. Then he spoke, or rather whispered, the

44

names of Marx and Lenin and looked meaningfully at me. He talked about the cause of the working classes. I realized he was a socialist like myself, and that made me happy, too. In this aspect of him, I hadn't been mistaken about his intellectual and human qualities either. But he saw a member of the secret police in every passer-by. At that time it was dangerous to discuss politics in public.

Much later that night, something very strange indeed happened, like a miracle. I had no idea whatsoever where I was, and neither did I care. I was in an alien world. I had recently witnessed the reality and everyday actions of a police state and the only living person keeping me in this hostile environment had let me down. I was upset and bitter. Drunk, too. I started planning my return home. Then he is suddenly coming towards me in the street. Juan. In his shabby jeans and a dark velvet jacket. The night was no longer oppressive, the air mild. He takes my hand and leads me home. He is my father.

He is good and considerate and friendly and decisive and calls a taxi and takes me home. I don't understand where he has suddenly appeared from, any more than he understands why I was where I was. I am feeling soggy and helpless inside, and instead of bitterness, I am quickly filled with great gratitude. I think he regretted letting me down, and was worried about me, so set off into town in search of me. And I think fate of some secret higher power finally brought me his way; it is like a confirmation of the two of us belonging to each other. Fate or predestination. I don't ask why he didn't come, why he broke our agreement. I ask nothing, only feel great gratitude. And he does not make the slightest attempt to apologize or explain himself. He is twenty-five years younger than I am and he is my son, but for this night hour it is the other way round; he is my father. And will remain so. He is Argentina and fundamentally it is all incomprehensible.

Later I was to learn that if you were to feel you were a real man in Argentina, you did what you felt like. From start to finish it had all been a matter of chance. He had been with Lilita because he preferred to be with Lilita rather than go to a match with me. And that was quite legitimate in his eyes. It was nothing. That's what it was like.

My faith in Juan was occasionally clouded by a distrust which was sometimes very strong. My faith was fundamental, but reality now and again gave rise to doubts to such an extent that my principles wavered. The same applied to Juan, of course. It was natural enough that he regarded some of my more far-reaching promises and pledges as airy, empty words from a man, decent enough perhaps, but a sentimental foreign oddball who was out of touch with reality. He did not expect reliability in middle-aged foreign tourists, just as I, at first, did not expect reliability in southern youths who more or less lived on the street.

His behaviour was sometimes so strange that I could not help being suspicious. He rummaged in my papers in my hotel room. He made swift secretive notes when he thought I wasn't looking. He was inquisitive about my friends – especially Q – in such an insistent and insolent way, the only conclusion I could come to was that he was looking for opportunities which he could later exploit. Blackmail? How would I know? But it was disturbing. I was convinced that he lied to me. That business of his interrupted career as a singer, for instance, that turned out not to be lies after all. He maintained he had made at least three singles. When? Well, not sure when, whenever, a few years ago. I asked to see at least one of the records. We could go back to Q's place and play it on Q's record-player. But Juan couldn't produce a single one of his own records. He hadn't got one. Lilita had had one, but unfortunately she had just lent it to a girl-friend. Claudio had them, too, but he couldn't find them. Really? Wasn't that a bit peculiar? Didn't Juan himself think that rather peculiar? No. Juan did not think it peculiar at all. Juan did not think anything about his own personal life peculiar.

Later on, I was to understand it all much better. But, at the time, I was sure he was lying. Just why was unclear. Perhaps because southern youths always lie? Perhaps because the whole race were liars and untrustworthy? My European or Scandinavian prejudices stuck like pins in my mind. He maintained he could accompany himself on the guitar. Did he even own a guitar?

I didn't show more than a fraction of my doubts openly, because I was afraid he would be hurt and leave me if I did so. But I asked him to bring his guitar with him to the hotel one day and sing for me, really show me what he could do. Perhaps one day, sometime in the future, I might be able to fix some engagements for him, in Finland or Sweden, I said vaguely. I was holding out the carrot to him, not even a carrot, really, nothing but an aerial root. He was much too clever to fall into that trap. He replied that he would like to sing for me, but only to please me, not to acquire engagements abroad. I didn't even believe that.

But he came. At the agreed time, to cap it all, and he had the guitar with him. It was a battered old guitar. His father had given it to him when he was nine. How could I know whether that was true? What did it matter whether it was true or not? He asked me what I wanted him to sing. He was best at tango. I said the name of the only Latin American composer I could remember at that moment. Victor Jara. His face remained expressionless. Didn't he know Victor Jara? Of course he did. Didn't he like Victor Jara's songs? I must have seemed dreadfully naive at that moment. He began to explain, with great solemnity, that it was impossible to sing Victor Jara in the present situation, and that I ought to know that. OK. I understood. Then he sang a tango instead.

He sat on the edge of the bed. I sat beside him in the rattan chair. It was a hot day, the curtains drawn back, the sun pouring into the room. After the first tango, he stripped off his shirt, the white one with blue on the shoulders, and sat there with the guitar pressed against his naked, brown, hairless chest, striking a chord and then singing. He went on for over two hours, alternating between tango and folk-songs; describing what he was singing in simple Spanish words so that I would understand, naming names which at the time were unknown to me: Carlos Gardel, Annibal Troilo, Ariel Ramirez, Edmundo Rivero, Mercedes Sosa. Later I was to learn to love them all. His forehead and throat and Adam's apple slowly began to gleam, damp with sweat, and small drops of perspiration ran from his armpit down his chest into his waist. A tuft of black hair in the armpit.

While he was singing, he kept his eyes on mine all the time, without turning away, those black velvet eyes; to know what they concealed and did not conceal. I was so moved my eyes kept filling with tears, which I had to wipe away with my fingertips. Naturally he saw, but he took no notice. I didn't know whether he was good or bad, amateur or master or young god, but in my eyes he was a young god. Sang like one. For quite a time, I had been feeling bitter in my life, hurt and tired of publicity which sometimes seemed terribly unjust and ruthless. But that all meant nothing now; he had wiped it all away with his voice and the dark surging emotion behind it, emotion like waves in the sea, rising, falling, rushing. He sang for me, just for me. He was David. And I was Saul. With his singing he annihilated my melancholy, awakened happiness, and a new sadness was born, more profound than what had gone before, but sweeter. Everything I had distrusted about him and all my doubts evaporated and became nothing, for my life was transformed and he became everything of value to me in my life, his proximity alone sufficient aim in life.

A few days before I went home, we took the night boat to Montevideo. Juan had difficulties with the passport police. His papers themselves were in order, but his identity card was worn, rather tattered and crumpled. The official on duty explained that he couldn't send an Argentinian citizen abroad with such a shabby identity card. Juan protested lamely, apparently diffident, not at all himself, and for the moment appeared to have lost his otherwise supreme ability to talk himself out of tricky situations. The official, a pudgy pink-faced middle-aged man with an imposing body and fleshy hands, just shook his head. But, as a token of decency, he promised he would take the matter up with a colleague. He disappeared with the identity card and the queue at the hatch was static for over ten minues. No one reacted. No one grew irritable. No one started shouting or creating a disturbance. This was routine. It was always like this. This was what happened in Argentina, and patience was an inbuilt, obvious quality in nearly every Argentinian. You must not be impatient, for if you were, you at once spoilt your chances. No one could be bothered with the impatient. We waited and waited. Juan was nervous. I had never seen him like that before.

He asked – almost shyly, I thought – whether I was thinking of going on alone if the passport police refused to allow him through. I was anguished at the thought of such a possibility and explained that under no circumstances had I any intention of leaving him behind. We could go to Mar del Plata instead, he suggested. I said I thought that a good idea, but things would probably work out. They couldn't be that small-minded, after all, not even in Argentina, I thought. Juan knew better.

Another official appeared at another hatch and beckoned Juan over to him. He asked what Juan thought the authorities in Uruguay would think of an Argentinian citizen arriving with an identity card in that state? He would put all of Argentina to shame. Juan flung out his hands. He apologized. He became helpless and humble, beseeching and pleading. The result was that the new official, who was considerably younger and slimmer than the previous one, as an extra-special token of decency promised to telephone his superior officer and ask him. But, of course, as it was Friday evening, he could not be sure he would be at home.

We waited for another twenty minutes. The departure time for the boat came nearer and nearer. Juan got it into his head that the passport police chief was none other than the supercilious father of his previous fiancée. That father hadn't liked Juan. So this could do

48

nothing but go wrong. But then suddenly we were let through after all. The senior officer had given the all-clear.

Juan had no luggage. He had come to the hotel with a shirt and a clean pair of socks in an old plastic carrier-bag from San Pedro, and these we had packed into my suitcase. He called himself a singer.

'Do singers always travel with no luggage?' the Customs official asked ironically.

'Yes,' said Juan gravely. 'We singers always travel without luggage.'

We were standing alone on deck when the boat sailed away from the quay, Juan in his jeans and worn velvet jacket. He seemed happy and relaxed. Darkness had already fallen. We gazed at the silhouettes of harbour cranes against the sky glowing faintly yellow and red from the lights of Buenos Aires. The blue harbour lights passed and disappeared.

'*Soy feliz*,' he says suddenly. 'I'm happy.'

'*Yo también. Soy feliz.* I'm happy, too.'

'I've never heard anyone like you use those words before. You're the first. I like you very much.'

It was a final confirmation to me that I was not alone in what I felt. For he had already taught me that he always said out loud what he felt, and on the other hand never said anything he didn't mean. A love was born then, and at that moment neither of us bothered to ask how or why. *Fuimos ambos felices*. We were both happy.

It was raining in Montevideo.

'*Llueve*,' said Juan. 'It's raining.'

'*Sí. Llueve*,' I replied.

We couldn't say very much more to each other. But looks, lips, hands. Not speaking, huddled close together, along the wet streets towards the centre.

Montevideo was not an attractive city. Palm trees, skyscrapers, clean air, but apparently empty, and the people seemed frightened, introverted, most of them poor and badly dressed. We saw no police anywhere, and yet it gave us goose-pimples all over, knowing we were in a city where the cruellest of all police ruled supreme. The streets were clean, but the smell of blood somehow obstinately remained, casting a dreadful air of gloom over the city. Invisible traces of human blood. Not like in Buenos Aires, where life continued regardless, but the contrary, as if in a gruesome way life had already passed by. Hopelessness.

49

As usual, I had with me a number of addresses of people I was to contact and who would help me. Nothing came of it. I was not interested in new acquaintances. Juan was all I wanted and needed. We stayed at a hotel Q had recommended, very elegant and comfortable, just out of the centre, on the shores of the Rio de la Plata. We hadn't been in our room five minutes before Juan undressed and took a hot bath, lying in the bath, singing on the top of his voice. The final chorus of Beethoven's Ninth, among other things. I reckoned that the number of times in his life he had had access to a real bath had been few, and so now he was 'as happy as a sandboy'. He called me in. I sat on the edge of the bath and looked at his young body, constantly moving under the water, his torso brown and hairless, from the waist down his skin a paler hue, his buttocks, thighs and calves all covered with coarse black hair.

He maintained that he had once been able to stay under water for over two minutes. He asked me to time him and plunged below the surface of the water, lying there with his hands pressed against the side of the bath. His black hair hovered like a shimmering water plant in a gentle current. Again and again he plunged, but each time two minutes was too long. 'All those cigarettes,' he muttered disappointedly.

That evening we went to the cinema to see Chaplin's *Modern Times*. He hadn't seen it before. I had seen it four times. I wanted to try him out. If he likes it, he is perfect, I thought. He liked it. 'Brilliant,' he kept repeating as we came out of the cinema. 'Brilliant.' He had passed the test. He was perfect.

Juan

It is a jigsaw puzzle and I have completed it. The picture is not only of Juan, although he is in the foreground. Behind him is Lilita, and Mercedes and Marcelo and Norma and Pancho and Claudia and Daniel, and a number of others. I am there too, somewhere. Behind me is my family and a few friends. My publisher is also behind me. It is actually a swarm of people, Creoles and Europeans, Catholics and non-confessors, working-class and bourgeois, rich and poor, dark and fair, blue-eyed and black-eyed.

The picture portrays two worlds, two spaces in the history of the world, endlessly distant from each other, two cultures, which largely speaking have only the sun and the human heart in common. The human heart as a symbol. And I have completed the puzzle, we have completed it together, Juan and I. But it was my idea.

There are so many pieces in our jigsaw puzzle. The picture has so many facets, so many dimensions. One facet, for instance, is class-difference. Another is called money. A third is called the unfathomable sympathy of souls. A fourth reveals a human intuition that defies all ingrained concepts of probability.

Juan's pieces, and mine. One of Juan's pieces is called Luján, because I don't just pretend to take an interest in Lilita, but have quite concretely shown that I genuinely wanted to get to know her. Another of his pieces is called Montevideo, where I convinced him we would stay together even if the passport police refused to let him through. A third is called Helsinki, the first time he visited my family home, my childhood home district, and he briefly sums up: *'Tienes sangre burgués, pero tu alma no es burgués.'* 'You have bourgeois blood, but your soul is not bourgeois.'

My pieces are largely of another character. One is called human beauty, another physical contact. A third is called loneliness.

In the correspondence which followed my departure from Buenos

Aires in December 1976, everything that happened later was already decided or presupposed. Juan was to come to Europe as soon as possible. He would live with us. As our son. My wife was understandably hesitant, but in principle had nothing against it. The children had no objections and seemed almost enthusiastic about suddenly having a Creole brother in the house. Juan would sing, perhaps be famous in our enclosed northern country, far away from his own native heath. We would write a book together. It would be about . . . well, about what? About Juan, of course. And Argentina. For there was something truly remarkable about our friendship, wasn't there? He was young, I was old. He was a Creole, I was a Scandinavian. He was poor, I was wealthy. Through our literary co-operation, in a useful and not humiliating way, part of my wealth was to be transferred to him.

I was all fire and flames. He saw a chance and did not hesitate to take it.

Neither of us could take in the whole situation, for how could we have done that? But if we could have done so, perhaps nothing would ever have come of it. Not because of him weighing things up, because he had nothing to lose, but because of me. I should have realized what I was about to do, before the stone had really started rolling, that I was attempting the impossible.

Our starting-points were quite different. Mine were sentimental, his the need to survive, and necessity knows no laws.

Now it was high summer, late July, and we are writing in the year 1979. Tomorrow, my son goes to stay in Ireland with his girl-friend for the rest of the summer. My daughter is at home, but clearly only in transit. She came back from Holland recently and in a few weeks will probably be going to the USA and Central America. She is working her way round the world. Travelling is a way of life. I am glad my children travel. It means preferring the vista to the security inside a narrow frame. It means choosing insight before ready-made norms. I didn't travel in my youth. It was less common at the time, but would of course have been possible. If I'd wanted to. But I didn't. I was looking for a spot to stand on. Maybe it was just fear. Later on, I found a spot, but that was in life itself, not geographical. At the same time, I realized how dangerous it was to limit your world to habits and day-to-day life, for when that world is used up, you have nothing left.

A letter came from Juan a few weeks ago. We have meat to eat today, he writes, but I know nothing of tomorrow or the next day, and the outlook for the future is not bright. But whatever happens, he says at the end, you will know you have two children in Buenos Aires who love you dearly. Isn't that widening your horizons? Isn't that a lifetime's work? Not just that my spot is anywhere, but that Juan's spot is in Argentina. My family is spread all over the world, but it is still a family and feels like one. We do not flee from one another. We admit that each and every member has his or her own spot, and that spot does not necessarily have to be so on top of each other that we daily tread on each other's toes.

What have I to offer? This is what I have to offer: a passionate report from an area of life which is never in newspaper headlines. A report on faithfulness, trust, from those who are fundamentally betrayed. And I myself, floating in the space between the betrayers and the betrayed. A love story, slap in the middle of the grandiose insanity which is steering us towards catastophe.

Within the course of a few days, the following information on the state of the world has reached me. Arming continues splendidly everywhere. Disarmament does not go on everywhere, or only on the impotent lecterns of innumerable conferences. The armament industry of Sweden is expanding enormously and Swedish armaments can be found everywhere where political tension suddenly explodes into military violence. Sweden is now the seventh biggest arms exporting country in the world. And what does the Swedish government say? Rub its hands? Wash its hands? For what else can they do when faced with such a superb source of income?

In Brazil, for the last decade or so they have been cutting down all the rain forests in Amazonas. The Brazilian rain forests produce about half of all the oxygen in the atmosphere. In other words, they are vital to our existence on earth. And yet it has been decided they are more profitable if transformed into paper or cellulose. The Brazilian government and private American and multi-national companies are responsible for those calculations. And what does the President of the United States say? What do all the presidents and rulers of the world say? Rub their hands? Wash their hands? For what else can they do when faced with such a superb source of income?

For weeks and weeks, oil has been gushing out into the Gulf of Mexico from a damaged oil-rig. At the same time as this is happening, two giant tankers collide off the coast of Tobago and over three hundred thousand tons of oil float out into the Caribbean Sea. What do governments say? What do governments do? Wash their hands?

Fling out their hands? For what else can they do? Oil is once and for all oil.

Then I read in the Finnish communist newspaper that Amnesty International is conducting a campaign against the socialist countries of the world. What? Well, in the Soviet Union four shoplifters or petty thieves have been condemned to death for their terrible crimes. Amnesty has protested against the death sentences. Oh, communists of the world, you who ought to be representing reason and humanity in a world of violence and injustice! How can you allow yourselves to be so degraded? Your devoted loyalty to the cruel legislation of a dictatorial regime has as much to do with human solidarity as beatings and strict discipline have to do with the love of children.

Power is what it is all about. Money is what it is all about. There are two kinds of people on earth, those with power and those without. The money is shared according to the same pattern. Occasionally power has a concrete aim, to change the world, to make a better world. Then power gradually becomes detached from every concrete aim and becomes an aim in itself. But when power has ceased to exist in all respects except for its own sake, when it is simply an aim in itself, then it has already been turned into its opposite and has become powerless. That is what the world is like now, or how it is becoming. For when power has perfected its institutions, it has created its own ivory tower, where plans and decisions are made without reference to what happens outside it, in real life, where human beings and animals and nature exist. That is what happened to the Christian Church when it finally refined its institutions for the exercise of political power. The church remained behind in the middle of the village, a remarkable fossil, but the voice of reason and the human voice came from quite a different direction and other circles have taken over the task of being the lodestar for human beings and making the world a better place.

Who holds the handle when the broom sweeps? Not politicians. Nor presidents or ministers or party leaders. For they have locked themselves into their ivory tower of power and are sitting there beside their hot-lines, mumbling incomprehensibilities to each other, irritated by the ingratitude of the starving millions and brooding on nitpicking party matters or the Pope's beard.

Doing something is less important than learning the ugly art of maintaining power, for it can happen that 'doing' goes against the art of maintaining power.

So thumbs are twiddled, awaiting considerations whether to dismiss or appoint or award or expose or appear on television occasionally, as if from a peephole at the top of their tower of ivory. All is politics.

But I no longer trust politicians.

They often speak, but what they say is but a thin curtain of words fluttering in an open window, behind which powerlessness and emptiness have their abode. They talk to avoid the necessity of saying anything definite.

Where does reason have its abode? Where does the will to better the world have its abode? Where is there a window lit by wisdom and the will to act? God knows. I don't. For the windows in the fortresses of democracy are blacked out.

The corridors of power echo, echo with stupidity, emptiness, lack of imagination and the betrayal of human beings.

Politics means to betray. Politics means avoiding things and blinding yourself. All is politics, but they who have politics as their profession are no longer responsible. Their insanity lies in the arms race and party tactics. We can no longer live on their conditions. The dog that whimpers with hunger has more to teach us about the meaning and importance of politics than the politician in his television cage.

And what have I to offer against this? One single human being, lifted out of the human ocean, an arbitrary species, brought into focus by love. Juan. With neither power nor money.

But it worked. Juan had a better life and my life acquired greater dimension. And our friendship persisted.

Argentina was in a state of economic and political crisis. Was it not my duty to portray this crisis? No, I say. Argentina is always in a state of crisis. That is the normal state of affairs in the whole of that continent, as the European press never fails to inform us. That is what it is like and why it is like that. There are hundreds of journalists who understand and can describe the economic and political power-games far better than I can.

Crises, crises . . . I am tired of crises, the whole hellish catastrophic course the world is on and with which . . . like some kind of moral duty . . . one is supposed to be preoccupied. Catastrophe is a matter for those in power. I went to Argentina with my pocket full of addresses of people with power and I didn't bother to seek them out. I know their vocabulary by heart, their prejudices, their ignorance, their amiable capacity to avoid everything essential.

How terrible the bourgeoisie are, equally unbearable everywhere.

I went to Argentina to meet the powerful and I met one single person utterly without power.

What is important or unimportant? What is constructive or destructive? The catastrophe and its opposite. I hold Juan up against the entire immense block of violence and want and threats of annihilation and let him glow. His knowledge, his will, his dreams.

Juan speaks. I listen. We sit up through the long nights back at home in Esbo and in our rented apartment in Stockholm. He tells me about his life, what it has been like, what it might have been like, what it was going to be like in future. Lilita has stayed behind in Buenos Aires. She is no longer his fiancée, but his wife now and he loves her. My Spanish is much better than it was in those first few weeks in Argentina. I understand most things, the main features at least. Yet the torrent of his words is sometimes like listening to a waterfall, or to music. Through my hearing, my brain (and my heart) registers a sequence of sound signals and I sense or know that each one of them contains something, and together they form a meaningful combination, that together they constitute a message comprehensible to the mind, but I cannot interpret them correctly the moment I hear them. Juan's language is to me like the language of music, and the language of music again is the opposite of the language of politicians; in the former, a cascade of in themselves unintelligible sound-signals, behind which is hidden an eternal landscape of experience with human contact and emotional meaning. While in the latter, the sound signals are wholly intelligible, every word in the politician's speech included in the arsenal of language meaning something, in itself comprehensible to the listener, but behind it is nothing, no meaning, no message, no consolation, nothing but emptiness.

I had a remarkable experience in Prague last spring. I have never been so close to the mystery of music, nor has the mystery ever been so close to its solution, I felt.

Daga and Honsa, our Czech friends, had managed to get us tickets for a sold-out concert by the Prague Philharmonic. When we got to the concert hall, we had no idea what was going to be performed. Music as music, I thought. Perhaps that was so. Anyway, I was not particularly prepared. It was nothing much more than a way to spend the evening. When we sit down and I glance through the programme, I see that we are to listen to Rachmaninov's Second Piano Concerto and Beethoven's Fifth Symphony. Highly conventional, in other words, I think to start with. The members of the orchestra come in one after another and begin to tune their instruments. We sit there, commenting absently on the audience and the lovely *art nouveau* hall, as one does at concerts. Then suddenly I hear within me, like a presentiment, the introductory chords of the piano concerto. I have heard it a hundred times before. I know it by heart, bar by bar, movement by movement. I loved it in my youth. I have hated it. I have despised it, but for many years I have been indifferent to it, played out, a passing phase in my music-listening life. But now it comes back, hurtling itself over me, from my subconscious, before the soloist and conductor have even appeared on the platform, seizing me, shaking me, falling on me. And before I've heard a single note of Rachmaninov, I am already so moved, so filled with what is to come, my eyes brim with tears and I say silently to myself, over and over again: 'I can't cope with this, I won't be able to cope with it.' I feel an impulse to rush out, to leave the hall as fast as I can, but I control myself and remain seated. Then the whole thing starts.

It is a torrent of emotions, and the sentiment and pathos are sentimental and pathetic, just as I have experienced a hundred times before, at times loving it, at times rejecting it, but this time and for the first time ever, overwhelmingly and utterly intelligible, or almost intelligible.

For the first time in my life, I feel that music, symphonic music, is a language in which the notes are letters, the chords words and the bars sentences, and I feel in some marvellous way that I understand the language, or almost understand it. Music is a waterfall and, like the waterfall, seems to conceal a mystery, as much sound as uninterrupted movement, the roar of the water, the roar of the notes, and the roar not just a roar but an endless combination of sound particles, each and every one distinguishable, intelligible, meaningful in itself as well as in its context.

(The passionate great waterfall at Iguazú in Misiones in northern Argentina, far up in the north on the borders of Brazil, and there among the enormous fat iguanas and millions of butterflies in clumps like scavengers, under the burning sun, in the damp suffocating air, Juan was close to abandoning me, the terror, the anguish, among the tropical trees, on the edge of the waterfall, in that tremendous noise, Juan as Hermes, the messenger of life, distancing himself from me, and the voice of death behind the foaming curtain of roaring water, calling me on, Garganta del Diablo, the Devil's Throat, and going in there, taking the step through the curtain of water, through the foam, right through the thundering voices of water, calling, urging, to pass through the curtain of water, at least to solve the mystery of life and death, but refusing this time too, because of Hermes, for the sake of Juan's face, his eyes, the hand that touched . . . like the magnet of life touching, continuously, again and again . . . the caress of life vanquishing the roar of death . . .)

. . . For the first time in my life I was on a level with the pathos and sentimentality of Rachmaninov and it is a question of experience and life. The language of notes, the language of experience. Now I know what you are talking about, at last I know what you are talking about; music is a code and the key is called experience. Behind your note-language is feeling and I recognize that feeling, for even if your experience is quite unlike mine, it has been accompanied by a feeling and that feeling is unintelligible, because we have it in common.

After the interval, on that remarkable but superficially wholly undramatic spring evening in Prague, as the orchestra thunders out Beethoven's Fifth, every bar also familiar to me since my youth, my receptivity has been sharpened to an extreme, although the emotional tension has already slackened considerably. He has a language of his own, Beethoven, and I understand that language, or almost understand it. The instruments converse, the violins indicating something, eagerly and stubbornly, like children or sea-birds on spring evenings, and the 'cellos reply, subduing, engrossing, with an admixture of thoughtfulness, adulthood. Again and again, the flute interrupts with an urgent message, and then suddenly the whole rushing torrent is off, borne by trumpets and kettle-drums, the conversing of many voices, the polyphonic discussion, the flowering of a hundred blooms, movement, counter-movement, final movement, question and response, counter-question and objection, hesitancy, afterthought, whim, final summary, conclusion. Applause. The language of sound, the curtain of notes. Parting the curtain of notes like a screen of glass pearls and finding behind it a human being speaking in a hundred voices, sounds, notes, a human landscape, the landscape of language.

We have grown into a landscape of language of our own, Juan and I, at first with hardly any elements of ordinary spoken language. It was the language of deeds, of emotions, expressed in eyes, lips and physical movements. In that way, we got to know each other, and knew each other so well that when we eventually had a common spoken language – Spanish – it became largely a means by which we could confirm what we already knew about each other, what we had already told each other about ourselves in the other way. The landscape went straight through us. We were both there. We had it in common. In Stockholm, Juan dreamt my dream. In Salta, he understood and reacted to my thoughts, on the other side of the borders of sleep, I awake, he asleep, but even in sleep attentive to what was going on in my brain, my silent agreement, in Swedish, to cap it all, as if my sensitivity responded to his feeling. A continuous conversation through perception.

Later, when we were to determine our common position in relation to the outside world, our language became necessary, indispensable, more important than anything else.

Juan speaks. I listen. At home in Esbo, in our rented apartment in Stockholm, he gets excited and cannot communicate. He draws me to him and our faces are so close to each other that his hair brushes mine. I hold his hand. He holds mine. I sit on the chair, he on the floor in front of me, resting his arms on my knees. He lies in bed, I sit on the edge, leaning over his naked chest. He speaks. I listen. I ask. He responds. It is the nights, the still nights, always at night, for the night is his time of vigil and emotional life.

His paternal grandfather came from Sicily some time at the end of the nineteenth century. His mother comes from Formosa, the northernmost province on the borders of Paraguay. He is Italian on his father's side and has an Italian surname. On his mother's side he is half-Indian, as his grandmother was Indian.

The human sea. The cross-currents, unceasing currents without end. Human beings like waves from one part of the world to another, people in currents, the currents created by need and the will to live and dreams of the future, that eternal dream. I might have gone to Sicily and met a Sicilian. I might have gone to Formosa and met an Indian. I went to Buenos Aires and met their combination. Blood ties. Mixtures of blood.

Juan's grandfather went northwards in his search for work, across La Pampa, through the Argentinian wilderness. Finally he came to Misiones and was made an offer he could not refuse. He was a handsome man of about twenty, strong, courageous and full of life. The Indians in Misiones, who felt their blood had been thinned out by generations of inbreeding, realized that the whole future of their tribe was in danger, and they saw in Juan's magnificent grandfather a chance of salvation. Consequently they asked him (politely? a little shyly, perhaps) whether he would be willing to stay with them for a while to inject some of his strong, fresh, European blood into the veins of their descendants. He is said to have hesitated, but only for a moment, for when he looked round, he found himself surrounded by beautiful young Indian women, in small groups, in long rows, a sea of young women standing in silence, gazing at him expectantly. He agreed without a second though.

Juan's grandfather stayed with the Indians in Misiones for many years and they were delighted with the fruits of his labours. A large number of children, slightly lighter in hue than their predecessors, were born to the village, and they were all slightly stronger, slightly more lively and slightly more intelligent than the children born before the appearance of Juan's grandfather. The Indians loved the light colour of their children's skin, for they considered that many of their difficulties and much of their wretchedness were due to their dark skins. It was like living the carefree life of a bull, taking each day as it came, and for quite a long time Juan's grandfather felt as if he had at last found his place in life. He was so appreciated in the exercise of his profession, so invaluable did the Indians think he was to the future of their tribe, that one day, to make quite sure, they cut his Achilles tendons, so that he should not disappear by mistake, or even take it into his head to escape.

It was at this stage that he began to grow thoughtful, and the women no longer seemed so beautiful; quite simply everything began to lose its flavour. And although his desire was still indefatigable and unfailing strength remained between his thighs, he realized that one morning he would inevitably wake up an old man. What would happen then? The women would no longer want to know of him, and the men would be aggressive and set about him with their weapons. So best to leave now, while the time was ripe.

One starry night, he left, limping on his semi-healed tendons, gradually making his way back to Buenos Aires, and from there to the little town of Chivilcoy, where he married and became a house-owner in his old age. Out of the legend of the wonderful youth of Juan's grandfather, some of Juan's own character was to take shape, more than half a century later. Juan's grandmother? Juan said nothing about her.

Juan's mother was called Mercedes. Today she is sixty-eight years old. What was her girlhood like? What was it like in Formosa when the First World War was raging in Europe and Argentina's affairs were being managed or mismanaged by the idealistic Leandro N.

Alem and the realistic Hipólito Yrigoyen? Juan does not know. Mercedes has told them nothing. Your maternal grandmother and grandfather, then, what were they like? Juan doesn't know that, either. Mercedes has said nothing about them. Presumably, even she doesn't know. It is hard to get Mercedes to talk about her childhood. She doesn't want to remember, as things are so much better for her now. She grew up in an asylum. She had an elder sister who died young of tuberculosis and general overwork, or malnutrition.

When the two girls were about fourteen, they were placed in domestic service with a well-to-do family. That was nothing much to remember, either. A hard life, little food and a great deal of work. Yes, there was one thing! If the girls did not do well enough, if they had been too slow, or careless, or in some other way had caused displeasure to the family, they were punished in a special way. The Señora strewed the seeds of dried maize over the stone floor. Dried maize is very hard and sharp. The girls were ordered to their knees on this bed of dried maize. There they had to stay for hour after hour, humbly, until they had changed their minds, had promised to improve, until the skin on their knees was reduced to bloodstained tatters.

Mercedes was nineteen when she married Marcelo, Juan's father. She gave birth in swift succession to two children, Rosa and Ramon. Then twenty years were to go by before Juan appeared. Rosa was for a long time a hairdresser in Buenos Aires in the working-class area of La Boca and then, at a mature age, she married a comparatively wealthy widower, Griseldo, who had come up the hard way. He was almost the same age as Mercedes. They had a little son called Gabriel, in whom was combined everything usually expected of children of older parents, a spoilt, precocious, charming little harum-scarum.

Ramon is a pilot. Yes? And more? Nothing more. Juan didn't want to talk about him. He broke off contact with his elder brother a long time ago. Why?

'Not worth talking about. He's no longer my brother.'

'But why, Juan? Can't you say why?'

'OK then. He's not worth having as a brother, because when he got married and had a family of his own, he stopped bothering about our mother. He started treating Mercedes condescendingly, or as if she weren't there, and I can't forgive him that. A son who neglects his mother, what kind of a person is that? Don't you see, I simply had to break off relations with him?'

No, to be honest, I don't really see, but neither do I get involved in

61

an argument about it, but accept it. Accept Juan. As always. Everything about Juan.

Marcelo was fifty when Juan was born. Now he is seventy-three. Juan, like his nephew Gabriel, was also a child of older parents, and that throws some light on his character, at least explaining why Lilita often accuses him of being spoilt. She thinks he is self-absorbed, temperamental and quick to demand service of those around him. But she loves him, she takes him for what he is. The relatives maintain that Juan is a faithful reflection of his father, and just as Lilita accepts Juan did later – preferred to live at night and sleep by day.

Marcelo is an old man, full of vitality. His thinning hair is quite white, he has a pot-belly and is rather short, much shorter than I am. His friends call him '*búho*', the owl. That is because he has always – as Juan did later – preferred to life at night and sleep by day.

The house in Chivilcoy is full of memories. Simple memories, but cherished, bright milestones in the grey ordinariness of poverty. Marcelo searches in drawers, in small boxes, and finds two photographs of himself, pictures from his youth or manhood.

In one, he is with friends in the park in Buenos Aires, beneath a eucalyptus tree, in the 'thirties or thereabouts. He is dressed like a dandy, a hat on his head, the brim well down over his forehead, cigarette dangling from the corner of his mouth. His expression is relaxed, but proud, challenging, a good-looking man, very self-confident. The three friends are almost exactly alike. Why do my thoughts go to Al Capone and his gang? It is Sunday. They are out on their Sunday round, strolling about for a while, having a good time. Workers in their Sunday best, and more, Argentinians, *porteños*. There they stand, four cheerful friends, and the Sunday sun is shining, an outdoor café just visible in the background. It is over forty years ago and yet a faint whiff of the big city world can be sensed, invisible and forbidden to the children of better families, but nevertheless a whole world and full of possibilities. The pickpocket has status there, and the pimp is king.

The other photograph has been cut in half. Something or someone standing beside Marcelo has gone and been destroyed. Marcelo fiddles about with the photograph and laughs smugly, looking round expectantly, hoping to be persuaded to show it. Mercedes sighs rather wearily, as she's seen all this many times before. Juan scolds his father, thinking him foolish. Marcelo takes me over into a corner and shows me the photo. In it, he is somewhat older than in the picture with his friends, but just as flashily dressed in hat and tie, a cigarette between his fingers. His expression is equally proud, equally self-satisfied, his look challenging, turned to the right, towards the missing part of the photograph. Then he tells me, out loud so that the whole room can hear. A woman was standing beside him, young, wonderfully beautiful. The trouble is that the picture was taken after he was married to Mercedes, yet he had felt a great need to keep it as a souvenir. What should he do? He didn't want to hurt Mercedes, as he loved her. In the end, he had arrived at this solution to satisfy all parties. Anyway, he still had the memory of the girl in his heart, and it's a good photo, isn't it? Mercedes sighs again and smiles wearily. It's a long time ago. She isn't the slightest bit jealous any more. Never was, actually. In Argentina, it is not a woman's way to be jealous. Nothing would work if that were so. Lilita has learnt the same lesson. Lilita looks at Juan in exactly the same way as Mercedes once looked at Marcelo. Men are men and it's up to women to adapt to them.

Marcelo had been a bus driver, *colectivo*, in Buenos Aires during the first years of their marriage. Every month, he had put aside a sum of money to be able to purchase his own bus and later on, eventually, become the owner of a whole bus and a line of his own, for in those days public transport was all privately owned. But just as he saw his dream beginning to come true, when he had saved enough money to be able to realize his dream of a bus of his own, bus transport was suddenly nationalized and his dream shattered.

Marcelo was both disappointed and angry, so decided to shake the dust of the city off his feet. He collected up his family, his few possessions and moved back to Chivilcoy and the family house, where he has stayed ever since. The *porteño* became *campesino*, the city-dweller became a countryman. He had a little chicken-farm and a garden, the profit from which was just sufficient for a living. Sometimes not even that. He has got rid of the chickens now and lives on a pension. He is not alone with Mercedes. There are cousins across the road, and his sister, a widow, now lives in a small farm cottage. Her name is Elena.

Mercelo's youth? That was just the same as for everyone else with no money or education. Survival was the most important aim. A day at a time. A day and a night at a time. Marcelo was a full-time poker-player, a ferociously successful poker-player, making his living that way for many years. He cheated if necessary, anyhow when he came across fools, foreigners, or inexperienced sons of rich men on the run or looking for adventure. He played with marked cards, aces up his sleeves and in his trouser waistband, a full flush under his jacket, nimble-fingered as hell, he was. Was he never caught? No, no, only the stupid get caught. Marcelo was not stupid.

Neither was Juan stupid. He was like his father, quick to learn, quick-thinking, constantly prepared to adopt to the demands of the situation, formed by an irrepressible desire to live, a tremendous will to survive.

Juan was born in Chivilcoy, grew up in Chivilcoy and went to school in Chivilcoy. He had left school when he was fourteen and, as he was a gifted child, both his teacher and his family thought he should continue in secondary school, better himself with learning, become something grand, anyway something better than a poker-player and chicken-farmer.

He himself wanted to. Or did he really? Did he know what he wanted?

He ran away from home the year he left school and was away a whole month without his parents having the slightest idea where he was. That was the first time, and he was no more than fourteen. When he was sixteen he had run away so many times he already regarded himself quite independent, a grown man with considerable experience, an independent entrepreneur in the big city of Buenos Aires.

Juan remembers his childhood as a happy time. Many of us do that, perhaps most people, often just for memory's sake, for memory is like that, and Juan knows it. So he doesn't say: 'My parents never quarrelled' or 'My parents were always happy.' Instead he says: 'I have suppressed troubles and difficulties, because I'm a person with a positive outlook on life and I want to remember the positive and good things.'

Even a very small child can also experience poverty in the home, poverty as an atmosphere; it can be sensed and a child can be imprinted by it even in the cradle, in the same way as a child is imprinted by love or violence or indifference. Juan has a picture in his mind, silent, wordless, clear though rather blurred at the edges, of being an infant in his cot and lying in the dark little room between the kitchen and the living-room, and he remembers the sense of want, a strong but indefinite feeling of want and shortage, that something was missing – perhaps it was hunger. Yet it was not a question of poverty as suffering, but poverty as a way of life, hard but bearable, a condition. For where poverty is compensated for by love, it must be almost total to be regarded as absolute suffering.

Later on, when he was about five or six, he remembers the same room and the same bed and the only window in the room, small and cut out of the wall high up by the ceiling. The window is open and a warm wind is blowing in. It is December, high summer and Christmas time, and he is lying there gasping in the heat and listening to the explosions up in the roof when the zinc plates warp in the heat of the sun. He lies staring at the window waiting for *los reyes magos*, the three kings, to appear – for in Argentina the three wise men come with gifts at Christmas. He is lying there in tense expectation, and like children at Christmas all over the world, he is dreaming about everything he wishes for, but his dreams are in vain. For Christmas is not for the poor.

The few times *los reyes magos* actually appear or pass by invisibly and leave something behind them, they leave only a small bag of cheap sweets or something Mercedes has baked, or something equally poor and modest and uninteresting in comparison with the harvest of gifts gathered by better-off neighbouring children and school-friends. Juan is imprinted by poverty.

One night it is so hot he cannot sleep. He lies tossing and turning in bed, trying to find a spot where the heat is less unendurable, and he stretches his leg over the side of his bed to feel the cool of the floor against the sole of his foot. Then the square of the window is suddenly filled with a blinding white light, a formation of light like a white ball, hurtling into the room and striking his foot on the floor like an electric shock. He doesn't understand what it is. Neither has he ever understood since. It is inexplicable. Magical. The powers.

They definitely exist in reality, the powers. There are definitely veins of inexplicabilities running through life, at least for those who look out for them. Reality is definitely charged with magic, with mystical force. Hadn't Marcelo himself in his youth, during his nomadic years in Argentina, far up in Misiones, where the humid heat is far more terrible than in Chivilcoy – hadn't he seen an evil spirit with his own eyes, a hideously forbidding creature coming towards him along the road at dusk, laughing mockingly and then disappearing, dissolving into nothing.

And what about José's goat, his father's cousin's goat, which was tethered on the grass just by the corner of the house? What about that? It got loose one night and José heard it and ran out into the moonlight to catch it and saw the goat disappearing round the corner of the house, its tether dragging behind it. José chased the goat round and round the house, but the goat was always too quick and the chain, wriggling and whipping in the gravel, kept slipping out of his hands. When José was exhausted, the clatter of goat's hoofs and the rattle of the chain suddenly stopped and there was complete silence. Gasping, José stopped and stood still for a moment, getting his breath back, leaning against the house. And there, in the moonlight, he sees the goat calmly grazing in its usual place, as if nothing had happened. When he goes over to it to tether it again, he sees to his astonishment and fear that it is still tethered in the usual careful way in which he had tethered it the evening before. The goat had been in league with the powers.

Everything has a soul. There are fine tracks of nerves along the railway lines, which make the rails feel pain when the train thunders along them. He is sorry for the rails. He is sorry for the tyres of cars, too, as he is convinced it hurts when they tear against the asphalt or strike stones on the road.

He doesn't laugh when he says this; on the contrary, he is profoundly serious, thoughtful. He doesn't disassociate himself from the childish mistakes of his past, doesn't even smile in a superior way; he is loyal to himself. Now. Always.

'How can I, when I was so terribly sensitive as a child, be so hard now I'm adult?' he asks.

'You're not hard, Juan.'

He is rather upset by this statement.

'Of course I'm hard! Do you think I'd have managed, do you think I'd have been able to be what I am, if I hadn't been hard? With a life like mine? Among people like that?'

'You made yourself hard, but you're not hard.'

He sighs. He agrees with me in the end. Perhaps it is as I say. He is not as hard as he wants to be.

One day when he is about five or six years old, he is sitting in the back yard of his father's house, playing with stones in the gravel. The sun is burning and it is oppressively hot. He is alone. He is bored. He holds the stones in one hand and throws them with the other. Six feet. Nine feet. With bored movements in bored idleness. Suddenly one of the stones comes alive. It doesn't stay where it has fallen, in the gravel with all the other stones, but takes off and flies back, hitting him on the cheekbone just below his left eye. He has never seen stones come alive before. But he knows what it is. He is living in a magical world and the powers are playing their games. The powers have been in an excited mood and wished to play a trick on him, because he was sitting there in the sun, apparently so sluggish and listless and indifferent. His cheekbone hurts. Reality isn't what it appears to be. There are forces in the invisible which people don't control. On the contrary, those forces control people. He is in contact with them, and feels their presence very strongly. Will always do so.

There are other forces controlling people. Even in infancy, he was aware of their presence in his body. Later he would be obsessed by them, obsessed to the extent that for long spells they completely determine his way of life. At the age of three, he feels desire for his mother when she takes him into her bed. He caresses her breasts and feels sweet satisfaction. Irritably but patiently, she pushes his small hands away, again and again.

At the age of six, he discovers his own sex organ. One night, sixteen years later, he confides in me that his organ is a trifle crooked when erect because he masturbated so much in childhood. I doubt it, but as usual he is difficult to dissuade from his beliefs. As a twelve- or thirteen-year-old, he attempts a sex act with a girl of the same age. Is she as keen as he is? Naturally. It succeeds beyond all expectations. He is astonished by an orgasm that fills him with an unspeakable sense of happiness. A colourless viscous liquid trickles out of his organ, which is still childish and undeveloped.

When he is fifteen, he starts an affair with a slightly older girl living in the neighbouring house across the yard. She comes from a different social class. Her parents are rather refined and count themselves among the bourgeoisie. There would be a terrible scandal if their relationship were found out.

In the darkness of the night, he climbs out of the window of his father's house, slips across the yard and makes his way up the drainpipe into her room, like any other Romeo. A light has been burning invitingly all evening in her window. But her parents' room is dangerously close. He helps her down the drainpipe and leads her across the yard to the henhouse, and there they carry out a jubilant sexual act, the hens cackling and carrying on.

The following day, the girl's mother is in the baker's shop, boasting of her daughter's diligence and splendid qualities, self-important and domineering in that insufferable way of bourgeois wives. She sits up late doing her homework at night, the dear girl, her mother explains in a high, self-confident voice. Last night, for instance, her light was on until dawn. She had stayed awake herself, the mother, so she knew for certain. But, she adds, slightly thoughtfully, at about one o'clock she really did think there were thieves in Marcelo's henhouse, because the hens were making a dreadful noise.

'I slept with her almost every night that summer,' says Juan.

'In the henhouse?'

'In the henhouse.'

'Must have been an exciting time for the hens?'

'The hens? In the end they went crazy with excitement as soon as they heard us creeping out into the yard, and they laid eggs as never before. To Dad's surprise and joy.'

'You were a good son.'

'I've always tried to help wherever I could. Not exactly in every way possible, but with the means within my control.'

'*Eres un artista cultural, pero yo soy un artista sexual.* You're an artist in the field of culture, while I'm an artist in the field of sex.'

'I've never been able to subjugate myself. What is the unbearable in life is not having a rough time, but being dependent. Freedom is a thousand times more valuable than security and prosperity. Happiness isn't found in material things, but in a clear conscience.'

'And you've a clear conscience?'

'My conscience is perfectly clear. That's why among other things, unlike you, I have no problems sleeping.'

Then he immediately starts telling me about the long and well-planned escape from the parental home.

He simply couldn't stay on at home any longer, simply couldn't. On the other hand, he didn't want to hurt his old parents, because he loved them and knew they loved him. It was a difficult decision to make. He was only fourteen. He decided to do it gradually, to let them get used to his absence in stages, deciding on a break in small portions, a gentle transfer. He thought that would be less painful for Mercedes and Marcelo.

He couldn't stand being a burden on his parents, and then there was also this business of freedom, how valuable it was? Buenos Aires tempted him as nothing else in his life had ever tempted him. That was where he was going. He had to go there. It was not only the city of opportunities, it was first and foremost where he could live. There was nothing in Chivilcoy. Chivilcoy was a dull town, a sleepy town, a town for people with no imagination, unable to perceive alternative or more exciting possibilities than the dreary day-to-day round, the petit bourgeois struggle for daily bread, fairly meanly apportioned at that.

Chivilcoy was a small town, musty and stagnant in the way small towns are. It was not possible to live there.

But worst of all were the sacrifices his parents made. He became desperate when he saw what they did for his sake, when he found out that they denied themselves so that he should benefit. He couldn't bear such self-denial by people he loved. There were needy days of shortage when Marcelo ate nothing, maintaining he wasn't hungry, just so that Juan should have enough to eat. He couldn't go on existing in that way, loafing about and exploiting their love. In poor homes, everyone who is able to has to do right by himself, or else leave, go out into the world to learn to stand on his own feet. That's what it was like. That's what it had always been like.

In any case, although he no longer felt like one, in his parents' eyes he was still a child. That was also hard to endure in the long run, exposing himself to consideration and care which began to feel increasingly suffocating because it corresponded less and less to his own ideas of himself as an adult.

So then it was a matter of taking the train to Buenos Aires, always as a stowaway. Each time he returned home, he was equally welcome, a beloved object of anxiety, while at the same time his bid for freedom and desire for independence was respected. He himself was grateful for their love and anxiety, while at the same time he was fully aware of the value of being respected for his need for freedom. In this way he came to experience something which on the whole was unusual, a harmonious rebellion against the older generation, based not only on mutual wisdom and mutual consideration, but most of all on mutual love, the love that is sufficiently strong and primordial not to be found wanting.

Juan wanted to take the train to Buenos Aires to go to the school of life. At first, he could always say he was going to see his older sister, but he no more wished to be a burden on Rosa than he had wished to be a burden to his parents. He wanted to stand on his own feet and was to learn very soon how terribly difficult and complicated that was for someone who had nothing and knew practically nothing worth anything to circles in which there was money.

When the guard came round to clip the tickets, Juan was clinging to the accordion-shaped connection between two carriages, the wind tearing at his shirt and hair. He had to regard it all as an exciting adventure, because if the thought of falling off and killing himself ever took hold, he was as good as lost. There was nothing much to stand on nor much to cling to, but he had learnt how to do it from an older friend. In actual fact the trick was well-known to all rail stowaways in Argentina. He had a fellow-criminal who warned him when the guard was coming, a thin little creature of about ten, one of the wretched ragged little urchins who populate the trains of Argentina, selling chocolate or aspirins or anything for a miniscule profit, forced by a human need so deep that it could no longer be counted in accepted social contexts. But he was a bright cheerful boy and Juan always felt greater solidarity with him than with the other rather more prosperous passengers on the train. One day, the boy wasn't there any more. Juan asked a small colleague in the trade what had happened and was told that his friend and confidant had fallen off the train and been killed in a desperate attempt to escape the police, who were after him. Juan will never forget him. He remembers him with pain, not only because of his friendship and loyalty, but because it was his first real encounter with the cruelty of human society, the grimness of life.

Buenos Aires is like a large, no, an immense head on a well-developed but somewhat neglected and ill-clad body. Buenos Aires is a severely overpopulated city. Over a third of the whole poulation of Argentina tries to make a living there. Over the centuries, people have poured into it from both the east, largely across the sea from Italy and Spain, and from the west, from the interior of Argentina. Argentina is a rich country and its reputation for riches has travelled the world, but the wealth is largely owned by people of the kind and class that have no wish to share it. Buenos Aires is only an ordinary big city as far as cities go. It is not easy to make your way in Argentina if you arrive empty-handed, however strong or persevering or willing to work those hands are. Buenos Aires is not the city of inexhaustible opportunities, as is perhaps thought and hoped in the wretchedness of somewhere far away in Chaco or Tucumán.

And yet every year, people in vast numbers move into Buenos Aires. They have so little to lose and things could hardly be worse than their poverty out in the country. Sometimes they are. It is not difficult to go under in a Latin American city. Thus Juan is in good company. He is no exception; on the contrary, from the start his destiny has been extremely trivial and ordinary. His depressing task is to make his way on exactly the same miserable terms that have applied to millions of others before him, and after him, in hopeless sequence. Hunger drives most of them, need drives them all. Juan was no exception. He came like hundreds or thousands of young boys come every year from the country to the city, finally driven by want and poverty, however much self-esteem asserts itself with arguments and talk of the need for freedom. For soon, very soon for many of them, even freedom shows its true face; that face is not beautiful, but a cruel grinning mask of hunger, exposure and humiliation.

There was so much to see, so much to experience, so much to learn in Buenos Aires. Juan was inordinately inquisitive and totally without means, but at the same time intelligent and flexible, charming and impatient. This soon, and almost of its own volition, gave his life its direction. Childhood in Chivilcoy slowly and imperceptibly began to become, or to be remodelled into, a bright memory, full of security, full of joy, full of magical experience.

He lived on the street. When he was first in the capital, he knew no one. He was alone. But gradually he became aware that there were other youths in the same situation as he was. His loneliness ceased and was replaced by something else, a hard-driven and for that reason a much more solid and valuable fellowship. Like him, they had come from the country, from other towns, from other parts of Argentina, with the same indistinct aim as his, to live and learn, or more purposefully to look for work. But it was the same for all of them, they lacked money and any contact with the section of society that had money. A brotherhood arose among them, the solidarity of need driving them to share everything equally. This gave them a kind of security, a kind of safety in their exposed position, and meant human warmth in a hard and hostile world.

'Was that when you became a taxi-boy?'

'No, that was earlier, in Mar del Plata, really, the first time I ran away.'

'When you were fourteen?'

'Yes, I was fourteen at the time.'

In Argentina, everyone talks about Mar del Plata. It is the holiday town, the tourist town, the summer paradise, where everyone goes if the opportunity arises. It is on the Atlantic coast, just south of Buenos Aires, a few hours by car from Chivilcoy. Juan had heard many wonderful stories about Mar del Plata; in his mind it was a place in the sun, his dream town, and he longed to go there.

After he left school, he used to stand on the street-corner near Marcelo's house and watch the stream of cars full of holiday-makers coming from the north and passing through Chivilcoy on their way to Mar del Plata. One day he was standing there with a friend of his own age, and the temptation was too much for them. They thumbed for a lift, a car stopped and off they went, travellers with no luggage.

For Juan and his friend, Mar del Plata was the first and determining confrontation with harsh reality. Hitherto they had never considered that the person who has nothing shall be given nothing, or that nothing is free in this world. Neither food, nor house-room. They spent the first day down on the *playa*, in the sun among people, and they felt no want, they were together, it was fun. But when night came, they had nowhere to go. They were hungry. Suddenly, they were quite alone. No one cared about them. They had heard about lovely days in Mar del Plata, with sun and warm winds and bathing in the blue Atlantic, but they had never heard about the biting night cold. They lay on the deserted *playa* in their tee-shirts and jeans, on the sand, under the stars, shivering and wishing they were back home. They were cold. They couldn't sleep. Perhaps reality does sometimes correspond to dreams for those who have money, but for those without, reality always has the same cruel awakening to offer in a cold and deserted world.

The following day, Juan and his friend made the acquaintance of an elderly man in charge of the toilets on the beach. He was kind and understanding, shared his food with them, and when evening came and the beach was closed for the night, after the tourists had long since gone off to their restaurants and nightclubs, their hotels and boarding houses, he unlocked the place for Juan and his friend so that they had somewhere to go. Sitting on the lowered lids of the toilets, leaning against the wall, each in his own cubby-hole, they slept night after night for almost a month. Among the smells. But sheltered from the cold and the wind.

How is it possible? I ask. A lavatory seat as a bed? For several weeks? Sitting too? Why didn't you go home? We didn't want to go home. It was as simple as that, he replies. For the person who has nothing, but is nevertheless determined to survive, everything is possible. It's as simple as that.

One night Juan is roaming round the streets of Mar del Plata on his own. He passes a car which has broken down, a large Mercedes-Benz. A distinguished-looking middle-aged man beckons to him and asks for help to get the car started. Juan pushes. When the engine starts, the man invites Juan for a ride. Juan gets into the car. The man makes a suggestion. Juan doesn't really understand, has never really even considered such a possibility. He hesitates. The man offers him money, quite a lot of money, too, to anyone who has nothing. Why not, thinks Juan, and agrees.

That was how it started. He was fourteen years old that summer.

Being a taxi-boy – *ser taxi-boy* – was his chief means of livelihood for many years to come. At first it was very difficult, not so much because it should have been shameful or distasteful, but because at the time he didn't know how or where to pick up customers. He had done his first apprenticeship in Mar del Plata and that had gone well. He had a little money in his pocket, and he and his friend had no need actually to starve any longer. Naturally his friend wondered where the money that suddenly began to pour in came from, and he cooked up some appropriate story. It never occurred to him to tell the truth, neither then, nor since. There were quite a few advantages in this way of earning money, and when all was said and done, practically no disadvantages, not that he could see, anyhow. But that was his business. He was determined to go on. He went to Chivilcoy for a while to rest, then set off for Buenos Aires, where the gates to the school of life stood wide open. He wanted to graduate in that school.

But he was new to Buenos Aires, hitherto unknown country to him. So at first he had to go whichever way his nose led him and take whatever chances arose. He grew thinner. He was nearly always hungry. He could never plan for more than twelve hours ahead at the most, and he never knew where he would sleep when he was tired, or whether he would even have a chance to sleep at all. Every day was as new as a day can be. Nowadays he has a thousand friends in Buenos Aires and he knows the capital like the back of his hand. But at that time he had no friends at all, or at least no one he knew sufficiently well to be able to trust. The only thing he knew with any certainty was that towards midnight he would be out on the street hunting for prey. Night after night. The same, year after year, and yet that was better than at home in Chivilcoy. It was freedom.

He went to the school of life. He learnt an enormous amount about human beings, the demands made by human beings, and the art of surviving. But he learnt practically nothing that might be of use to him later on in the working world, the 'real' world where society functions.

For a year, he went on a course to train as an electrician. Griseldo managed to persuade him to do it. He had no difficulty mastering the techniques and the actual craft; on the contrary, he was good with his hands and liked messing about with meters and electrical apparatus. But he didn't want to be an electrician. So he abandoned the course without any papers to say what he had learnt and what he was able to do. That was his education. Only reluctantly would he open a book. But he signed his name self-consciously with a great many scrolls and flourishes. He preferred to read the book of life.

Despite all this, in time he became a professional, but at an activity which no society cared to count as an 'honest job', and which all upright citizens everywhere always regarded with contempt or at best with compassion.

Juan accepted neither the contempt nor the compassion. He was proud and self-confident. He signed his name with a great many flourishes. He did not demand much of his fellow men, but he did demand to be treated like a human being, worth neither more nor less than others. He maintains I was the first to do that without reservation. That was the beginning of our friendship, and the end of his career as a taxi-boy.

While Juan was in Europe, we talked almost every day – or every night – about this. Not surprisingly, he liked philosophizing about prostitution, indeed, was sometimes utterly obsessed by the subject and able to talk about it for hours. It was clearly the first time he felt he could talk freely from the heart, with no risk of reprisal or reprimands. I had gained his confidence, I listened and accepted. I neither moralized nor screwed up my nose. When Claudio realized what Juan had got up to at night, he had been so upset that they had come to blows. He had hit Juan, his young friend and protégé. That was a painful memory. And naturally Lilita, always so outwardly calm and matter-of-fact, deep down was both miserable and much affected. She was magnificent, understanding everything and forgiving everything in her love, but she was a woman, his fiancée, and had some claim to consideration; the reality had to be dressed up a little for her to be able to endure it. It was different with me.

At first he talked about prostitution exclusively as a matter concerning women, talking only about female experiences, female activities, which finally became confusing. Did he really not regard his own activities as prostitution? And if not, how did he regard them? When I finally asked him whether *ser taxi-boy*, being a taxi-boy, was not prostitution just as much as *ser puta*, being a whore, he was silent for a while, staring at me, his beautiful black eyes suddenly appearing even blacker, and I presumed he had either not really understood my

74

question, or else had been upset by it. When he answered, it was with one single world. 'Naturally,' he said, refraining from any further explanations, and I realized that despite his openness, this was because it was a difficult and painful subject.

To be able to talk about his life as a prostitute, he had to maintain a distance from it and the only logical and natural distance to hand in this case was the distance between his male sex and the female sex of his prostitute colleague. For prostitution meant, and generally had always meant, selling your body to a man, a genuine female activity, but usually a heterosexual function. Although it was disparaged everywhere from a social and moral angle, it nevertheless had a certain status as a heretosexual function, a certain nimbus; it was never good to be a whore, but as a whore one could nevertheless refer to history, whether your name was Madame Dubarry, Madame de Maintenon or Isabella Perón. On the other hand, there was no romantic aura about homosexual prostitution or boy-prostitution and never had been; from start to finish that was simply obscene and degenerate. In other words, it was easier to preserve your self-respect and talk about your experiences as a prostitute if you did so as if it were really a question of female activity, for in that way they seemed less of a social and moral burden. At the same time you had a chance of protecting to some extent your own severely strained male identification by transferring part of your experiences to female experiences, thus thrusting them aside on to a female experience level, which you imagined was not really your concern.

The primary concern of a prostitute who wishes to survive is generally just the level of development of her ability to protect her personal integrity, her identity as a person. In boy-prostitution, it is also always a question of how well you managed to protect your own male sexual identity. Many do not manage to. Juan has.

Night after night, he emphasizes that, in his opinion and in his experience, it is not primarily financial or social need that drives a woman on to the streets. This may be so in certain cases, but it is usually something else, a profound and uncontrollable sexual need. I doubted this. According to my social-moral upbringing, prostitution was essentially a direct result of the social injustice of a class society.

'Why is there prostitution in Sweden, then?' Juan says immediately.

That was the autumn when we were living together in Stockholm. We had an apartment on the south side of the city, by the water below

75

Hornstull. At first Juan was frightened or unwilling to go out into town on his own, but I finally persuaded him, and on the very first evening, as if attracted by an invisible magnet, he had made his way up to Malmskillnad Street and had at once understood what was going on there. He had stood there for quite a time, observing the girls disappearing with their customers and then returning, only to vanish again. He had even spoken to one of them, when it turned out she knew a little Spanish. That was his inquisitiveness. And he was – so to speak – on his mother's street. I protested that the girls in Malmskillnad Street were mostly drug addicts practising prostitution to pay for their drugs. He just smiled and shook his head. He knew there were other variations and not just what happened in the porn clubs.

We went to porn clubs a great deal, in fact so often that in the end we were both bored rigid with this soulless form of pastime. And yet it was practically the only form of entertainment Juan's unilingual state allowed us. There were no Spanish films on in Stockholm. The theatre meant nothing to him at all, and my Swedish friends did not speak Spanish. I was too old for discotheques, so it came down to endless goggling at sex organs and live sex shows. For a while we tried to establish aesthetic and philosophical viewpoints on it all, to make it more meaningful, but in the long run that also seemed shabby. We watched striptease and sex-act artists in action. We appraised and praised. We compared. But the variations were not great and in the end it was not possible to conceal that this pleasure was fundamentally totally hollow. When I asked Juan whether he would perform publicly if offered money to do so, he replied 'yes' without a second's thought, yes, he surely would. He had no inhibitions in that respect. He had no inhibitions in general in that world.

I noticed that as soon as he entered a porn club he changed in an amazing way, his self-respect increasing quite dramatically, his movements quite unaffected by the artificial velvet-draped murkiness typical of such places, among the heavily made-up professional women in their peculiar professional clothes. He was neither embarrassed, shy, loud-voiced nor haughty, as most men become in such surroundings, myself included. He appeared at home, calm and self-confident, and I realized that at last he could feel he was among friends in a real sense, a kind of companionable fellowship, a security in what was recognizable and familiar, a counterweight to the cold inpenetrable alienation he experienced with my circle of intellectual friends. He was imprinted. He knew a great deal about his trade.

'It gets like a drug in the end and you can't stop,' he says, still talking about female prostitution. 'On the contrary, the need grows and you demand larger and larger doses. Paid sexuality.'

He was talking about prostitutes who earned enough to live on, indeed more than enough, in three of the seven days of the week. Where were they on the other days? At home resting with a cup of strong tea and a good book? Not likely. Out on the streets, on those days too. You just can't stop. You have to do it. Not just because of physical need, but also because of the irresistible temptation of easily earned money. And easy come, easy go.

Juan knew a great many prostitutes in Buenos Aires. There were intelligent ones and foolish ones, beautiful and less beautiful, younger and older, well-adjusted ones and neurotic ones, happy and desperate, they were all sorts. Now and again, he had worked together with some of them, as certain kinds of customers, rich, middle-aged men, sometimes wanted to try something extra and have sex with a young woman and a young man at the same time.

'How does that work?'

'He screws her and I screw him.'

'How?'

'Use your imagination.'

On the whole Juan did not like to describe his work in detail, partly because for him it was a matter of almost de-dramatizing the obvious, practised manipulation and body movements, not incomparable with those of a stoker or engineer on a ship, but also partly because it was a protective mechanism. Going into the details of homosexual sex was like being tempted into a sense of degradation, which it was possible to keep at a distance if spoken of in general terms, like a job, any old job.

It was primarily lazy, indolent women who became prostitutes, Juan thought, women who in their teens hadn't become caught up in secure marriages, women who lacked a stable anchorage in reality, who lacked realistic ambitions, who lived in a dream world, dreaming of an easy life, easily acquired riches, the happy luxurious life of the film star. These women constituted the group most at risk.

But another thing united them all. They had climbed out of poverty. They existed against a background of material need and severely limited social opportunities. They had all been born into the working class. Their clients, on the other hand, usually came from the middle classes or the upper class, where there was money. So up to that point prostitution was indeed a consequence of the unequal division of wealth in a class society. Juan had not read Marx. He had read no political literature in general and lacked any kind of political education. He also fundamentally lacked any genuine interest in politics. But he knew what a class society was. There was no reason for him to doubt or even discuss its existence, because from birth he had felt its presence and ruthlessness in his very skin. He was loyal to the working-class, always, a loyalty that was self-evident, in his very blood. He knew where social difficulties and distress came from, where the evil originated. The bourgeoisie. In his mouth, 'bourgeois' was a term of abuse.

Behind all Juan's philosophizing on female prostitution lay signs of himself. But you had to listen carefully, for he often answered direct questions evasively or not at all.

'Describe a day in the life of a taxi-boy,' I ask him one night, rather officiously. 'From sunset to sunrise.'

'*Bueno*,' he begins. 'Purely physically speaking, being a taxi-boy is less of a strain than being an ordinary manual worker, but from a mental point of view it is considerably more demanding. You have to be mentally very strong to cope with being a taxi-boy.'

That's all he says. How could he say more? He has not answered my question because basically it was a stupid, naive question. He knows as well as I do that he could never transmit to me 'what it was really like'. His private experiences are his private experiences, just as mine are mine, and on the whole our lives have been so vastly different that similarities are almost imperceptible, thus true and genuinely mutual empathy is more or less unthinkable. The only way we can understand each other is simply to accept each other, everything, without reservation.

Juan regrets nothing. He has been a prostitute from fourteen to twenty-one, and in that time has learnt more about life and the condition of man than he would have learnt in a hundred years at school or university. He never ceases to emphasize this: he has learnt! He has learnt so much. In the school of life.

Why should he have any regrets? Certainly, he has spent seven years of his life on the edge of the law, but he has never committed a crime. He has never stolen. He has never robbed anyone. He has not committed murder. He has not even blackmailed anyone, although he has had plenty of excellent opportunities to do so. He has been in a service occupation, a private enterprise man in the service trade. What was there to regret about that?

'I'm twenty-two and I have more experience of life than a seventy-year-old who has lived a sheltered bourgeois life. Sometimes it surprises me that I don't collapse under the weight of all that experience, that is doesn't finish me off.'

He lived on the street. He possessed nothing. At the age of twenty-one he possessed a pair of jeans and two shirts, which he changed every day, one white with blue on the shoulders and the other red-checked with short sleeves. But he always gave the impression of being neat and tidy. He never appeared in a dirty shirt. That was all part of the professional image. You mustn't neglect your appearance. You had to be attractive, maintain your attraction, even if you were poor. Many taxi-boys forgot or couldn't be bothered. They were careless about their appearance, clothes and personal hygiene, and that soon told. They found it hard to capture clients. They were amateurs and amateurs inexorably went by the board. They had never really understood or sorted out for themselves what the real point was. You had to do that if you wanted to survive the competition. It was a ruthless trade and not for the unintelligent. The unintelligent went by the board. You had to be intelligent. Like Juan.

He possessed nothing except his youth and beauty. Except his body and his sex. His body was beautiful and his sex organ efficient and infallible. For seven years he had lived by selling his body and his sex, building up round them a small enterprise. He was a one-man business.

It was having your cake and eating it. It was being a commodity and at the same time its salesman and distributor. It was like voluntarily treating yourself as an object, but at the same time being aware that you were a human being. If you wanted to live with some dignity, and Juan definitely wanted to do that, not for one moment could you waver from the conviction of your own humanity. If you did that, you were lost. Sometimes it was hard not to, because to most clients you were nothing but an object, a commodity so constituted that for certain financial recompense it would produce a certain measure of enjoyment. Selling your body over and over again could in the long run instil in even the strongest person the idea that he really was only a thing, a plaything, a pleasantly shaped piece of flesh, with which men with certain tendencies, for payment, amused themselves in their free time. Juan was perfectly aware of this temptation. When he was younger, he had taken little notice of it and had lived for the day without reflecting on it, wholly occupied as he was with his overwhelming sense of being alive. But when he was older, nineteen to twenty, that is, he discovered where that was leading. That was when he became philosophical. Not until then did he start mentally forming a protective layer against what was being slowly forced upon him, that fatal sense of himself as a thing, an object.

He was a taxi-boy and as a taxi-boy he found himself somewhere on the borderline between the merchant who sells a commodity and the ordinary worker who sells his labour. His activities had a social function, he was convinced of that, but unfortunately it was a social function that neither the authorities nor public opinion approved of, accepted, or even remotely respected. He was to a great extent outlawed. This did not affect him, for the choice had been his. But the risk of what is called 'objectification', a kind of spiritual and emotional paralysis, or petrification, was nevertheless always there like an imminent threat.

If he was successful in regarding himself less as a merchant selling a commodity and more as an ordinary worker selling his labour, perhaps the threat automatically became less imminent. So he started regarding being a taxi-boy as a service profession, not quite, but almost comparable with that of a hairdresser, for instance, or a waiter or a hospital orderly. Even if his clients usually regarded him as an object, as a commodity, he on his part began to regard them, his customers, as something more than customers, something more than purchasers; he started regarding them as human beings, and when he did that, he was sometimes able to see the chasms of human need and wretchedness behind the rigid superficial mask of physical desire. That helped. When things were at their best, he felt he had carried out a kind of social service; he had been a moment of joy and relief to some unknown man, who had stepped out of his private sea of endless loneliness for a few moments, only to vanish back into it.

Being a taxi-boy meant that you lived at night and – at best – slept by day. For people like Juan, with nowhere of their own to live, sleep was a constant problem requiring solution every day. At certain times, he might move in with some lone wealthy man who fell in love with him and whose bed and board he shared. But that generally ended in fear, humiliating suspicions, mutual recriminations and painful scenes of jealousy. Juan's pride and need for independence meant that he was neither able nor willing to subject himself to simply anything. The affluent men who kept him were sometimes very generous, but they nearly always made the mistake of demanding humble gratitude and total obedience in exchange, making no allowance for Juan as a living human being with needs and desires of his own. So after a while this entailed leaving and slamming the door behind him. On the whole, Juan preferred brief, temporary contacts, even if they weren't quite so profitable. There was something repulsive and in the long run unbearable about homosexual love-affairs, and as on Juan's part it could never seriously be a matter of reciprocal emotion, the signs of mutual exploitation finally became so obvious that it was impossible to go on.

For a short while as a beginner he had hung about the public toilets on the Retiro railway station, but the clientele there was unsatisfactory in every respect and the police so troublesome that he was always running the risk of being caught. So at a very early stage he transferred his activities to the centre of Buenos Aires, the pedestrianized Lavalle, the block round the main street Carlos Pellegrini and finally Charcas (now renamed Avenida Marcelo T. de Alvear) where the wealthiest men hunted in cars.

He went out at about midnight and worked until dawn. Every night, month after month, year after year. Yet it was never the same, each night different, no night like the others. That was what bewitched him, his experience of people, the stream of people, the people of the night who were quite different from those of the day. There are two quite different races, says Miguel, a contemporary colleague of Juan's, and Juan agrees. There are night-people and day-people. Night-people are gentle, sensitive, imaginative, or to put it briefly, human. Day-people are hard and efficient, but empty and uninteresting, or to put it briefly, inhuman. One should beware of them. Fundamentally it is not possible for an honest person to live except at night. In Buenos Aires.

We went walking together one night, Juan and I, in the boy-prostitute area of Buenos Aires, the boys hanging around in groups, or young loners prowling along the pavements or standing on street-corners, smoking, waiting. Juan is slightly uneasy. All this is behind him nowadays. He seems almost ashamed on behalf of his younger colleagues, or perhaps he is feeling sorry for them. Yet he can suddenly exclaim in tones that reveal pride bordering on self-satisfaction:

'In my great days, I was the best-known taxi-boy in the whole of Buenos Aires.'

I believe him. Everyone knows him here. He greets people right and left, ex-clients and ex-colleagues and other representatives of the people of the night. There is a kindness and natural respect in the way they all treat him.

'Everyone loves me,' he says.

It is true. I share him with many others. At that moment, it doesn't matter. I feel a kind of delight in being in his company, being seen in his company.

It is Friday, or actually Saturday, because it is already past midnight. There are a great many people around, crowds along Lavalle. Two youths in the white uniform of the Marines are standing outside a cinema in the glare of the neon lights. Juan gives them a quick glance and then explains to me what is happening. They're waiting for a catch. But they're not full-time prostitutes and never have been. They belong to the relatively large group of Argentinian youths who have discovered that this is a simple way of earning money for the Saturday dance or a night out with their girl-friends. They'll sleep with a man tonight in order to be able to sleep with Maria or Laura tomorrow night.

An endless stream of cars flows along Charcas, each with a lone man at the wheel. Sometimes a car glides over to the pavement and stops. As if from nowhere, a youth appears and stands for a moment talking through the open window. Then the door opens, he gets in and the car is driven away. It is all over in less than a minute. They have to be quick, because since Videla came to power the police have tightened up considerably on street prostitution.

Juan demonstrated to me what you do. I fell back and he walked about twenty metres ahead of me. Suddenly he was moving differently from before, sauntering more, but at the same time extremely alert. He did not want all the passers-by to know what he was after, but he did want the ones who were on the hunt to know that here was prey (or vice versa, for the prey to know that here was a hunter). He signalled constantly with his whole body, but I knew that the determining signal came from his eyes, that seeking look, totally expressionless to the uninitiated, but challenging, meaningful, for whoever knew and wanted the same thing, the look that met another look and lingered for a moment, fastening on each other and explaining everything in less than a second. Every deal in this trade depended on that look.

A car slowed down within five minutes, gave a responding signal with its indicator and turned down the next side-street. Juan followed. By the time I reached the street corner, he had already checked out on the man and was coming towards me. The man in the car started up and disappeared. He would drive round the block and pass us again if we chose to continue up Charcas. Again and again, until he was successful in what he had set out to do.

'You see how simple it is?' said Juan.

'Night in and night out. Didn't you ever get sick of it?'

'Sick of it? Sometimes when I went out I felt like vomiting. It was so disgusting it turned my stomach.'

'And yet you went on doing it.'

'I had to. It was my way of surviving.'

He made a sweeping gesture up towards the façades of the apartment blocks.

'I know all the blocks in this part of Buenos Aires,' he says, 'the lifts, the stairways, the apartments. This is where the middle classes live. Once I had to climb the fire-escape to the eleventh floor and get in through the window to his bachelor room, because his mother was in the living-room waiting up for him.'

'You took terrible risks.'

'Yes, but I needed the money. He was a young man, that time, very unhappy, and I didn't want to disappoint him.'

It was always like that. The secretiveness, the reciprocity. No one was to know anything, for it was all shameful, the sweet desirable deeds carried out illicitly, the most private of all private enterprises, an almost underground course of events, but eternal and ineradicable, for it was part of human kind, a human form of expression. Discretion was the main thing. And in Juan's case, a good heart always whispering something inside him.

The sordidness, the tristesse, the most indigent form of human proximity.

'The number of times I've been in a lift, halted between two floors, or on a stairway right at the top, by the attic door, my trousers round my ankles and a man on his knees in front of me, slobbering, his wet lips round my sex. Everywhere here. Everywhere in Buenos Aires.'

'Without feeling degraded?'

'Sometimes I laughed, roaring with laughter, but silently. So that I wouldn't cry. Naked in a strange bed with a stranger, his head between my thighs and his hands fumbling over my body. Sometimes I thought I'd never make it, that I'd go crazy, like lots of my friends – some went crazy, others took their own lives – I've told you, you have to be strong, and I was strong, but lots of the others . . . I never cried. I roared with laughter, but silently.

'I was liked by everyone because I wanted them to have value for money. I was very active, always, during the actual act, I mean, not only because I wanted to give them the greatest measure of sexual enjoyment I could, but also as a kind of antidote to the sense of degradation, of being unjustifiably exploited. I was doing a job and I did it as well as I could. I listened to them, sometimes feeling almost like a psychiatrist. I suppose it's a kind of therapy for them. You've no idea how much human need and despair there is in this city, and not just here, but all over the world. Perhaps I've been able to alleviate that a little, in my way . . . there are taxi-boys and taxi-boys. Not all of them are like me. Some of them are just out to get it over and done with as soon as possible and to cheat people of as much money as they can get . . .'

'And you? Weren't you doing that?'

'Of course I was. But there are limits. There has to be fair play within certain limits, otherwise I don't want to be part of it. I'm like that, a little un-Argentinian, perhaps because of the Italian or the Indian blood in me. Most Argentinians think of nothing but themselves, their own profit. I can't really be quite like them . . . which is why I'm still poor . . .'

'Were you never afraid? I mean, of coming to some harm?'

'No. What do you mean? I'm strong. I can defend myself. I've no need to be afraid of anyone. I'm not afraid of anyone. I've learnt that I don't need to be. I know people.'

'Didn't you ever differentiate between client and client? I mean, did you just get into any car that stopped beside you? Did you go to bed with any man who asked you to, regardless of what he looked like or what kind of impression he made?'

'Of course. There was no difference. I gave myself to every man who asked for it, as soon as I was sure he could pay. It was business. And business is business.'

Juan tells me that he could have up to five paying clients a night. Five completed sexual acts, that is, with five different men, all utter strangers? Exactly. Coming five times in one night under such peculiar circumstances, how can it be possible? It just was possible. It was a question of earning your daily bread, of surviving, and it was a point of honour not to disappoint your client. But sometimes it didn't work out, he was indisposed, he was too tired, flaked out, exhausted.

Then he discovered a trick that might satisfy both parties. One night in Stockholm he showed me how it worked. He cupped his hands in front of his mouth and coughed up some phlegm about the length of a match. Then he swiftly ran his hand over the rigid penis and the result was almost perfect, impossible to believe other than that he had come. 'They don't care a fig about me, they're only occupied with their own enjoyment – at my expense – so the risk of being caught is almost negligible,' he says drily, for once with a faint but evident touch of contempt in his voice. 'Sometimes they thought I had produced a remarkably small amount but then I used to say I'd slept with a girl just beforehand.'

The sordid details, one of the many unmentionables in a ruthless life.

But he still had no regrets. He learnt to care about the good sides of life and avoid the bad sides. He went on feeling himself a disciple in the school of life. He was strong and persistent and had a relaxed and totally undramatic view of his own body which made it easier for him to live as he lived. He had a muscle between his legs, a muscle among other muscles which required no special treatment, as all muscles were there to be used. In his view of himself and the human body, he was unusually uninfluenced by the Christian taboos which make sexuality so difficult and problematic for so many people.

Life was hard enough, all the same. To mitigate its worst blows, for a short while in his early teens he started on drugs, largely following the example of his friends. He smoked hash and sniffed cocaine. But it wasn't good for him. As soon as he noticed that drugs by no means enhanced his vitality, as he had imagined, but on the contrary dulled it, he decided to stop. That's the end of that, he said to himself, and it was; it's a long time ago, and he hasn't once fallen for the temptation since.

'I've a very strong will,' he says. It's true.

He learnt to distinguish between good people and bad. There were good people everywhere, but the bad people were mostly to be found in the upper classes. The richer, the worse. The more distinguished, the higher up the ladder of society, the more insensitive, the more selfish, small-minded and indifferent they were to the destinies of others. Yet over the years – as a taxi-boy, on the street – he became acquainted with many men reckoned to be from the top layers of society, and in some cases a friendship developed which would clearly be for life. But they were the exceptions, the good exceptions.

When he was at the height of his career, which must have been when he was between nineteen and twenty, and just before he met me, he had from eight to ten regular customers whom he met regularly once or twice a week, after making a date with them over the telephone. Among them was at least one doctor, a judge, an industrialist, an ambassador, a senior civil servant and a police commissioner. They were all men in their middle years with no money worries, some married, others bachelors. They usually owned several apartments in Buenos Aires, and the married men naturally consorted with their families in one place and with Juan in another. All of them led double lives. But for Juan this was naturally in many ways advantageous.

He had them carefully categorized in his brain together with their addresses and telephone numbers. His memory, like his sex organ, was infallible. He telephoned Arturo on Mondays, Marcelo on Tuesdays, Claudio on Wednesdays and so on. They invited him to lunch or dinner, sometimes even to the Jockey Club ('I am the only person who gets into the Jockey Club without a tie,' says Juan proudly) and they enjoyed his company and liked talking to him. Juan is an excellent conversationalist. He was not only born quick-witted, but in a way was born educated, or with an intuitive social adaptability which means that he can merge in a fairly natural way into even the most sophisticated bourgeois social scene. No one ever need be ashamed of being seen in Juan's company, not even at the Jockey Club. He himself says this is due to a supernatural quality with which benign Providence has equipped him. Sometimes it frightens him just because he believes profoundly it is something supernatural, and yet he never hesitates to exploit it. He knows nothing about medicine, nothing about law, almost nothing about international politics, and yet – a miracle – he is capable of carrying on an intelligent conversation about medical problems with his doctor friend, about legal problems with his lawyer friend and about international politics with his ambassador friend. How can that be possible? I could have told him it had nothing whatsoever to do with the supernatural, but was instead his intellectual capacity and his attentiveness which sometimes allowed him to assimilate the thoughts and opinions of others so quickly that he never even noticed how it had happened. But I let it go.

In a strange way, Juan lived an unusually sheltered life at this time. Through his doctor friend, he was protected from illness, his

86

friendship with the police commissioner guaranteed that he was free from harassment by the police, and his legal problems could always be referred to the lawyer. He had managed to arrange things for himself in this way. And yet it was not good, for when it came to the point, this circle of friends was always unsatisfactory, because the conditions were always set by his older friends.

Even so, in many ways everything was better for him then than a few years earlier. *Sleep* was no longer the overriding problem each dawn. There were several fruitful beds in which he could stay in the mornings, and should one not be available, he had usually managed to scrape up enough money during the night to be able to afford to take a room in a cheap hotel. He no longer needed to think up tricks to satisfy his need for sleep as he had had to do in his early youth.

In those days, he had often bought a cheap matinée ticket at the cinema and slept in the seat through several showings until evening came and work summoned him. In the summer he could sleep in the parks, in the shade of the palms and holly trees, or on the sands of the Rio de la Plata beach. But that was too cold in the winter, when he was forced indoors. He found he could sleep in buses too, *colectivos*. He would ride from terminal to terminal and back again, on certain routes that took up to an hour and a half, so he had three hours sleep altogether that way, and if that were not enough, he could always repeat the journey.

If he were quite broke, or almost, there was always the Academia, the tavern and billiard-hall on the corner of Corrientes and Callao, which was open all round the clock. He had dragged himself there on many a morning and spent his last centavos on a place to sleep by perhaps buying nothing more than an expresso coffee. He had sat on the narrow wooden bench along the wall in the part of the hall containing the billiard tables, his expresso functioning as his entrance ticket or assurance of sleep against a kind of small wooden bracket which at regular intervals broke the length of the bench. Leaning against the wall and the bracket, he had slept there for hour after hour in all that thick tobacco smoke, billiard balls crashing and waiters calling out the orders. Regardless of the time of day or night, there is always someone in Buenos Aires who wants to eat or drink or play billiards.

'Didn't anyone come and chase you out?' I ask him naively, familiar as I am with Scandinavian orderliness and its thousand and one welfare regulations.

'Never,' says Juan. 'There's solidarity among the people of Argentina, and it's accepted and respected. The waiters at the Academia let me sleep on because they knew and understood what it can be like for a fellow human being, often from their own bitter experience.'

Juan's relationship to money gradually became more and more problematic. He wanted money because he knew no one could live without it, but at the same time he didn't want money because he had some idea of the destructiveness and demoralization of money and its influence on the personality. In other words he wanted to be like his wealthy well-born clients, but not so insensitive, not so self-satisfied or blinded by the doubtful pleasure of possessions. Juan wanted to be good, and his experience told him that money never makes anyone good.

'If there were no bourgeoisie, there wouldn't be any prostitution either,' he would say, and then add: 'If you call our book *Taxi-Boy* and *Taxi-Boy* is on the cover, then there should be *Burgués, burgués, burgués, burgués* . . . on the back, all over the back, because the one presupposes the other. It's the bourgeoisie that keeps the taxi-boy system going, and the whole bloody prostitution system, too.'

'But it was your own choice. And quite voluntary, too.'

'For lack of anything better, yes.'

'And what would be better?'

'If we earn a lot from the book, for instance, I could perhaps consider importing a sauna to Chivilcoy and setting up my own small business, so that I could earn enough to keep body and soul together. The main thing is to be my own boss, because I couldn't stand being dependent on anyone else.'

'A lot of your contemporaries work in factories. Miguel works in a kiosk for ten or twelve hours a day. Why not you?'

'Factories! Salesmen! Never again! I've tried it. It doesn't pay. Look at Pancho. He's got three jobs on the go. He works at least sixteen hours a day, and even so can't make ends meet. It's exploitation. I refuse! I refuse to sell myself to the capitalists for such an atrociously low price! Wear myself out physically and spiritually for someone else's profit, and yet never have enough to be able to live a reasonably decent life. No thanks. Not for me.'

So that was honest labour. It doesn't pay. Juan and his friends had rebelled in their way, by putting themselves outside. There were others, politically more aware and socially more ambitious, who rebelled in another way and often for their own sakes and with more disastrous results, through political and union activities. But for them all it came to the same thing, fighting against a class-society which defended its bourgeois privileges and the established order with a terrible obstinacy and also often with exceptional cruelty.

So naturally as a result the main issue was nearly always only money. Conversations, what one did. Very soon after we had got to know each other, I noticed that Juan dealt with banknotes in a way that seemed to me strange and unnatural. I myself and most people I had mixed with until then didn't think about what we did every time we handed over or received notes; on the contrary, it was part of the basic framework of life that required no thought, in taxis, in supermarkets, at the cinema, as little thought as moving the left leg in front of the right when walking. But it was not the same for Juan. He appeared to think about what he was doing even when he handed over a small note, as if every note meant something quite special and so required thinking about, as if every banknote, even the smallest of them, had a content of its own: eating, sleeping, clothes to wear.

There was a concealed aggression in Juan whenever he had money in his hand, a craving, a kind of held-back hunger or anger when he handed it over, like when you take food away from a hungry dog. A violence in the movement of the hand, always controlled but noticeable all the same. He loved counting money. He was a monomanic note-counter, the moment he had more than one. And he did it with the kind of eagerness, a sensual empathy, almost lechery, that I have only come across before in crude jokes about Jewish money-lenders and other misers. But Juan was not miserly, only poor. The note was in the hand of the poor.

No, Juan was certainly not miserly. On the contrary, he was extremely generous. Sharing had always come quite naturally to him, self-evident in the world he had grown up in, and finally becoming a cornerstone of his philosophy. He helped wherever he could. He might give away nearly all his night's earnings if at dawn he happened to meet a younger colleague, a beginner in the trade, who had had less good fortune than he had and was tired, hungry, unhappy and had nowhere to go.

Lilita's family were hard up. There were days when there was not a centavo in the house to buy food for dinner, and Pancho and Norma and their four children had to go hungry to bed. When Juan was first engaged to Lilita and became part of their family, he sometimes allowed himself the pleasure of dispersing the gloomy atmosphere round the bare dinner table by playing the part of a magician. He took the bus into the centre, made a swift inventory of the bars in Carlos Pellegrini and continued along Charcas. An hour or so later, he would be back with his arms full of food and no one could understand how he had done it. They were all pleased and no questions were asked, for not asking questions was one of the rules of the game. But Lilita had some idea. She disapproved, but said nothing and kept her thoughts to herself, for that is what women in love do. In Argentina.

But all this was not just generosity and a spontaneous desire to help as best he could. It was also that the money burnt in his pocket. Easily-earned money was not for hoarding. It was unclean money, profits from prostitution. In the long run, life and a future could not be based on that, and even Juan, with his highly elastic morality and his experience of the contradictions of life, could occasionally see what was lunatic and absurd about earning food for seven people in the course of a few minutes by allowing a total stranger to massage his sex in a lift halted between two floors.

There were economic values and human values, but, oddly enough, they often appeared to be quite incompatible. Money flowed back and forth through the body of society and no society could exist without money; money was the blood of society, keeping the social organism going. For this reason it was also impossible for an individual person to live his life wholly without money. Living a life worthy of human beings or living your life with dignity was, or should be, an obvious aim for everyone, shouldn't it? On the other hand, money in itself does not seem to be a condition or a presupposition. You only have to glance at the rich at the top of the social pyramid to see that all too rarely do they live their lives with true dignity. A poor person is often better than a rich one. And more dignified. Juan knew that, because he personally had known both sorts. The value of money was relative, regardless of the aims you had set yourself in life. If nothing else, death at least finally destroyed everything you had built up through money. No one could take his wealth with him to the grave. Money was more than just a doubtful base on which to build human happiness. Money was nothing, really, paper in the fire of life and ashes in the stillness of death. There were more stable, truer values on which to build your happiness: love, friendship, a clear conscience. So he never stopped saying: 'I don't want to be rich, I want to be happy.'

Juan had actually thought all this out during his brief days of glory, when he was between fifteen and sixteen. He had been an 'in' pop-singer then, a well-known figure in the city discotheques of Buenos Aires, quite a prospect, yes, and very promising. He had a small group with whom he appeared in nightclubs, he made recordings and his voice echoed round the walls of the record shops in Lavalle. Everyone loved him, and he lived like a king, the girls practically queuing up for the pleasure of going to bed with him. His pockets were bulging with money which never came to an end. He had a large apartment with plenty of rooms and he drove around Buenos Aires in a white Mercedes. He signed his autograph for the little girls who surrounded him and clung to him like leeches. He was drunk with success, but it was false success, a doubtful happiness, and it wasn't long before it came to an end.

He had a stage-name. He called himself El Puma.

Juan could sing, there was no question about it. He had a good voice and perfect pitch. He also had personality and he did not sing just anything in any old way. As a nine-year-old, he had won a prize in a singing competition at school, he had sung as a soloist with the school choir, and general opinion had always been that he was musically talented, in fact, could easily have taken up singing as a career. But when the eulogies suddenly arrived, like almost everything else that happened to him at the time, they had a doubtful background and were in reality wholly dependent on his function as a prostitute, a taxi-boy.

During his roamings in Charcas one night, he had come across a wealthy director of one of the largest record companies in Argentina, a homosexual who over the years had launched a number of young male singers in the world of pop, of whom not a few became real stars. Now Juan was to have the privilege of counting himself one of them. On condition that he shared his bed with his patron. They all did that, and as for Juan it was a professional job, he had no objections. There were probably others who found it harder to subject themselves, who to a far greater extent saw it as degrading.

So Juan was suddenly the central character in a ruthless publicity campaign. He was launched, not especially originally but effectively, as the poor boy from the street with nothing but gold in his voice. Songs were written specially for him and his records distributed all over Buenos Aires. His first song was a hit, and it must be said that it was not bad. He sang in his rough adolescent voice, slightly sentimentally and with melancholy, but very purposefully, roughly 'why don't you want to love me, is it because I am poor and have nothing?' Suddenly

91

it looked as if Juan had a future, and his parents were proud of him. He was permitted to sleep with Sylvie Vartan.

It was about this time, or slightly later, that he first met Lilita. He had been performing on television one evening. Lilita and her sisters at home had seen him and her heart had started thumping in a strange way. Later that evening, the girls had gone to a dance and Juan had suddenly appeared there, like a king, a local Travolta of his day. He had spotted Lilita, they had danced together and immediately taken a liking to each other, so had agreed to meet again. From that day on, Lilita was faithful to Juan, although she knew the same did not apply to him. Juan stuck to Lilita over the years, because he noticed very soon that she was not like the others. She did not love him because of his success, but for himself, and she was unswervingly loyal even in times of failure and degradation. That was how both engagement and marriage came about.

The record company director was given short shrift with a vengeance, for one day Juan had had enough. The man was an unsympathetic character, not only outwardly unattractive, bald, pale and flabby, but also very much the rich bourgeois, authoritarian, domineering, smug, cynical and class-conscious. Juan should know his place. The man had provided him with money, a Mercedes-Benz and a large apartment of his own, but in exchange demanded obedience and subjection, and Juan would neither obey nor subject himself.

At first, Juan refused to go on sharing the director's bed, reckoning that he could afford to now he was a name and a potential profit-factor who couldn't be treated in any old fashion. The man agreed, but allotted Juan another task, that of decoy. Juan went into town with the man in the evenings, and when the man caught sight of a good-looking youth whom he felt like having, he would send Juan off to persuade him and make sure a deal was done. Juan often succeeded beyond all expectations, as he lacked inhibitions on this level and never had any difficulty talking people into things. In the long run, however, it was an unpleasant and slightly humiliating task, although better than having to be of service himself.

What turned out to be more difficult to overcome was that the man demanded the right to come and go at Juan's as he wished. He remarked on the state of the apartment and was pushy and small-minded. Not for one single moment did he let Juan forget who was the true owner. Or of the car. Or where the money came from. Juan held court. It was open house all day and friends came and went in an unceasing stream. The man did not like it, not at all. Juan used to put his rooms at the disposal of homeless young couples for moments of dalliance, friends and their girls, first one then another. They came and made love and went and came back again. The director forbade it. That was it. Juan had had enough. He simply went and never returned, left his lover and patron, broke his contract, left his career as a singer and his fans, the nightclubs, the spotlights and a cheerful and in many ways trouble-free life. He was like that. Swift to make decisions and unbending when once the decision had been made.

So he was back on the street again. He was no one again and possessed nothing. But he had Lilita. He had come to the conclusion that became the lodestar of his life: he didn't want to be famous. He didn't want to be rich. He wanted to be happy.

Taxi-Boy

Juan and Lilita were married on the first of April, 1977. She was twenty and he had had his twenty-first birthday a few months earlier. With practically no money, they went on their honeymoon to Carlos Paz in Córdoba. That was what you did; all newly-marrieds went to Carloz Paz after the wedding. When they came back to Buenos Aires, they stayed in a cheap little hotel as long as Lilita's wages lasted out.

On the third of August that same year, Juan took a flight to Copenhagen, where I met him, and a few days later we took the boat to Helsinki. Juan stayed with us until February 1978, almost seven months, and Lilita came over in November. We spent Christmas together at our home in Esbo.

Juan was no longer a taxi-boy. He had promised himself that. He had promised Lilita. He had also promised me. Never again sex for payment. But such a violent and total change in his way of life was no easier for him than for anyone else. With his ability to make smooth transitions and his undogmatic view of life, he allowed himself relapses now and again, anyhow when he considered the whole financial situation definitely demanded it. But on the whole, prostitution was now to be a closed chapter in his life.

He felt great responsibility for Lilita. He had a very definite view of what was demanded of the male partner in marriage. It was the husband's task to look after his wife and children. He was quite determined to do this. He wanted to live an honourable life and support his family with honourable work. But up to now, things had not looked promising. He lacked any kind of education. He still stubbornly refused to take any work going, just for the doubtful pleasure of receiving a monthly wage which would not even be sufficient for the necessities of life. Going to Europe to resume – perhaps – his interrupted career as a singer under less psychologically oppressive and humiliating circumstances, was not only a temporary solution of the problem, but also quite simply a fantastic chance, more than a poor Argentinian and ex-taxi-boy could even imagine. Juan's romantic ideas of his own specialness suddenly seemed to be confirmed in reality. He did not hesitate for one moment, although it was hard to be separated from Lilita.

I myself was too overwhelmed by my feelings for Juan to take into account serious difficulties. My ideas on the possibility of making Juan's visit to Europe happy and fruitful were quite unrealistic. I loved him. I was like an insanely ambitious father, seeing all the opportunities of life and success combined in his son. I was the Godfather. I was Daddy Long-Legs. Juan was nothing. Through me he would be able to become everything he wanted to be (or I wanted). I loved listening to him singing. Nothing gave me greater inner satisfaction, such peace of mind, such enjoyment, as his singing. I knew he was an amateur, but at the same time I knew that some of the greatest singers in the world, Caruso, Jussi Björling, Frank Sinatra, had at some time in their lives all been amateurs. If they could, why not Juan? Through me.

But Juan did not want to be famous. He wanted to be happy.

When Juan came to Europe in August 1977, we knew each other almost as well as we do now, and yet we didn't really know each other very well, because hitherto we had hardly been able to talk to each other. Almost without ourselves knowing how it had happened, we had slid into an emotional relationship which we were both convinced would last for ever. But we knew very little about each other as individual people, as individuals with individual standpoints and individual histories.

That was where the difficulties began.

To me, Juan was unique. In reality, he was not unique. In Juan's mind, I was . . . I don't actually know what I was, but it was equally divorced from reality. And when reality collided head-on with illusion, with the romantic dream, with the misunderstandings of ignorance, then the difficulties arose. They crept up on us slowly. I don't really know when they began. Or when they ceased, if they have ceased now. Or ever will cease. For they have not ceased. I still carry him with me just as much, in my heart. Just as he carries me, in his.

When Juan came to Europe, we had known each other for no more than a month. In relation to me, he had been a taxi-boy for most of that month. The point was that I had never directly sought him out in that capacity. He had from the very first been a human being to me. In the end, I became the same for him, despite all the differences between us, which were a constant obstacle.

Naturally I was perfectly aware of his means of livelihood, the first time I met him that night in the tango bar. I knew he was . . . an ugly expression . . . out to get money out of me and that he was offering his body as recompense. Or would do so. But that had no effect on me. It seemed neither repulsive nor especially tempting. Least of all did it seem morally challenging or cause me moral misgivings. For me he was . . . obvious . . . something different right from the start, original, just a human being, *un ser humano*, a human creature. That made me invulnerable, at first. When he thought he was being clever, he was being just what I expected him to be.

I knew he was a taxi-boy, but I was not entirely aware of his scope or how long it had gone on. All this did not become entirely clear until our conversations at night in the living-room in Esbo, and in the little apartment in Stockholm. We wrote a book together. He gave me the material and I wrote it down, at that stage only in my heart. My heart was overflowing with happiness. Everything he gave me was pure happiness. What he told me was all turned into happiness as things were turned to gold for King Midas. It was like a dream, and yet utterly real.

At the time, I was still convinced Juan was unique. It wasn't until my second visit to Buenos Aires in the autumn of 1978 that I realized he was not that at all. My feelings for him did not change in any way as a result, but deepened. That was what was strange. I couldn't have enough of him. We couldn't have enough of each other. There were days of silence and despair, days when we almost hated each other. But hatred, what is hatred? The black lining of the cloak of love. And whoever rips off the cloak of love makes himself bleed.

There were a number of lodestars in Juan's life, rules of thumb, boundaries beyond which he did not go; a way of existing and a way of behaving towards the outside world, a perception of life . . . as a man. A philosophy of life. For a long time I thought he was alone in this, that he had thought it all out on his own, a function of his own nature, his individuality, his special individual needs. But it was not so. During my second visit to Buenos Aires, I realized that he was but one of many. He was Argentinian, the prototype for a certain type and not an especially unusual type at that.

Yet naturally he was unique in the sense that there is only one 'Juan' on this earth. Who is like Juan. Who looks like Juan.

It was his freedom. Being his own master.

It was not subjecting himself to the rules of bureaucratic society except in situations when refusal might involve a direct threat to freedom itself.

It was being clever all the time.

It was not obeying orders from any kind of authority except when his life was at stake.

It was his persistent class-antagonism, not being servile to the upper classes or accepting disgraceful conditions, but, on the contrary, using the upper classes and exploiting their weaknesses.

It was his pride, always safeguarding his own dignity.

It was his internal solidarity, his demand for unconditional loyalty, never betraying a friend.

It was the insuperable contradiction between the night person, the good person, and the day person, the bad.

It was loving Buenos Aires, the unceasing life of the streets, the starry sky above the city, the moon above La Boca, home of the anonymous oppressed masses of the Earth, having his roots in Buenos Aires and never being able to pull up those roots.

It was being a man and every moment defending your manhood, satisfying your need for women and food, constantly, constantly in pursuit.

It was being together, many people at once, meeting, talking, experiencing the passing of life, making plans without every time seriously reckoning on realizing them.

It was presenting the joy in advance of the difficulty.

It was loving Argentina.

Finally it was living a more or less asocial life, by conventional standards at least, not so much being above politics, but still not having arrived at a political way of seeing life, almost like living too political a life.

Today I know so many of Juan's kind in Buenos Aires. They are not at all alike as people, I don't mean that; on the contrary, they are very different in themselves. But their fundamental view of life and their own personal standpoints are remarkably similar in many aspects. They are Miguel and Sergio and Ricardito, Chiqueline too, although Chiqueline's life, in a melancholy way, is more of a tragedy than a defiant fiesta.

'I never lie. I can't lie,' Juan says. Sergio and Miguelito say the same. But their idea of lying is quite different from the lying Protestant puritanism taught us in northern Europe. Their concept of lying is more elastic. A lie is useful, and as it is useful it should be used at least in situations in which it has obvious and immediate advantages and does not harm anyone else. A lie is morally justifiable in the fierce struggle for existence.

But as lying in certain situations is morally justified, human hypocrisy automatically has less elbow-room. The untenable puritanical demand for absolute truth, which in Europe has created the image of the Protestant priest in his inflated hypocrisy, has no equivalent in Argentina. For in Argentina you lie when you lie, but not as in Europe simultaneously and piously maintaining you are really telling the truth.

Juan knows very well that nearly everything he has done to earn his living has strictly speaking been against the law. This applies not only to his activities as a prostitute, but also to his selling of smuggled liquor and other contraband, and, for a limited time, drugs, and to the fact that, over the years, he distributed quantities of banned pornographic films and publications. Both Miguelito and Sergio have done exactly the same, but it does not make them feel in the slightest that they are criminals. When they have broken the law, it has always been a matter of foolish laws brought about to persecute the individual rather than protect him, making life more difficult for a huge number of people rather than easing it. But they have all avoided more serious criminal activities. On principle. Sergio and Juan, anyway. Not only on principle, but also from a sheer, innate, organic instinct for self-preservation. They have never stolen. They have never robbed anyone. They have never broken into premises, least of all taken anyone's life, despite the fact that they have spent a large part of their lives at the bottom of a social scale, inevitably the resort of regular criminals, and despite the fact that their environment has often been one of regular crime. Miguel's life, on the other hand, has not been quite so consistent when it comes to abstinence from criminality.

Juan has an amusing story about his secret friend and ex-client, the homosexual police commissioner. He laughs whenever he tells it and he is a little proud of it, too. This was at the time when Juan was selling smuggled liquor. The police commissioner had implied that he would have no objections to a bottle of genuine Chivas Regal. That was not difficult for Juan to acquire. The police commissioner asked him to bring the bottle to the police station during working hours, which Juan did. But before he did so, he had the nerve, or the courage, to empty out the contents for his own use and replace it with an equivalent quantity of Old Smuggler, the cheapest native whisky that could be bought in Argentina. He handed over the bottle, on which there was no trace whatsoever to show that it had already been opened. The police commissioner was delighted. He paid the price and caressed the bottle tenderly with his hands and eyes. Genuine Chivas Regal is a great rarity in Buenos Aires, reserved for the most select circles. The police commissioner was so pleased he immediately offered a couple of colleagues a glass, there and then. Juan grew nervous and tried to leave, but the gratitude of the police commissioner was so overwhelming he insisted Juan should stay and drink to the health of the Argentinian police force, the best police force in the world. That's what happened. There was Juan, who was nothing and possessed nothing, who was hunted as a vagrant by the police at night, and there were three middle-aged senior police officers formally raising glasses to their lips and taking a sip. Juan was so frightened his knees were knocking, but the police commissioner simply smacked his lips and said 'Aaaaaaah' slowly, exclaiming with glowing eyes: 'Lovely, lovely . . . the genuine article.' The other two men agreed. Soon they were all involved in a long and expert discussion on the poor quality of Argentinian whisky in comparison with the genuine Scottish original.

Juan had cheated them, and that made him happy, without the slightest twinge of conscience. All three of them were there to be cheated. They were also boorish and not a little self-important. With mock surprise, he talks about the amazing suggestive power of bottle labels, but he really feels slight contempt for the police commissioner. He has played a few tricks with the bottle and yet everyone is pleased. In different night-time contexts, the police commissioner has exploited his misery and social victimization. They are quits, to say the least. He has played a trick on an influential man, a well-deserved little trick, and he neither can nor wishes to do more. He is quite prepared to leave great fateful national frauds to others to carry out, those in power, the high-ups, the police commissioner and his kind.

A taxi-boy must have the capacity to fall in with almost every demand of his profession, without hesitation. He must not say 'no'. He must be good and attentive. Juan is good and attentive. So are Sergio and Miguelito. Always willing to do almost anything.

A taxi-boy has to be good-looking, otherwise no one will want him.

Juan is good-looking. Sergio and Miguelito are also good-looking, and they are all aware of it. They can exploit their physical appearance and they know how to flirt with a man – in a manly way. That is not quite the same as flirting with a woman. They know how to ingratiate themselves and offer themselves, with their eyes, the smile on their lips, their handsome features, chests and shoulders. They know how to talk to a homosexual, how to arouse what is homosexual in a homosexual man.

Juan is convinced that he is more intelligent than average. Sergio and Miguelita are both convinced of the same thing. You have to be intelligent to manage as a taxi-boy. You have to be more intelligent to manage as a taxi-boy. You have to be more intelligent than the others to be able to survive between the Scylla of the law and the police and the Charybdis of the fierce competition. Juan and Sergio and Miguelito are more intelligent than the others. In fact all of them are more intelligent than all the others. That has to be believed. It gives them a kind of security, a security in the only place a taxi-boy has the chance to find and expect security, in himself.

Juan and Miguel are both twenty-three years old. They feel rather old and tired, and know that whatever happens they won't have many more successful years in the trade. You have to be young; that is the cold reality. You have to be able to offer the devastating charm of youth, otherwise no one wants you. So they will stop, breaking out of the magic circle of prostitution for ever. Juan has already succeeded. He has Lilita. He has been to Europe. Nowadays, he has an apartment of his own to live in. Miguel makes brave attempts to establish himself in a respectable job and succeeds for a while, but then sometimes slips back into the old routine. He wants to be a taxi-driver, from taxi-boy to taxi-driver. Juan has implied the same hopes. It is an independent and lucrative profession. But taxis do not grow on trees.

Sergio is younger, only nineteen, and he can reckon on a few more years, but he also knows that this kind of life cannot last for ever. He wants to be an actor. He acts in a small amateur dramatics society and dreams about going to drama college. He occasionally earns some pocket-money as a model, *modelo*. He likes doing that.

There is something else which unites Juan and Sergio and Miguelito, and that is the softness underneath the often bone-hard, tough, male exterior – a concealed need for tenderness, a suppressed pleasure in expressions of tenderness from older men. Perhaps it is one of the keys to why they have lived as they have lived? For surely it is not simply need and the fierce laws of life; there is also this aggravating, unmasculine longing for tenderness. To be caressed by an older man, the security, usually furiously denied or kept a shameful secret, but in rare moments of complete openness, confidentially and trustingly admitted.

There are parallels. The often cynical, sometimes crude and one-sided sexual satisfaction homosexual men seek in young male prostitutes in the streets of Buenos Aires (and in the streets of the whole world) is amazingly similar to the one-sided sexual satisfaction the same predominantly heterosexual young male prostitutes seek in girls and women, in the same streets, discotheques and cafés. An expression of manhood: the sexual tray held out for you to grab whatever is on offer, to pick according to desire, according to means, according to varying tastes and inclinations. A man screws; it is his right because it is in his nature.

A man is not like a woman, gentle, yearning. A man goes straight to the point. The prick keeps the wheel of life going for a man. Women swoon in virgin cages.

All men need tenderness.

That is the reality. That is the truth. Men are like women. They yearn as women do. But that is not part of the Argentinian image of manhood, nor of the image of manhood in general. For tenderness is weakness and man is not weak. In Argentina it is the man who wears the trousers, Juan says. It is the man who decides.

And yet every man yearns for tenderness.

So you have to find it via circuitous routes; in provocative tearful moments, weak false moments of reconciliation or in the sheltering darkness of the marital bed. Or by paying. Under the brutal, callous mantle of boy-prostitution.

The members of Juan's family have no idea whatsoever that he has been a prostitute since he was fourteen. Neither have the families of Sergio and Miguel. All three of them have lived a double life down to the last detail ever since their early teens, not only because of the nature of their activities, but also out of consideration, affection, a kind of goodness of heart – not to cause their nearest and dearest any more pain or worry than life normally has in store for all of us; the justification for lying, lying as goodness, a motivated double-morality or double-morality as a moral quality. Being yourself without harming others. Choosing the least repugnant of the wretched possibilities available, but at the same time showing a pleased and confident façade in the context where it is most desired, most sincerely expected, the childhood home. That demands personal integrity and strength. That demands judgement and courage, *courage civil* on a level that the rulers of the world in general could not even dream of. For such are the conditions of life for some of us, not just severe, but sometimes also extremely hard to decipher.

Sergio is not yet twenty. He nearly always appears happy and unconcerned, and like Juan and Miguel, he also started earning his living as a taxi-boy at the age of fourteen. His mother's widow's pension has never been adequate, so for many years he has supported his mother and himself by street prostitution.

Sergio is a well-brought-up youth with a pleasant manner. He is polite and attentive and makes pleasant conversation, enjoying talking openly about himself. He has the kind of spontaneous radiance of a child of fortune, and if one did not know better, one would never believe any worry in the world had ever burdened his mind.

He lives alone at home with his mother, in a suburb far away from the centre, a journey of almost an hour and a half by bus. He comes home every morning at dawn, between six and seven. He sleeps all day and wakes in the afternoon. In the evenings he meets his friends, goes out with girls or goes to rehearsals at the drama society. From about midnight, for the next few hours, he works earning his daily bread. But he takes the whole thing lightly and his earnings are, accordingly, often quite modest. He is not like Juan. He likes to have a good time, and he often stays with anyone he likes being with. What does his mother say? She doesn't ask. But about his way of life in general? Sleeping all day and being out all night? She doesn't say anything. She did so earlier on, but now knows better. She says nothing and consents. He makes that Argentinian gesture meaning 'then I'm off', a waving movement of the hand vertically beneath the ear. She knows he will leave as soon as she starts asking questions or complaining about his way of life. He has done so before. Many a time. And stayed away for several weeks, sometimes months. So now she accepts everything and minds her own business.

He loves his mother and feels great responsibility towards her.

Sergio was once engaged to a girl of good family. Her father was a wealthy industrialist who had a large apartment in the smart part of Buenos Aires, between Santa Fé and Avenida del Libertador. Sergio could not visit his fiancée in a sport shirt and jeans. No, jacket and tie were obligatory, for in those circles the formalities are rigidly adhered to and that applies to teenagers as well.

The girl's parents did not approve of her running around with Sergio, nor of her running around in general, but least of all with Sergio, who was not of the right social background. They distrusted Sergio because he was neither a student nor had a job. And yet he always appeared to have access to money. They thought he was involved in some kind of criminal activity – not without some justification, for that matter. Stealing, they thought. To find out what the situation was, they employed a private detective who tailed Sergio for a while without his knowledge. The detective did not take many days, or rather nights, to find out the kind of murky business or dark deeds that provided Sergio with the money in his pocket. This was reported back to the fiancée's parents, who confronted Sergio with it. It was a turbulent encounter, which Sergio miraculously managed to talk himself out of, telling them a pack of lies which was finally so inspired, so detailed, so moving and believable, the parents climbed down and apologized for suspecting him. How could they have believed anything so hurtful and so dreadful of poor Sergio? Of course he was no taxi-boy. He was a good honest boy. OK?

A brief time of happiness followed for Sergio and Teresa. Sergio continued to live his own life on the side as if nothing had happened and Teresa started her studies at the Commercial College, for she was a modern Argentinian woman who believed in independence for women. She wanted to stand on her own feet. But her parents started thinking along the lines of marriage, because all Argentinian parents of good decent Argentinian girls do that. Sergio was to get a job and make a career for himself in Daddy's firm and the wedding was already planned down to the last detail. No one asked Sergio or Teresa what they thought. Father and Mother knew best. But Teresa was more than hesitant, because even if she did love Sergio, she would actually rather study than stand at a stove and bear his children. Sergio didn't want to marry at all. Tie himself down for life? At nineteen? When the whole world was still waiting to be explored? No, thanks. So he withdrew. They parted friends. But a few months later, Teresa's parents had found another and better husband for her and the wedding bells began to ring after all. She had finally submitted to those who knew best what a girl's life should be like.

But Sergio was free. He was still doing what he wanted to do. That was the main thing. Although he missed Teresa. Very much.

There is a freedom.

There is an indomitable refusal to submit, to bow down, to follow the current, to approve of those in power.

There are bandits, and tramps, and outlaws. There are filibusters and Robin Hoods, freedom-fighters and noble robbers. The loved and the hated. The forgotten and the legendary. Doc Holliday, Emilio Zapata, Lalli, Victor Jara, Wolf Biermann, Che Guevara and Mao Tse-tung.

Laws are passed but laws are not there to be abided by. Norms are created but norms are there to be broken.

What have Juan, Miguel and Sergio to do with these freedom-fighters and troublemakers? Nothing. Nothing more than a sense of life: that freedom exists, and that it exists for everyone, even for me, and that I sacrifice anything to acquire it and keep it. On the extreme edges of the class of people for whom Mao is god and Zapata king, Juan and Miguel and Sergio live their silent, anonymous, unknown, semi-underworld life.

Perhaps it is not like that at all. Parallels are hard to draw, contradictions difficult to find. The bandits and the freedom-fighters use violence as weapons and aggression as their mainspring. But what unites Juan and Miguel and Sergio, their kind, is ultimately something quite different, the opposite, their lack of aggression, their complete inability to make their way in life with violence as an instrument.

What is there left, then, in a world in which violence frighteningly often *is* the law, and blood flows daily, in the streets, in the sands of the desert, over the forest clearings? Tenderness? An instrument of love or a distorted picture of love? An open hand instead of a clenched fist, a caress instead of a razor? Doing no harm to people, but giving people enjoyment, pleasure?

There are millions of homosexual men in the world; there always have been and always will be. But Juan and Miguel and Sergio are not primarily homosexual. They receive their pleasure and take their pleasure through women. And yet. Part of them is homosexual. Juan counts in percentages. Ten per cent of me, he says, is homosexual. It is a drop of something, hard to get the better of, which has fallen into his consciousness and made him human, taught him to see the world in human terms, not as a battlefield and place of execution, but as an amusement park and market-place.

He sees people as people and does not judge, except their obvious visible evil, for he knows how people's loneliness corrodes, and he also knows, as Sergio and Miguel do, that for the desperate, he can sometimes be a brilliant, soon-to-be extinguished flare of light and warmth and pleasure in a desolate sea of darkness, loneliness and pain.

When Sergio was in Brazil, he took part as an actor in some pornographic film productions, films of sex acts intended for hetero-sexual consumption. When I ask if he found it difficult or unpleasant, he says, 'No, why?' and shrugs his shoulders. Just another meal ticket, an opportunity, and he had taken the opportunity. He was prepared to take on any temporary job to earn a bit of cash. In this respect Juan had always been more particular. A Danish pornographic magazine publisher had once offered him work as a nude model, but Juan had refused. The fee offered him had been negligible, an insult in human terms. He saw no reason why he should travel all the way to Denmark to live under the same reduced circumstances as at home. He would rather starve in Buenos Aires, where he belonged, than in Copenhagen, about which he knew nothing.

In other words, both Sergio and Juan, alongside their own private enterprises, had had superficial contact with the multinational sex industry, with its turnover of millions, making a few big crooks rich at the expense of many underpaid and exploited labourers. It was an underworld business, with secret branches in the business world above ground. It was also business on a genital level, a genital business, however you want to put it, and yet on the whole depressing-ly like the much-cherished and overshadowing business world which is the basis of human society, its maintenance and development. Alike, that is, in that the huge profits never go to those who do the hardest and dirtiest work.

Otherwise, Juan and Sergio and Miguel are just like other people and in their free time, they are exactly like other people. They don't read books or newspapers (Juan does occasionally). They watch television. They go to the cinema when they can afford to. They go dancing on Saturday nights and find themselves a dolly-bird if that's the way it goes. Miguel plays football with his friends in Palermo Park at least once a week. And they have an underlying interest in everything everyone else is interested in.

When Juan realized where my political sympathies lay, he im-mediately brought up Marx and Lenin and Trotsky. In fact, at that time, he knew nothing about Marx or Lenin or Trotsky. When I say to

Sergio that Argentinian tango fascinates me both as folk-music and as a musical form, he at once dredges up a song from his not particularly well-stocked store of tangos and apparently spontaneously sings it from the depths of his heart and at the top of his voice. When Miguel discovers I am a writer, he says without the slightest hesitation that he has also made a few attempts at that trade. He writes poems. 'Often? A lot?' I ask. 'We-ell, three or four, perhaps,' he admits. But this is not in any way a matter of lying. It's a game.

When Juan hears I am socialist-inclined, he also becomes socialist-inclined, because he knows that will increase my interest in him. When Sergio hears about my interest in tango, he at once demonstrates his own interest in tango, because he knows that will increase my interest in him. And when Miguel hears that I am a writer, he hunts out evidence that he is, too, because he knows that will increase my interest in him. But Juan is not interested in politics, Sergio's tastes in music are in fact rather dreary disco music, Travolta and the latest hits from the USA. And Miguel is illiterate. But he has written three poems in his life, to relieve the emotional pressure, which at one time must have been excessively strong.

It is a professional trick, one method among the many taxi-boys use to make clients swallow the bait. A way of pleasing, of making yourself attractive and interesting. But not only that. It would be both wrong and unjust to regard it simply as a gesture of commercial calculation, a variation of the clever salesman's sales patter. A taxi-boy is more human than a business man. Always. That is his strength and his limitation. He has to look after what he is because it is all he has. That's himself. But the man who sells himself is not like other men. He is an outlaw. He belongs or is dangerously close to the dregs of society on whom people spit. And that is not good; it is terrible.

To be like other people! That's it. To be like those who have succeeded in life. Not suspect, harassed, looked down on. But respected. Equal. To be equal. If I share the interests that have brought them success, I am at the same time a little more like them. To be like them! To live a life of dignity! Like them!

Juan in Europe

When Juan came to Europe, he was full of expectations. When he went back to Latin America seven months later, he knew Europe was not for him, but he would remember Europe for the rest of his life. He had seen Finland, Sweden and Denmark. On his way home, he had been to Paris and Madrid. All good in their way, but different. They were certainly not Buenos Aires, and he had his roots in Buenos Aires. Essentially, that was argument enough. He could not imagine living and dying anywhere else.

But before he was quite convinced of this, a great deal had happened. He was to have made a singing career in Finland. But nothing came of it. He was to have acquired a sound musical training in Finland. But nothing came of that, either. He was to have acted in Stockholm in a play partly written for him. Nothing came of it. He was to learn Swedish and stay in Stockholm for a few years to study. But even that was impossible to achieve. Misfortunes and adversities piled up on top of each other and, at certain stages, this made me so desperate I felt like putting an end to myself. I had deceived him. No question about it. I had lured him across the Atlantic with false prospects, and all I had been able to offer him in reality was disappointment and defeat.

But Juan did not reason in that way. Misfortune was the air he breathed. He was acquainted with it and knew it inside and out. The only thing he had truly mastered in life was overwhelming misfortunes. Life had taught him that, because for anyone who has to think about survival all the time, overcoming misfortunes is his daily, recurring, primary task. He was not surprised. In fact he had reckoned on all of it, and was not even bitter, certainly not desperate. So when things went wrong, it was usually he who consoled me, not him needing consolation from me.

Days went by and nothing was known about the new day before it had come to an end. Life was like a pearl necklace of new opportunities which kept appearing then disappearing again, appearing and dissolving. Some of the opportunities were splendid, a few unique and fantastic, but most were minor and insignificant, to be taken up or discarded. But there were always opportunities; there was certainly no lack of them, anyhow at least two could always be counted on.

My philosophy was a philosophy of progress – to succeed. I had been born with it, as that was what prevailed in bourgeois Europe. His philosophy was different from mine – to live and let live. He had been born with it, because that was what prevailed in poverty-stricken Latin America. He did not allow himself to be influenced by me, for he was convinced that as a human guideline his philosophy was worth more than mine. Thus, in the end, he was not the one to learn something important from me; rather I learnt something important from him.

In every situation, man is worth more than the position in which he finds himself. Man himself is always worth more than his material props and technical extensions. As a factor in life, the simple combination of 'you and me' is in the end infinitely more important than the glittering combination of 'you and me and the car and the bank account'. That's what Juan says, though he expresses it more simply and in a less sophisticated manner.

When Juan came to Europe, that was a unique and fantastic opportunity, which, although indeed realized through me, was in his mind a fortunate consequence of rare luck and unusual cleverness on his part. For Juan, I represented that one-in-a-million chance, and anyone who didn't take it was simply stupid. For me, Juan was an assignment which in good time would bring material blessings to us both. Neither of us really took in the extent to which it was purely practical deliberation on the other's part.

Juan thought I was acting entirely from an overwhelming feeling for himself as a person, which in itself was true, and I imagined that, from the start of his relationship with me, he acted less with cleverness and more with spontaneous affection. In actual fact, both of us had been calculating, acting according to plans made beforehand for advantages that could be gained at the other's expense. We did not know each other. But as what he wanted out of me in the end coincided almost exactly with what I wanted out of him, we managed to avoid a catastrophe at that level. My feelings for him were the kind that are blinding, but on the other hand his feelings for me were sufficiently strong to disrupt cold calculation. So we met at last at the point where our feelings more or less harmonized. And stayed there. Juan wished to be respected as a person. I wanted to be appreciated for my own sake.

What if Juan had been a woman?

If Juan had been a woman, there would have been nothing to write about, no more than the usual old story of love and anguish and marriage crises and slamming doors and suffering, dissolution and farewells.

But Juan was not a woman. And although what I felt for him was in many respects the same as I would have felt had it been a woman I had fallen in love with in Argentina three years earlier, it was still not the same. It was something more. Juan was my son. He became my son. He is my son.

What is good and successful, what is beneficial and has been benefited from, in fact almost everything good in this human chain of events, is based on this fact. Juan was a young man and he became my son.

But I thought all this out very much later, because from the very start my feelings for him were so strong and obvious that there was simply no room for careful consideration, reflection or hesitation. Juan was a human being, that was enough. All the complications and doubts that are part of a loved person's sex, regardless of which sex is in question, did not on the whole exist in my mind. Juan was Juan and he was to have a better life, and the happiness I felt was recompense enough for all my efforts.

Juan had been in Europe for over three months and the two of us were on our own in Stockholm when I had the first inkling that something odd and peculiar was going on, something I ought to treat in a special way, outwardly dismissive, smoothing it over.

I remember it very clearly. It was a Sunday afternoon at the end of October or the beginning of November, at three or four o'clock. We were lying beside each other in Juan's bed in the apartment in Stockholm watching television. It was football and consequently something Juan could relate to. He often stayed in bed all day, and I was free because it was Sunday. The doorbell rang. Outside, the autumn sun was shining, a lovely day. I decided we were out for a walk and whispered to Juan that we wouldn't answer the door. But the doorbell went on obstinately ringing over and over again, making Juan jittery, although it could not possibly have had anything to do with him. Finally he got out of bed, pulled on his brightly coloured long pants and went and answered the door. It was Frej Lindqvist with a bundle of newly typed manuscript pages of the play we were working on at the time. We didn't ask him to sit down. He stood there in the middle of the floor and we talked for a while about what we had written over the last few days and how we should go on, but without the slightest sign on either side that the situation might be regarded as ambiguous. Not a raised eyebrow, not a tremor in the voice. Juan stood slightly apart, wearing nothing but his long pants, listening without understanding, apparently quite unconcerned. I had to stay in bed as I had no clothes on.

Not until after Frej had left did the thought occur to me that I really ought to have reacted with some kind of shame, or with eager explanations. But, oddly enough, I hadn't. Neither had Juan reacted in any way. We were in that sphere of accumulated affection, and what the world about us thought or didn't think was nothing to do with us.

But I didn't know what Juan was thinking. Juan had no means at all of appreciating the extent of my happiness. Consequently my happiness was to a great extent pure illusion.

Yet at first everything went like a song. At home, Juan had no perceptible difficulties in adapting, and neither did we. He soon became great friends with our son. They were like brothers. He did his best, and that was not a little, to charm Selinda. He cooked Argentinian food. He was polite and pleasant, cheerful and attentive. He was discreet and well-behaved. He was part of the family.

That was what was so remarkable. From the very first, he was one of the family, and when Lilita came, so was she, and they remained so, both of them. Perhaps Lilita most of all quickly and easily accepted her rôle as the adult daughter of the house. If that were so, then it was no more than natural, as for her there were no concealed emotional complications. And yet it would be a lie to say it was not sometimes difficult.

It would be a lie, for instance, to maintain that Juan was not occasionally a considerable annoyance to Selinda. She had not asked to have him under her roof. I had more or less forced him on her. Naturally I had discussed it all with her before his arrival, but in a way that meant she had very little choice. I had given her little chance to say 'no'. When he finally arrived, she really had very little reason to complain. Juan behaved perfectly. But for her, he was nevertheless an intruder and it wasn't only his presence that disturbed the habitual family routine. What I felt for him also meant a constant element of uncertainty for her, a perpetually uneasiness. We were all aware of this, not least Juan. This meant that we could neutralize emotional dangers and avoid emotional quagmires into which it would have been so easy to fall. Especially for me, Juan was a son, Lilita was a daughter. Selinda was *mama*. I was *papa*. Jerker was *hermano* and Nina *hermana*, brother and sister. And so it became, despite a number of near-accidents occurring now and again.

Juan was different from us in many respects, but he was a human being and none of us needed anything more as a starting-point for lasting companionship and affection. Many of his habits were unlike ours, but we accepted them and tried not to impose ours actively on him. On the other hand, he made attempts to adapt, without succeeding particularly well. We thought differently on many matters, and continued to do so. We never tried to compete actively over the question of which human values were best, Scandinavian or Latin American. In this way, Juan remained Juan and we remained ourselves, mutually accepting personal identities and basic national characteristics; at the same time, it was an expression and prerequisite of affection, in the long view. It was also the only way to retain affection in the heart, despite social difficulties and superficial antagonisms in daily life.

The worst stumbling block for us all was language. I was the only one who could communicate in any way with Juan in his native language. Selinda and Jerker went off to Spanish classes, but the result, at least on Selinda's part, was somewhat unsatisfactory. Jerker learnt more quickly and towards the end was able to converse quite fluently with Juan and Lilita about the things young people talk about, everything in fact. Juan made brave attempts to learn Swedish – and Finnish – but the pronunciation of Swedish caused him almost insuperable difficulties and, as far as he was concerned, what he learnt amounted to nothing but a few scattered words and simple expressions.

Our conversations at meals were at first limited mainly to cheerfully establishing what this and that was called in Spanish and Swedish. 'Garlic' was '*ajo*', '*ajo*' was 'garlic'. 'To boil' was '*hervir*'. '*Zanahoria*' was . . . well, what the hell was '*zanahoria*' . . . long and the colour of an orange . . . oh, yes, 'carrot', '*zanahoria*' was 'carrot', and so on. It was fun for a while, as a communicative life-belt in fact quite invaluable, but in the long run it became rather boring and clearly unsatisfactory for all of us as a linguistic basis for family existence.

On the other hand, perhaps this lack of a mutual means of expression saved us from the more serious confrontations and sharp differences of opinion which would otherwise have been unavoidable. Selinda simply couldn't accept Juan's Latin attitude to women, and Juan couldn't accept our nonchalant, insensitive, northern European attitude to the institution of the family. If one opinion had really been tested against another, perhaps imperceptibly and quite against our own wills, feelings of incurable disappointment, of insuperable estrangement, at worst suppressed contempt, would have crept in, and would inevitably have clouded or actually destroyed the harmonious sense of family we all felt or pretended to feel, because we so profoundly desired it. The opposite is also possible, of course . . . that views would have been adapted to others, incompatibilities admitted and accepted and solidarity strengthened and deepened even further.

What was difficult for Juan was his loneliness, his social and linguistic isolation, and not least his sexual isolation. We were at home among our friends and everything we were used to and thought important to our comfort and our physical and spiritual well-being. On Juan's part, he was separated and far away from all of that. He was a stranger, wholly at the mercy of our goodwill. Everything he really valued was on the other side of the Atlantic. Nothing that truly meant anything to him was where he was. He totally lacked the habit of travelling. He even lacked any genuine desire to travel. The only time he had been outside Argentina before was in my company, for a couple of days in Montevideo. His roots were very deep in the asphalt of Buenos Aires, so deep in fact, that every move caused him considerable mental pain.

It took a long time for me to realize this, and even longer before I could bring myself to admit it as an inevitable fact. In actual fact, Juan's situation was the situation of the immigrant, albeit in the most pleasant possible circumstances. His problems were faithful reflections of European immigration policies affecting millions of people all over the highly industrial countries of our hemisphere. In our enclosed and secure little family environment, we could have, in other words – if we had had the sense to do so – gradually come to understand all the torment, suffering and mental tension millions of people experienced to a greater or lesser degree as a result of the new migrations that world capitalism had released. Juan was an exception in that his situation was more voluntary than compulsory. He was no 'guest-worker' in the current cynical sense. On the contrary, he was to a great extent simply a 'guest'. In our home. He knew he could and would return to his own country within the foreseeable future. Yet the symptoms were the same. Those fiercely painful symptoms of the immigrant.

Juan was uninterested in getting to know the new countries he went to. Apparently uninterested. The only thing that really interested him was living his own life. He lacked the joy of discovery. He was no Columbus. He didn't even have anything in common with the roaming youngsters of the hippie variety that populate both Asia and Africa as well as his own part of the world. Anyway, he was not European in the expansive meaning of that word. His mobility was a local mobility and he at once ceased to feel at home in a setting in which the cultural tradition inoculated into his blood in childhood was no longer valid.

In relation to Buenos Aires, Montevideo is roughly what Helsinki is in relation to Stockholm, as close geographically and as close in social and political structure. But smaller.

Yet when we arrived in Montevideo, Juan behaved like a stranger. He noted that young people behaved differently and dressed differently from in Buenos Aires, much worse, more sloppily. He had no idea what one could do or where one should go to find out just what was typical of Montevideo, almost like a Finn in Stockholm. On his first visit. Abroad. Presumably he wouldn't cope in Santiago, either. He thinks of Chileans the way many Swedes think of the Finns. In his own environment all pickpockets are considered to come from Chile.

We liked each other; that was the simple human basis of Juan's experience in Europe. A basis of that kind may appear very brittle, but all the same, in our case, despite all the strains on it, it held. I liked Juan and Juan liked me. My family liked Juan and Juan liked my family, but this was not so spontaneous or self-evident that we didn't occasionally need to reassure each other. It was a moral duty, and to a great extent the result of a conscious emotional process, because if we did not like each other, we all knew it would go wrong. Sympathy cannot be made compulsory if there are no prerequisites for it, but if there is a seed somewhere that grows, sympathy can burgeon into a great many branches. That is what happened in our case.

Liking something also involves being loyal and showing respect, even in situations that superficially seem perfidious and hurtful. That was what we always tried to hold on to, loyalty and respect, and, on the whole, that is probably what anyone needs to survive spiritually, even when in his mind his surroundings largely appear to be a desert. A few drops of humanity in a life's brew as bitter as witch's milk.

But then nothing was ever that cruel for Juan.

In Buenos Aires, I often had a feeling that Juan was in control of everything that happened, anyhow at the grass-roots level on which he lived his life. His alertness never slackened, his senses registering everything happening around him. He knew most things. He was acquainted with a million people and for that reason had contacts he never hesitated to use. In many circumstances he behaved like a highly privileged person, seldom standing in queues as others did. He hardly ever paid entrance fees. All this was lost to him when he came to Europe. He was transformed, the air going out of him. He became another person.

His still retained his sharp watchfulness, but it had become aimless and unconcentrated, as if he no longer knew to what he should direct his attention. I took this to be a lack of genuine curiosity. When I went to Argentina, I wanted to get to know Argentina. When he came to Finland, he appeared to have no special need to get to know Finland. On the contrary, he avoided the unknown. His primary need appeared to be that of a tortoise, to creep in under his shell, and the longer it went on, the more both Finland and Sweden became a kind of Siberia to him, a place of exile.

From the very beginning he was unenterprising, but instead of his lack of enterprise decreasing, as new things became less new and more familiar, it appeared to increase, so that finally he allowed himself to become completely dependent on my initiative.

He could do nothing on his own. He spent day after day in bed, apathetic, sluggish, staring up at the ceiling. He hardly answered when spoken to, and when he did he was angry and aggressive. His depressions were profound and hopeless, and the irritation I felt at first finally turned to despair. At times I was convinced I had failed.

It was better in Stockholm. There he finally got used to going out into town on his own. But he could make neither head nor tail of Helsinki, though that probably had a great deal to do with the climate. When we were in Stockholm, it was autumn. When we got back to Finland, it was winter. He could not stand the cold and in the end it almost drove him crazy, and yet his lack of enterprise and initiative was still puzzling to me. Indifferent to everything unknown?

Was he really that? Or afraid of the unknown? How can a person change to that extent, becoming sluggish and passive in an alien world? When his life and habits at home had been so full of activity and *joie de vivre*?

Is that universal? Does it apply to us all? Myself included? Is it a question of mentality? To some extent, a degree of education in adapting. For the person who knows little or nothing about the world beyond the horizon does not know how little he knows and has no spontaneous need to know more. But the person who knows a little soon sees how little he knows and wishes to broaden his knowledge. Knowledge is power? OK, over one's own destiny, anyhow. Knowledge is a factor in life. Curiosity is a driving force in life. Well, what knowledge? Curiosity about what?

Ever since I was at school, I have occasionally met young people from the USA, and when we have talked about the future, almost without exception it has appeared that their dream of the future, their aim in life, has been no less than one day to be the President of the United States of America. My own ambitions have never been aimed so clearly at greatness and fame, but have nevertheless always presumed the need *to be something, be someone*. That is our European heritage, each individual a King Karl XII, a Louis Pasteur, a Hans Christian Andersen, a Garibaldi or a Winston Churchill; the spirit of competition, happiness seen in terms of honour and fame, each and every one of us the forger of his own happiness.

Juan has never given a thought to becoming the President of Argentina. His happiness is not the same as European happiness. It is simpler: love, friendship, a roof over your head, food for the day and the freedom to do what you want within comparatively modest social limitations. Juan was once famous, or at least well-known, but the price he had to pay for it was far too high, including unacceptable limitations on his own personal freedom, so he preferred being poor and free to being rich and famous and dependent.

Prostitution in the ordinary meaning of the word was nothing, simply one way among many of earning a living. But to prostitute yourself in more elevated financial contexts, nearly always inevitably in order to rise in life, to become rich and famous, to sell your soul while trampling on others and on those weaker than yourself, that was too much. Juan could not bring himself to do that. Even in prostitution there were limits, and prostitution in the wider context which goes under other names, financial competition, or development of the community, or defence of the nation, in which ideas and human values were really sacrificed for money, or advantages and comforts were bought at the expense of the weak and the exploited masses, that kind of prostitution was far beyond what Juan could ever allow himself. A press baron or an arms manufacturer, or a director of a multinational firm or a servant of a machine of political violence, not Juan, no, never!

He was unable to compete or even function as a one-armed bandit in the jungle of the musical entertainment industry. He lacked the desire for power. In this he was very un-European and in this he was different from North American youth. They had also inherited their compulsory social ambitions and longing for power from a way of life stemming originally from a European tradition. Power is a European trauma and the drugged, alcoholic and childish collective neurosis today experienced by European youth is surely to a great extent connected to this enforced and almost complete powerlessness, the shattered dream of power, which is almost the only thing the industrialized welfare states have succeeded in giving to their youth.

Unlike young people in Europe, Juan was not frustrated in his desire for power and social ambitions, everything society suddenly lacked the prerequisites to satisfy.

On the contrary, contentment was the basic foundation of Juan's life. He was content with very little. He wanted only to live and let live, and in contrast to his European and North American contemporaries, he felt no need to trot around, bowed with anxiety and confusion, searching for vanished or unattainable instruments of power, still presumed to be a temptation for everyone to some extent. That was why his lack of curiosity was so incomprehensible to me for so long. That was why the kind of knowledge he sought was so alien to me for so long.

In Europe, man is man's greatest enemy. Don't deny it! I know it to be so. Every person who approaches us we meet at first with concealed aggression and suspicion. Fellow man is not fellow man, but the opposite, someone whom it is primarily a matter of neutralizing and vanquishing. In Argentina – for safety's sake let us say in grass-roots Argentina – man is first and foremost a fellow man. For Juan, man was first and foremost a fellow man, whom he approached with openness and a spontaneous desire to make contact. But in Finland and Sweden he came across all too many people who seemed to him closed and frightened, who seemed reserved and formal, who seemed false and unreliable, because they did not go straight to the point; they said one thing and meant another. Juan was not like that at all. That was the difference. That was the basic difference. That was why he always longed to go back home.

He was used to living his life surrounded by people, constantly surrounded by numbers of people, in the daytime, at night. That was as it should be, his world was like that. A hundred conversations a day, with a hundred different people, about anything, about this and that, but conversations, being together. When he came to Finland, he suddenly met people who wanted to be alone, who quite simply loved being alone. That was unfathomable. It applied to me, too, my need to be alone. For the first time in his life he was afflicted by loneliness, and he could not endure it.

That was one of the reasons why Lilita came to Europe in November; she was summoned to Europe, so that Juan should not die of loneliness. It helped for a while, but it was not enough. Lilita was his beloved, but she was not the constant stream of people on the streets of Buenos Aires. Not even her presence was sufficient. He could not live if he did not feel himself one of hundreds who felt as he did and spoke the same language as he did, literally as well as symbolically. One among tens of thousands, a minute dot among millions, the great warm mass of humanity; he had to feel the pressure and security of the masses.

Naturally it would have been easier if everything had gone according to plan, as we had planned or dreamt about, and he had found work, earned money and been successful. He came to Europe as a singer. He introduced himself as a singer. I introduced him as a singer. That alone. It was true, but he was not a professional. He was no Mick Jagger, and I was no demon impresario. So what happened happened. I was partly blinded by my love for him and for that reason sometimes badly overestimated his musical abilities. He himself was perfectly aware of his limitations and deep down suffered doubts and uncertainties which he tried to hide as best he could, but which were finally perfectly evident. On my part, I occasionally felt out of my depth, the whole business a kind of insane *Münchhauseniad*, holding oneself up by the hair, quite suddenly establishing oneself as a con-man by trying to make someone out as a great singer, not because he was especially good, but because he was so deeply loved.

And yet behind all this was a good thought. I have never had a guilty conscience about anything I've done in connection with Juan, and there is nothing I ought to regret. Juan was a drop in the ocean of mankind. He was on his way from nothing to nothing, and I was the only person in the world with the means of changing that situation. A great many chances had arisen in his life, and he had taken them, but they had nearly always been dubious chances, on dubious conditions. All right, he was '*un artista sexual*', but that was no way to earn a living in the long run. He himself knew that. Singing was the only thing he could do, his only real capital. I was to give him an honest opportunity to sing, so that at least the necessities of life were secured.

It all started with a real disappointment and ended with a semi-success, but in reality nothing went as planned.

By chance, a few weeks after his arrival in Finland, he was given the opportunity of performing far out in the Finnish countryside. A parish somewhere up in the Arctic Circle – ambitiously and praiseworthily – was to put on an evening's programme on Latin America and Juan was to contribute with examples of Latin American folk music. It was something, anyhow, we thought, a start to his career, and it would presumably bring him in something.

He set off by train on his own in the best of moods, and returned a few days later, superficially happy and contented, but remarkably silent about what he had done. Gradually it emerged that really he was disappointed and deeply hurt. He had been offered a sauna, and some of the Christians had made physical advances. That was nothing unusual, but in this particular context it had been humiliating and disturbing, not simply because it was wholly unexpected, but also because he had come to Europe expressly to start a new life, because he had expressly put an end to his old life. The actual programme, on the other hand, had gone well. He had sung and been warmly and gratefully applauded. But then, from an income point of view, no more. The church organizers had given him a handful of small change as an honorarium, eleven marks altogether.

I was as upset as Juan, or rather actually furious. I felt doubly humiliated, both on his behalf and on behalf of my countrymen. I was prepared to ring up the church potentates and the bureaucrats to demand an explanation and to tear a strip off them, but at Juan's request I refrained. He didn't want any trouble. He was used to veiled insolence. He was used to being treated like dirt, as a human being with a lower human value. For me, it was a shock. Either you say beforehand that it is a question of charity, or else you pay full fees according to the going rate. But not this, not a handful of small change, like a serf's child at the gate in the last century. But when it came to an unknown black-haired youth from Latin America, clearly it was not that important. Not in Finland, nor to God's chosen people. It was simply the Church's attitude to money and immigrants, pure and undisguised. *Mierda!*

There were others who were more helpful and obliging. One evening we managed to gather together some of the big names in Finnish musical life for a musical evening at which Juan was to show that he was good enough. Also present were Atte Blom from Love Records, M. A. Numminen and Esko Linnavali. There was also a singer from Cuba there, on a temporary visit to Finland. This was flattering for me, but unfortunate for Juan. Both of them sang, Juan first, the Cuban shortly after him. Amateurs and professionals should never be mixed, for in that way amateurism is painfully shown up. Juan kept up a good front, but realized clearly enough what the inevitable conclusion would be. The Cuban was a master on the guitar as well as a singer. Juan simply sang. There was nothing wrong with his empathy, but he had little command of technique.

So there were no LP recordings by Love Records of Argentinian tango or other folk-music. Neither was there a television show, nor a solo concert at the Arts Centre. Instead, he gradually started staying in bed all day long, apathetic, despondent and out of sorts. There were accusations and counter-accusations, sleepless nights and sharp exchanges in the evenings. Juan felt that his whole being was changing, that he was losing his identity, and it was all my fault, because for some damned stupid reason I had dragged him all the way across the Atlantic. I regarded his listlessness, his passivity and melancholy as the blackest ingratitude. Thus things were beginning to go really wrong. But it was all right in the end. The winter was long and dark and cold, the silence terrible. Juan felt he was freezing to death. His soul was iced up. There was no cure but to return to Argentina.

But Finnish musical experts had vouched for his promise, a promising young talent. That was surely honestly meant and anyhow no exaggeration. Because that was just what he was. Or is. Promising. What he lacked, what he ought to aim at first of all, was training, schooling. That was unfortunately easier said than done, for Juan's weakness was just that he found it so insuperably difficult to allow himself to be taught.

A few days before he went back home with Lilita in February 1978, he was at last given the chance of a concert in the Old Student Hall in

Helsinki, to be broadcast simultaneously on the radio. Rehearsal facilities had been unsatisfactory and he was dissatisfied and nervous. We sat in the front row, the whole family, keeping our fingers crossed, Lilita, and Selinda and Nina and Jerker and I. We were all equally nervous. It did not go especially well and he sang less well than usual. It was perfectly clear that he was frightened. Lilita and I exchanged troubled looks. His voice did not carry and was tense and pressurized, then occasionally he loosened up and we were able to heave a sigh of relief. But overall, the impression was rather more than mixed, and we knew he could do better, though the reviews in the *Helsingin Sanomat* a few days later were exhaustive and indulgent, indeed positive without reservations. So there was a semi-success after all, in the end.

Late in November, the bay outside our house froze over. As yet no snow had fallen. The days were crystal-clear with sunlight and a few degrees below zero. We took skates and a scooter-sledge and went out on the ice with Juan and Lilita. We taught them to skate, an exotic experience for both of them. Lilita enjoyed herself immensely and so did Juan, although it wasn't Buenos Aires. Afterwards they went into the sauna with our son. Lilita soon picked up Scandinavian habits and overcame her Catholic shyness, noting that it was neither terrible nor remarkable to show yourself naked in front of men other than the one you were married to. She would have had no objection to staying on longer in Finland. It didn't take her long to find out how much better things were for women in Finland than in Argentina, how much freer their position and how much greater their opportunities.

But Juan was the one who decided. She loved Juan and was loyal to him, not just to his habits and desires, but also to his opinions. In the end she always thought as he did, even if at first she had thought quite differently. It was sometimes irritating, and troublesome for her, too, although quite in line with her upbringing. Should she express herself as Lilita, as a woman, or as Juan's wife? In the end, she always expressed herself as Juan's wife.

Christmas was celebrated in the name of peace and goodwill. Juan and Lilita were each given knitted mittens and socks as Christmas presents from my mother. They had not expected anything and were both clearly moved. The atmosphere was warm and relaxed. We danced Viennese waltzes and Argentinian folk-dances. Never before had we had so much fun at Christmas. But a few days later, melancholy once again descended on Juan, like the ice on the sea round the islands. There was nothing else to do but gradually start preparing for their return home.

What was it that was so difficult? Truly difficult? Not being at home? Only that? I found that hard to understand, for I myself like being away from home so very much. Naturally there was something else which made the whole thing worse. The involuntary inactivity. The unbearable climate. The dark winter days. The silence where we lived. The snow. Living like a parasite in my home, living off me, not only for my love, but naturally also on my charity.

That was what was truly hard. That was also why we felt bound to discuss it, point by point, over and over again, so that no misunderstanding should arise, stealthily, clouding our relationship. For Juan was indeed used to living off other people, a parasite on the goodwill or weakness of others; he had done that for most of his life. More or less. But in my case it was different. For it was through me, or with my assistance, that he had at last managed to free himself from his old life. I was the one who was going to give him the opportunity of starting again, of starting a new life. So it was important to keep things separate. I was his friend, for real. He was my friend, in the true Argentinian sense. I was also his father, though make-believe, not for real, or slightly more than just make-believe. He was my son. That was the only reason why he accepted money from me. He was no taxi-boy in his relationship to me, and never would be. For me, he was not for sale. And what on his part he did for me, he did exclusively within the framework of friendship, the overwhelming friendship I sometimes preferred to call love. Within the framework of the family. The make-believe family. Or more than make-believe.

There were my drinking habits, too. Juan used to drink watered wine with his meals, but otherwise wine and spirits played no part whatsoever in his life. He was also very Argentinian in this respect. With a few exceptions, people don't drink to get drunk in Argentina.

It is more than likely that the decisive culture shock on his part was caused by Finnish drinking habits. As early as in August, a few weeks after his arrival, one Friday afternoon in a small country town, he had seen some twelve- or thirteen-year-old youngsters, girls too, staggering totally drunk round the streets, helplessly, and horrible to see. He was terribly upset. He maintained firmly that the whole Finnish nation would collapse within less than thirty years because of drink. I tried to argue that we lived within a Nordic drinking tradition which had its roots in Viking times or even further back. Even more reason to worry, was his only reaction. He simply couldn't bear the sight of drunks. What he felt was not simply distaste; he was also frightened of them.

Occasionally it so happened that I came home drunk. I didn't mean to. Alcohol was not good for me, and I had known that for a long time. I also knew what Juan thought about drinking and had decided to give it up for for that reason as well. And yet things sometimes went wrong. Juan was terribly upset. He didn't recognize me. My whole personality changed and certainly not for the better. After I had sobered up, he wouldn't speak to me, except to inform me that he was going to pack his bags immediately and leave for home. He kept on making the Argentinian gesture that means 'I'm off'. Again and again. He was disappointed and desperate.

But he finally agreed to talk about it. We talked for hours. About alcohol. About him. About me. And about us. He made brave attempts to understand me. He imagined that I found it just as hard to give up drinking as he found it to give up women. In other words, drunkenness was unfaithfulness in the same sense that adultery was. I was not pleased with this comparison. For me, the one was no compensation for the other. All the more incomprehensible, then, in his opinion.

It always ended by me making a solemn promise that this time would be the last. Never drunk again! Just like in marriage! And just as false and impossible to keep to. And yet it came from the heart and was so infinitely honestly meant, in actual fact, much more honestly meant than in marriage. In other words, it was somehow more important to keep in with Juan than to keep in with one's own wife! How on earth could that be? In marriage there was a constant need to keep one's own end up, which was wholly absent in my relationship with Juan.

There was also this business about women, his sudden enforced celibacy. Juan had been used to sleeping with women since his early teens. Regularly. Daily. Preferably several times a day. Like a hawk constantly hunting for food, he was constantly searching for women willing to sleep with him. On the streets of Buenos Aires. Though not prostitutes. They were his colleagues. He never paid for his pleasures. On the other hand, there were some women, usually of grandmother age, who offered money. To make sure. Then he was once again a professional. Then he accepted what was being offered. In the bedrooms of luxurious apartments, in the fragrance of perfume, among the rattle of jewels and pearl necklaces, from frustrated, distracted widows and stay-at-home wives, whose anguish drove them into doing things which would then always remain sweet, aching secrets in the darkness of memory. At these times Juan felt his therapeutic task very strongly, that he had given sexual service, a public service in an area of neglect, a straw someone had grasped at above the ocean of loneliness.

He was never either aggressive or importunate. He was matter-of-fact, eager but courteous, tactful but totally uninhibited. When he saw a woman who aroused his sexual desire, he made an offer which she could either accept or refuse. It didn't matter if he were snubbed. All he had to do was to keep his eyes open over the sea of women until the next one appeared. If she accepted, it was a matter of finding a peaceful place where the act could be carried out, no more complicated than that. Despite Catholic sexual taboos, there were many women who did accept, for the sexual climate in Argentina is different from that of Scandinavia and cannot be judged strictly according to Scandinavian values. Double morality? Naturally. Just as in Europe. But simpler, less intellectualized. More of it, yes, indeed, but as a double morality regarded as less mendacious, all the same. For double morality is double morality in Argentina, where in Europe it often has other labels, sometimes 'complete honesty', for instance, or 'realizing oneself'.

When he came to Europe, Juan was suddenly shut off from all this. He kept on nagging at me that I should find him women to go to bed with. When nothing came of it, he accused me of egoism and envy, and there was a grain of truth in the accusation. Naturally I could have found female companionship for him if I had really wanted to. But I didn't want to.

Jealousy, that fatal thing, was always lurking round the corner. Although I understood perfectly well from my own experience how unbearable the situation would become for him in the long run, I could not bring myself to lift a finger to alter it. Here in Europe, he was my discovery and my property, i.e. that was just what he wasn't and mustn't be. But was all the same. I couldn't bear the thought of him being out in the evenings and at nights for the sake of someone other than me. The amazing thing was that he understood without my having to explain. Up to a point, his loyalty to me was greater than his urges. The only solution which finally satisfied us both was to send a ticket to Europe to Lilita in Buenos Aires.

Juan had a strongly developed sense of his own irresistibility. He was convinced not only that most women desired to sleep with him the moment they laid eyes on his beautiful self, but also that, after a while, they fell in love with him. This was a judgement based on experience, and yet, viewed quite factually, it obviously contained considerable strains of exaggerated self-absorption and vanity. He himself thought he was beautiful. Sometimes he would ask, with a hint of genuine anxiety in his voice, whether I thought he was a narcissist. If I then replied 'yes', he hurriedly explained that he had only been joking. Narcissism was something abnormal, wasn't it? But he wasn't abnormal, not in any respect, I couldn't believe that, could I? No, no.

Juan soon started seeking sexual objects even in our own surroundings, but – and this was typical of him as a person and of the kind of relationship between us – he felt he first had to ask my permission. Or as in the film by Pasolini, *Theorem*, Juan's rôle. He mentioned it himself. Whether he would be a similar force in our family.

'May I sleep with Selinda?' he said.

If I had then answered yes or not answered at all, so that he would have been able to regard it as silent agreement, he would have unhesitatingly and at the first possible opportunity seduced my wife and gone to bed with her, and in next to no time we would have landed in an emotional complication which could not have ended in any way but unhappily. Consequently I answered, 'No, you may not sleep with Selinda,' and he concurred with no further comment. No harm in trying.

'May I sleep with Nina?'

That was trickier. In Argentina it was natural and justified, for there a father decides about his daughter's life in quite a different way from in Finland, where there is still a kind of sexual property-right over one's marriage partner, but definitely not over one's children. Yet I felt almost instinctively that, in this case, I was more less forced to behave like an Argentinian father rather than a Finnish one. For I knew that Juan – in the full vigour of his Latin cultural tradition and whether conscious of it at all – would slowly but irrevocably be taken over by a sense of contempt, not only for the woman he was sleeping with, but also for me. If I agreed to his sleeping with my daughter (or my wife).

It was a difficult situation. I explained that I had neither right nor desire to make decisions on behalf of my adult daughter, and at the same time I let him see how profoundly and honestly I disliked the idea. I appealed to his compassion. I asked what he thought it would be like for her the day Lilita arrived, should Nina really seriously fall in love with him. He seemed somewhat uninterested in imagining such a possibility. Just as this development, according to the inevitable logic of the emotions, started going in the direction in which the end result could only be one thing, the offer from Stockholm City Theatre suddenly came like a gift of the gods. I had a reason to stay in Stockholm for quite a while, and that Juan came with me was only natural. Self-confidently I explained that he would get a part in the play we were writing. Tailor-made for him.

It would also have been utterly absurd! Competing emotionally with one's own daughter! Jealous of one's own daughter!

On the other hand . . . what right had I to act so arbitrarily? An old man like me standing in the way of the happiness, however brief, of two young people? What was Juan to me? Son? Balls! More! Infinitely more!

(It was in the small hours. I had a dream about the Devil. About me and Juan and Nina and the Devil, that someone was to be sacrificed and it was neither Juan nor me. I cannot articulate this, or it is irrelevant, for it is no more than a fragment and perhaps immaterial, or like the boat with the white sail which tacks round and shows the black side of its sail with the bloodstains, and I couldn't tack round because I had to keep on course, the designated course, which I myself had designated and decided on and refined, keeping on course, keeping on course . . .)

After we had been in Stockholm for a while and Juan had begun to find his feet and started to go out on his own in the evenings, after he had met Spanish-speaking friends at the Arts Centre and was going to the Arts Centre almost every afternoon, he once asked me on his way out, newly-showered, his hair brushed, and wearing a clean shirt and his good, virile, fawn leather jacket from Argentina, he said:

'Have you any objection if I bring a girl back with me, if I meet one, if it works out that way, I mean, would we be disturbing you, I mean, if you're asleep . . .'

What could I say? I loathed the very idea. I loathed myself for loathing it. After all, everything was based on Juan having a life of his own and I having mine. I had my freedom to do as I wished and I did not allow him to intrude on that freedom. He had all the right in the world to expect the same of me. And yet. I answered as it was. That I neither could nor would stop him, if he wanted a woman in his room. But that, on the other hand, I didn't like it and he probably knew that, and also why.

He had been cheerful and unmoved when he had asked, expectant, perhaps slightly on his guard. Now his face darkened. He stood silent for a moment, staring down at the floor.

'You mustn't say that,' he mumbles. And he is angry.

'I'm telling you how it is.'

'Either you agree, or you don't. It's that simple. In Argentina, we go straight to the point. There it's yes or no. There we say what we think.'

'I've said what I think.'

'On the one hand, and on the other hand, yes, but how am I to know what you really think, and anyhow it's no fun bringing a girl back here if I know you're lying there in the other room not liking it!'

'This is all slightly complicated, Juan, and you know it.'

'Feelings! I hate such feelings between men!'

'I can't help that. It's how it is.'

'We won't talk about it any more,' he says roughly.

Then he tears off his fawn leather jacket and rushes into his room. He is terribly upset. So am I. I feel like grabbing his hair and throwing him out of the door, and shouting after him that as far as I'm concerned he can bring a hundred and fifty girls back here at any time of the day he cares to, but I control myself. I know it's not worth trying to talk to him now. I go into my room and close the door behind me. I try to do some work on the play, but that doesn't work at all. I sit listening, expecting to hear the outer door opening and being slammed. It doesn't happen. It is deathly silent in the apartment. My brain gradually overflows with Spanish words I want to say to him, to explain, to apologize (for what?), to take it back.

The hours go by. Just before eleven, I can't stand it any longer and go into his room. He has undressed and is lying on his bed, staring up at the ceiling. The room is dimly lit, the light from the hall and the street-lamps outside giving only a faint glow. Pale as moonlight. He is lying quite still.

'I've been thinking about it, and of course you can bring girls here if you want to,' I say. It takes a great deal of will-power to say it.

He doesn't react.

'You must give me time to think things over. You know I'm slow. To be sensible, I need time to think.'

Then he looks at me, his black eyes glittering in the dark. Suddenly he smiles and stretches out his hand.

'I've been thinking, too,' he says. 'I understand. I won't do it. Not here. Ever.'

I take his hand and sit down on the edge of the bed, his hand in mine. We look into each other's eyes and both of us smile.

'I want you to do what you want to do. I don't want you to have a wretched time out of consideration for me.'

'It's not that important. I see how you feel. We're friends, aren't we?'

'Yes, we're friends.'

He raises both arms and holds me and we embrace. Then we sit up all night talking and talking, about anything, everything. At dawn, when the garbage collectors come, we're still awake.

Juan tells me about a film he wants to make, if he had the money, if he ever gets a chance. It would be about the drifting homeless children on the streets of Buenos Aires. The poor children, the children relentlessly condemned to poverty from the start. The children with no future. The little beggar children. The little flower-sellers and the little orange-vendors and the small shoeshine boys. And the slightly older ones who have already become prostitutes. As Juan had done. And the even older ones, who have turned their backs on the law completely and live by break-ins and robbery. It would be a social document and at the same time a devastating appeal to parents and the authorities. He had already found a name for his film. It was to be called *En esta hora, exactamente, un niño esta en la calle.* 'At this very moment there is a child on the street.' I said there already was such a film, or a film with a very similar theme, a film made by Buñuel and called *Los Olvidados.* Juan had never heard of it.

Then Juan tells me a story, a story about eight street-boys in Buenos Aires being chased by the police, sometime during the first few months of the military coup, and the police are savage and crazy. There was nothing, at the time, one needed to be more afraid of in the whole world than the police. They were more dangerous, more brutal and more ruthless than all the robbers and evil spirits put together. Juan thought a whole book could be written about his experiences. But it would also be pure reality.

There are eight boys escaping from the police, who have automatics. The boys' only guilt is their poverty, and their only crime is their will to survive. They have done nothing wrong, except stealing some bread or fruit from somewhere, or selling themselves to a rich man for next to nothing, or losing their identity papers. Or they have a brother or sister in the guerillas. The police catch up with them and shoot them down, one after the other. Blood spatters against the walls and flows into the gutters. One after another, they sink down on the street and die, covered with blood. One of them is eight years old, another twelve, another eighteen, but none of them had yet reached his twentieth year. And few people or no one will miss them. When their small bodies have stopped jerking convulsively, those half-grown bodies, dressed in rags, now bloodstained, when death has irrevocably occurred, their souls slowly float up towards heaven. Eight dead bodies, eight souls, eight street-boys, missed by few or none. And while they are floating up towards the roofs of buildings in the city of Buenos Aires and disappearing into the blue which is heaven, which is nothing, the souls speak. The first says: 'I'm the one who was going to discover the ultimate cure for cancer.' The second says: 'I am the one who was going to create a new world order, who would make war superfluous for ever.' And the third says: 'I was going to make solar energy so cheap that no one would ever again ask for oil or nuclear energy.' And the fourth and the fifth and the sixth . . . all indispensable improvers of the condition of mankind, murdered by political violence, by stupidity, by social cruelty, the primary crime and failing of mankind.

He looks at me. Our faces are very close.

'Wasn't that a good story?'

'An excellent story, Juan.'

'Young people are so very different in different countries.'

Juan cannot make out the young of Sweden. He thinks Swedish young people are infantile, immature and depraved. Even when they are in their twenties, they behave like small children. He has not been in close contact with any of them, but he has seen what many of them are like, at the Arts Centre, the government cultural centre in the Parliament building, in the Underground, in Sergel Square and in the big department stores. He has seen them with their beer-cans, their amphetamine syringes, their skateboards. He himself has been called spoilt by Lilita. But here is a whole generation that not only appears to be totally spoilt, but at the same time in a horribly indefinite way to be wholly rejected.

Young people in Stockholm are not like those in Buenos Aires. Compared with young people in Buenos Aires, the young of Stockholm seem spineless, aggressive, noisy, hopelessly childish, and not only without contact with the adult world, but also consciously excluded from it. In Argentina, regardless of their place in society, children learn very young to take responsibility, to show consideration, to be a functional part of a collective. In Sweden, it appears to be almost the opposite; they never learn. Juan is not at all used to such sharp antagonisms between generations. In Argentina, it is natural to be courteous to older people, but equally natural for older people to be considerate to the young. In Argentina, they don't shout at each other or say nothing whatsoever across the generation gap. On the contrary, in Argentina, there is a natural, warm, encouraging communication between generations.

It is the lack of contact between people in Sweden – and Finland – which frightens Juan more than anything else. He thinks it is because of the dissolution of the institution of the family in these countries, for where there is no active family collective, at all levels, the possibilities for love are also strictly limited. And love is what we live off and develop from in the end, isn't it? Where there is no openness and warmth between members of the family – and not only between mother and son and father and daughter, but also between uncle and nephew and aunt and niece and so on – the missing openness is soon replaced by aggressiveness, the warmth by the cold loneliness that nurtures anxiety.

In Juan's mind, Swedish young people are lost youth, not just because most of them have no good family relationships in which to feel secure, but also because most of them are too well-off, and have always had too much, far too much, materially. No one has had to struggle to survive, as Juan has, and whoever has never had to make an effort to acquire what he wants, cannot really have any real idea of the value of goods and possessions, all goods and all possessions, crusts of bread and handfuls of rice as well as bicycles and slalom-skis. In itself, there is nothing wrong with material well-being; on the contrary, it is good and worth striving for, but material well-being which neither presupposes nor demands a corresponding concentration of personality, a corresponding development on a mental level, such well-being can in the long run become destructive. Juan knows that. He thinks he knows it. To be well-off materially can be a means or a route to happiness, but it can never be happiness itself.

Poverty demands responsibility. Poverty teaches you responsibility. Affluence tempts you into irresponsibility and irresponsibility leads to alienation and destruction. When Juan left his childhood home at fourteen, it was largely because he had to take responsibility for his own life and future, but that did not prevent him, deep down, at the same time, from also feeling natural human responsibility for his mother and father, and his whole family for that matter, if and when the need or circumstances arose. When his uncle suddenly died in Chivilcoy in December 1978, he did not hesitate to leave Buenos Aires in the middle of the night, hitching his way back, to be at his father's side in his grief and helping with the practical arrangements for a quick tropical burial. That was the difference. That was how he saw the difference. For it was clear that the young people he saw in Stockholm, in the Underground, in Sergel Square, in Farsta shopping centre, had neither the strength nor the ability to take responsibility for their own destiny.

We often roamed round Stockholm in the evenings. At the Central Station he saw what I didn't see, noticing everything that on my own I would never have noticed. That was his experience and my inexperience or innocence. We stood there in the echoing central concourse among other people standing there like us or passing by, and he pointed out to me with unerring sureness where the drug deals were going on, where prostitutes were striking bargains. Discreetly, unnoticeably. He was my mentor in a field in which I was a novice. He opened my eyes to what happens within what appears to happen. He taught me about the secret life that is constantly lived right in amongst us, the darker side of the trivial life called everyday routine.

This was his world and he would recognize it, regardless of whether the city were called Stockholm, Buenos Aires or Singapore. There were other things he did not recognize, which frightened him, which caused him terror, which he could not grasp.

Outside the Central Station, in the evening darkness, a taxi stops. A drunk scrambles out. He stands there, uncertain, confused, swaying as if on a ship's deck in the North Sea. Almost simultaneously, the taxi-driver also gets out of the cab. They exchange a few words, but we cannot hear what they are saying. Suddenly, and without the slightest warning, the taxi-driver hits the drunkard a couple of fierce blows in the face. The drunk sinks to the ground and lies there, while the taxi drives off and vanishes down towards Vasa Street. Juan stares at me. He is scared and disgusted and just can't understand it.

'Why?' he keeps repeating. 'Why?'

I have no answer for him. I don't know why any more than he does.

One afternoon in Sergel Square, we witness a fight between two inebriated girls. This time we understand what the quarrel is about, a plastic carrier-bag from the liquor store and its contents. One girl is large and strong, the other small and frail. Strands of hair toss about like brown grass in a storm, oaths drown Maria's one-man band in the corner of the square. The large strong girl is wearing wooden-soled shoes, the smaller girl already lying whimpering on the ground. The larger girl is beside herself and goes on and on kicking at the smaller girl with her wooden-soled shoes, right in her face. No one intervenes. Neither do we. Everything happens so quickly, or it is so incomprehensible, paralysing and unreal.

This is violence, unmotivated violence. Juan has never seen it before, never in the metropolis of Buenos Aires. Never like this. He did indeed come from a country where violence was an everyday matter, where torture was part of the system, where people disappeared and then were found maimed, dead, or were never seen again. But that was another kind of violence, directed from above and politically motivated, not as here, violence between human beings, totally meaningless violence, between people who should really stick together, people in the same boat, subject to the same oppression or the same solicitude, the same authoritarian indifference or the same authoritarian equality. In Argentina, people helped each other out of difficulties, spontaneously, without being called upon to do so or expecting compensation. In Sweden, they knocked each other down in the street and what in Latin America was class loyalty or simply human loyalty, Sweden's welfare state transformed into personal aggression, suspicion, egoism and unfriendliness.

I could not really see this as Juan did. I had known Sweden for a long time as a friendly country on the whole, in many respects considerably more friendly and kind than Finland.

One evening we go to see Sylvester Stallone's film, *Rocky*. Juan has seen it before in Argentina, so he knows what it's about, although this time there will be no Spanish sub-titles. But he would like to see it again and I haven't seen it before.

'I cried,' he says, as we emerge on to Svea Road into wet autumnal Stockholm.

I had seen that he had cried, and I also understood why. It was not only that the film was so close to his own life and his life's dream. The character himself, Rocky as a person, was also so close to Juan. The experience must have shaken him. Juan wanted to be hard. He was a man. It was unusual for him to cry and even more unusual for him to admit it without explanations. When I had to tell him he would not be given the part in the play at the City Theatre, as I'd promised, I wept with despair and disappointment over the failure of everything. To console me, and as evidence of his great and genuine friendship for me, he did not react with distaste or repugnance, but simply accepted it. That I wept.

When Rocky was out of work, he acted for a time as a henchman of the Mafia; threatening reluctant shopkeepers with violent reprisals, he extracted money from those who refused to see what was best for them and failed to pay the sums that the Mafia demanded for them to be left in peace.

'I've done the same,' said Juan.

'Worked for the Mafia in Buenos Aires?'

Well . . . not exactly, but extracted money with threats of violence, all the same. He replies evasively. Usually to help some younger, weaker and more timid colleague in the taxi-boy trade, someone who had come up against a barefaced bourgeois bastard refusing to pay up after the completed act. As a kind of professional loyalty then, almost? Yes, roughly. But not in any larger context, Mafia context? No, no. Yet there was still something vague about Juan's relations with organized crime. Rocky had been given the job because he was very strong. Juan was certainly not as strong as Rocky, but quite strong all the same. Strong enough.

Two films upset Juan, because they exposed him to profound, bitter and emotionally-laden identification. The second was *Midnight Cowboy*, with Jon Voigt.

After a while, Juan went to the Arts Centre almost every day. At first he sat reading Argentinian newspapers and thus got to know other Latin Americans in Stockholm, political refugees, guest-workers and youngsters who had left home for reasons with which Juan was in absolute agreement. He had learnt a Swedish phrase, and to be quite sure, had written it down on a piece of paper. 'May I go back home with you for a screw?' Whenever he caught the eye of any Swedish girl roaming around, he just held out the piece of paper and smiled his most charming smile. I don't know how often he succeeded, or indeed whether he succeeded at all, as he told me only about the times when it hadn't worked. One day he ran into an old friend from

Buenos Aires, whom he had not seen for several years. His name was Pepe and he at once became a new, exciting element in our life.

Pepe had also worked off and on as a taxi-boy, which was how Juan had got to know him. Pepe's father was a comparatively wealthy small business man. Pepe had taken himself off to Europe after a violent quarrel with his father, who had accused his son of theft, not entirely without justification, for Pepe had indeed tried to augment his income by selling antiques he had stolen from his parents' home. He had been in Europe for almost three years now; he had come by boat to Spain, stayed there for a while, but had not got on especially well with the Spanish police, so had made his way across the border to France, staying there, but drifting northwards all the time, to Amsterdam, Copenhagen, Malmö, finally landing up in Stockholm.

He didn't like Sweden. None of the people Juan met at the Arts Centre liked Sweden. They all wanted to go home, but nearly all of them lacked the means to do so. But Pepe did not want to go back to Argentina so long as his father was still alive. Generally speaking, he didn't know where in the whole world he would like to live.

Pepe had no job. He lived with a Swedish girl who had a small child. She kept him, and his main task was to look after the child while she was at work. He did not like doing it at all. He was also without any positive contact with Swedish society, mostly because he had failed to learn Swedish. When he wasn't at home looking after the child, he was out stealing in town.

Juan's and my pleasant little home on the south side of the city thus became transformed into a veritable thieves' den. Goods of various kinds gathered in the corners or wherever there was space; clothes, cameras, transistors, expensive perfumes and God knows what else. Naturally Juan asked my permission before they set about this seriously. I was appalled to start with, but couldn't help admitting I was also amused. In a way. The appalling thing was that I was quite incapable of seeing the immorality of what was going on. My grandfather had been Attorney-General in his day, the most senior guardian of the law, and now his grandson was unprotestingly allowing his home to be filled with stolen goods! Incredible! Or to be more truthful, it was simply and unequivocally exciting, stimulating and extremely entertaining.

At first I tried to remain aloof, preaching rather feebly to Juan about right and wrong and respect for other people's property. He laughed scornfully. His ideas on the right to property of the rich and the total lack of rights of the poor had been shaped for ever long before on the streets of Buenos Aires, and when he finally noticed my – to say the least – ambivalent attitude to it all, all his inhibitions vanished. Pepe was a very skilful thief. We laughed.

Juan assured me that Pepe and Pepe alone carried out these dubious deeds. He himself was merely a spectator, or at the very most a passive assistant, if necessary. He said this to placate me, as I had stated that under no circumstances did I want any trouble with the police on his behalf. Despite this, he took with him no fewer than seven pairs of elegant trousers in his luggage – all honourably stolen – when we went back to Finland in November. He would keep some for himself and the rest he would sell at a high price in Argentina. Lilita was already with us by then. She had also been bitten with Latin light-fingeredness and went to Finland wearing a smart blouse she had lifted from the NK department store.

As they had no money of their own, this did in fact make things cheaper for me.

Pepe mostly stole to have something to do, both as a protest and a way of passing the time. It was also a good, simple way of acquiring some nice clothes. When he needed cash, he stole anything, and there was no shortage of buyers. I was offered a brand-new camera to take home as a present for my wife. The original price was round about four thousand kronor and I could have it for seven hundred and fifty. I refused, but more out of cowardice than from moral misgivings, because I was afraid of what might happen at the Customs.

Pepe clearly did not approve of the way I dressed, for he also suggested he should acquire a new suit for me. All I had to do was to give him my size, the favoured colour and quality, and then be patient for a while. It might take a few days, as a whole suit was bulky and quite hard to steal. You had to wait for the right opportunity, and the right opportunity always arose sooner or later. I did not accept that offer, either. There were limits. In practice I was by now already a receiver, even if passively and somewhat reluctantly. If I had actively concerned myself with Pepe's stolen goods, I would have been a criminal in a more definitive sense, and I also lacked the necessary courage and desire. To that extent, I was still the grandson of Finland's old Attorney-General.

It was all based on a small but decisive difference in speed of reaction between the staff of Swedish stores on the one side, and Pepe, Juan and their Latin American friends on the other. The Swedish brain was a few tenths of a second slower than the Argentinian. When it registered what had happened, if it registered at all, in ninety-nine cases out of a hundred it was already too late and the black-haired thief had vanished into the crowd. Pepe rarely ate anything except stolen food. We often found ourselves in the kitchen at home, stuffing ourselves with steak, rice and vegetables and ice-cream for dessert, all stolen from the counters of Åhlén's.

Juan was not such a fool that he didn't understand perfectly well what it all entailed. Symptoms of social maladjustment, psychic disharmony, social isolation and rootlessness. He maintained that there wasn't a single normal healthy foreigner in the whole Arts Centre. They're all mad in some way, he said. He knew what he was talking about. On my part, I knew which way things were going when Juan was irresistibly driven into the same compulsive petty crime in protest, despair and homesickness.

One afternoon, we're standing by a display-case of beautiful glasses, he and I, surrounded by people buying and selling.

'Beautiful glasses,' I say.

'Which one do you want?'

'None.'

'That cut-glass one there?'

'No, certainly not. You mustn't!' I say, utterly petrified.

We stand there without moving, side by side, and he stares at me, defiant and slightly mocking, to show that he does not intend to obey me this time. As we stand there, something incomprehensible happens; the glass vanishes from its mount. I see it has gone, but it happened so swiftly I didn't have time to see how. He has it underneath his leather jacket, hidden beneath his scarf. When we get out on to the street, he gives me the glass, which would have cost eighty kronor.

'There you are,' he says ironically. 'A modest token of my gratitude for everything you've done for me.'

This was his blatant way of telling me that he couldn't stay in Sweden, that he had to return to his native country, to Argentina. There you didn't have to steal to feel you were a human being among human beings.

There was no balanced proportion between my indestructible feeling of happiness and his growing unhappiness. His proximity, the very fact of his constant presence in my life, filled me almost continuously with a giddy sense of gratitude, for the goodness of life, the fullness of life, the generosity of reality. Juan was my happiness. That feeling was spontaneous and uncontrollable. But at the same time, it was part of a plan that was less spontaneous and which, on the contrary, presumed control to succeed. Juan was my happiness, but he was also a literary project and a human project, and both cases involved an imperative condition that no emotional catastrophe should arise in our relationship. There was no lack of alarms and excursions, neither at the time, nor later. But as his irritation grew and the disharmony between us became more evident, in an amazing way so did our mutual readiness again and again to put things right.

One night we have a violent quarrel about what love is. The quarrel is really about us, about his unhappiness and my feelings of guilt. But at the time we're avoiding the point. It's a substitute argument. Juan tells me that in Argentina there are women who can love a man so much and so unconditionally that they agree to prostitute themselves to acquire for the man the money that will give him a trouble-free life. I am very upset. I say I consider him both romantic and cynical, and that if that is the case, it is not a question of love at all, but something else, an icy exploitation of a woman's weakness and an exaggerated emotional dependency on her part, or broadly a slave-situation rather than a love-situation. He protests, aggressively, or almost in self-defence, that I am bourgeois, with no experience of life, that I don't know what it's all about, that in fact the greatest sacrifice a woman can make on the altar of love is to sell the last thing she has, herself, to the advantage of the man she loves. A fraction of this is about himself. It is also about the different female and male experience between informed Europe on the one part and backward Argentina on the other. We get nowhere.

He thinks I am foolishly bourgeois. I think he's a childish and ignorant pup. Raging, I go to bed, but sleep badly. I've never been able to sleep well after an unresolved quarrel with anyone close to me. My wife, Juan. The following morning, he calls me into him, lying there in bed in a good mood, laughing. That was a good quarrel, but stupid. We both think that. He pulls me to him and we embrace, whispering in the embrace that nothing can break our friendship for good, and that our friendship is so strong, it'll last until the end of our lives.

Our quarrels are often about insignificant bagatelles, just like in marriage. They often arise from linguistic misunderstandings, his lack of knowledge of Swedish usage, my continued lack of fluent Spanish.

At the Arts Centre, he has learnt the expression 'damned shit' and he assumes it's an unusually horrible swear-word. People are restrained in their use of swear-words in Argentina. If you say something crude to another person, you really mean it as an insult and have to be prepared for the consequences. In Sweden and Finland, people aren't nearly so pernickety. You can say almost anything without meaning it and without offending the opposite party. It is morning and Juan is in bed as usual, very obstinate. Something has gone wrong somewhere with Lilita's ticket, and Juan, with temporary abandonment, is refusing to help clear it up. I lose patience and for once raise my voice. I yell at him 'damned silly infant!' or something like that. He stiffens and turns silent, and remains silent for twelve hours. Late that night, we are once again on speaking terms. But he is icy and maintains I have behaved unforgivably and that he finds it difficult to forgive me. I find it very difficult to understand why. He finds it very difficult to say why. I make a great effort to get him to explain, because I don't feel particularly guilty. Finally it comes out all the same. 'You shouted "damned shit" at me.'

One evening in Västerlång Street, after having dinner at Rodolpho's in peace and quiet and complete accord, Juan suddenly starts talking about 'homosexuality', maintaining that it's a disease and a sign of genetic decay and human depravity. I'm surprised and upset, as he has never, for obvious reasons, said such a thing before. I protest that as he has lived with and exploited homosexuals for years, he should be the last to express such narrow and prejudiced views. Now it's his turn to be upset and he maintains I haven't understood what he meant, but he nevertheless sticks to his opinions. Gradually we find ourselves in the middle of a real quarrel. I am morally indignant, he more and more annoyed. He brings the Tsar's family into the conversation, and I say I didn't know any of them were homosexual. In the end, Juan is thoroughly upset and angry, and, as a final salvo, says it's no good discussing things with me because I don't know Spanish! I can't make head or tail of anything. We go home in oppressive silence. We say nothing all night. Much later, it turns out that he was talking about haemophilia, the bleeder's disease.

I begin to wonder how many misunderstandings and unresolved conflicts have arisen because of language oddities and straight mistakes at the level where statesmen from different cultures and different language areas meet and sign agreements of world historical importance. In the course of history. For statesmen are no different from Juan and me, are they? And their interpreters? What is that Russian saying when he says something? What is the American saying? And the Chinese? 'Damned shit'? What do they mean by that?

Three months later, we are in Denmark to talk to my Danish publisher about the book we are doing together. One evening, we visit some old friends of mine. As we seldom meet, we like talking about things we have in common, mutual memories, mutual acquaintances. Juan cannot take part, he is outside, and for long spells he sits in silence. He doesn't understand what we are saying. We give him an occasional resumé in Spanish or Italian of what we are talking about. But that doesn't help the situation all that much; he is not one of us and feels it, and he sinks into a depression which gets steadily worse.

'What am I doing here?' he says despairingly, when we are alone for a moment. I don't know what to say to him, as I know only too well how he feels.

'You're my friend, and they are my friends. It's only natural for my friends to get to know each other,' I say later, and he admits that is true. But it is little consolation to him at this moment.

Once or twice during the evening, he tries to be his old pleasant, social and companionable self by making witty remarks about food and drink, or by showing conjuring tricks to the household's astonished and enthusiastic youngsters. It works for a while, but then he can't be bothered any more and sinks back into depression. He cannot live here. Not in Europe. He must go back to Argentina, although he really has nothing to go back to. Except his family and his friends, the streets of Buenos Aires, the sun, the warmth, everything of which he is a natural part. He longs to be back where his roots are.

We spent the night at my friends' house. They've made a bed up for us on the living-room floor. After the others have gone to sleep, we lie there for a long time, talking and smoking by the light of a small night-light on the carpet beside us. As we talk, his depression lifts. As so many times before, he is suddenly very open, very eager, and in that way of the young, he is filled with a desire to talk. He talks about Denmark and Finland and Sweden, where life is so unlike life in Argentina, and so difficult to adapt to. As so many times before, we then become very close to each other. It starts with the words and out of the words grows feeling. His eyes meet mine, and a warmth goes from him to me and from me to him. We talk about ourselves, about our friendship that is friendship but could be love, and circumstances decide the words. We talk about tenderness, living through tenderness, not in the hard way but in the soft way, and that some people can, like us, and other's can't. We're naked beneath the bedclothes and, as an obvious consequence of what we feel for each other, he moves over to me, creeps down under my blanket and puts his arms round me. We go on talking. About the book we're writing together, and that the only important thing is to tell the truth, and that the only important thing is to keep our friendship so that there will be a happy ending.

'You're very tactful.'

'What do you mean?'

'You're doing the writing. I only tell you. Anyone can do that. In reality my share doesn't correspond to what I get in exchange, but you've arranged it this way so that I'll be able to take money from you without feeling humiliated.'

'Without you, there would be no book . . .'

We put the light out. His head is against my shoulder. I hold him and press him to me, stroking his back while his hand moves slowly in my hair.

'You're my brother and my father and my friend and my son, everything a man can be to another man . . .'

'That's it, Juan. Me for you . . . and you for me . . .'

We fall asleep. When I wake, his head is still on my shoulder.

Then we're back home in Esbo again, and relationships are again balanced on a family level. The two of them are soon to leave. Lilita does not want to go, but Juan does, so Lilita does, too, in the end. We go with them for a bit of the way, the whole family travelling with them over to Stockholm. The last day in Stockholm. We have lunch at Sarajevo's in the Old City. Lilita leans her head against Selinda's shoulder and weeps. In the evening, they take the train to Paris. We say goodbye to our adult children on their way out into the world.

The house is empty. After we had returned from Stockholm, and I am at home, it is horribly empty. The room Juan and Lilita had is empty. It is quiet and empty everywhere, the pale winter morning light coming through the windows. I stand in the middle of the living-room floor and feel the silence and the emptiness and put my hands to my face and scream out my loss.

Scream like an animal. I never believed that such loss could feel like pain.

And everything that has happened since, everything I have thought about and planned and everything I have done, has had one single aim, one single goal, to see Juan again, to re-bind the family ties with Juan and Lilita.

Unfinished Notes

Today, Tuesday, 3 October, 1978, great heavy clouds hang over Buenos Aires. Drizzle succeeds pouring rain and the temperature is fifteen degrees centigrade. It is spring. Last night, the temperature fell to ten degrees. We froze, my foster-children and I, on our way to and from the restaurant where we had had an early dinner at about half-past eight. I live in the centre of the town, in Avenida Rivadavia, on the fifteenth floor, with a magnificent, rather exciting view across the endless array of buildings and roofs of the metropolis, stone, stone, stone. At night, the lights and neon advertisements glimmer beneath the dark sky. Like mysterious night-swallows, bats dart back and forth outside the window. They make me think of flying-fish in the Atlantic.

The rain pours down. It is half-past twelve.

Late last night, a tremendous thunderstorm broke over the city, the sky rent incessantly by lightning, transparent blue like a warning light from God.

I am at home in Buenos Aires. Where does this rare feeling of being at home come from, flickering so faintly, so seldom felt these days where it should really be felt, far away in Europe, where I have lived my life? The absence of trivial responsibilities? The absence of a social context familiar to the point of boredom? The legitimate human need to create a new world or to broaden the horizons of one's habitual world? I have my children here, two adult children out of four, living in Argentina, adopted, but loved as much as if they were my own. That is not quite enough to explain my sense of being at home. The people are different. The people *are* different. In Argentina one feels a security on the human level, which has now vanished in the excellent social organization of Scandinavia. Swings and roundabouts. It depends on one's preferences.

Today, Wednesday, 4 October, the weather is beginning to be more normal. According to information on the television, it is eighteen degrees outside and the time is seven minutes to eleven. Cloud-cover is very thin. The sun is coming out. In the district of La Boca, by Rio de la Plata, there were floods the day before yesterday, eighteen inches of water in the streets, and friends of mine who live there had to be good and stay at home and go without food. All day yesterday, the rain poured down. I was afflicted with depression, with a number of personal complications as a result. Life is often a dubious affair, anyway, but my life is especially dubious. Everything I write is a lie; everything I write is the truth.

He came to see me yesterday afternoon, as we had agreed, and it all went wrong from the start. In a certain kind of human relationship there is a distrust that is fatal. I immediately lapsed into this distrust. He began to play tango on the gramophone. I imagined he was – consciously – building a wall between us with his damned tango. But it probably wasn't so. Why should it have been? I pretended to sleep and after a while went into my bedroom and lay down on the bed. He sat for a long time in the living-room, singing to himself. We were to have had dinner together back at their home. I did not go with him. I practically drove him out. He was upset. My anxiety was slowly transformed into malice. I felt he quite consciously wanted to hurt me.

Almost so that I hated him.

The gossamer-like foliage of the jacaranda tree. Soon the *avenidas* will glow blue with jacaranda trees in bloom.

It is half-past twelve. Television information says that the temperature is twenty degrees centigrade, but heavy rain clouds are gathering again over Buenos Aires. He is coming to see me in an hour's time; we agreed before I drove him out yesterday. We must settle this thing that has happened between us. It is not the first time, either. Nor the last, for sure. This is the strangest, most difficult, most comprehensive and most wonderful human relationship I have ever experienced. He is my son. He *is* my son. But so infinitely more than that. That's what is so inexplicable.

The godfather.

On Friday, 6 October, the sky is still covered with clouds. The temperature is fifteen degrees centigrade, according to the television a moment ago. The time is a quarter to eleven. Late on Wednesday evening, when I returned home after dinner with some of the Vivero family and switched on the radio, the last movement of Sibelius' Fifth thundered out into the room through the stereo speakers. There was nothing special about it apart from the fact that it pleased me to be able to hear Sibelius even in Argentina. Why have I noted that down? Because I thought it might arouse patriotic feelings? But then it didn't.

He came on Wednesday afternoon – oh, miracles – a whole hour earlier than we had agreed on. Concern about our argument? Mutual concern? I don't know. We had a rather long but somehow still unsatisfactory conversation, which ended in the physical expressions of tenderness I had missed ever since mid-February when he visited me for the last time in my temporary workroom in Helsinki. It was different then, the warmth, melancholy and honesty of farewell. Now it was actually more like starting again from the beginning, like the first time in Buenos Aires in November 1976.

'*Tu eres un niño,*' he says to me. 'You are a child.' Even if he is right in certain respects, it is somewhat worrying all the same, as it makes me think that perhaps he does not know me very well after all; I am far from being a child in the vital areas in which adults mainly function. But he says he understands me. I think we understand each other. Was that only '*un grand illusion*'?

Love is the strangest phenomenon in the life of a human being.

On Wednesday evening, Lilita invited me to dinner. Present, apart from Lilita, were Juan and I, her mother and father, her sister and her fiancé, and then the younger brother, or more familiarly, Norma and Pancho, Claudia and Luis, and young Gabriel. They arrived two hours later than arranged, so we did not sit down at the table until about ten o'clock. I was very hungry. Somewhat earlier, I had been shopping with Lilita in the nearby market hall: two large chickens, bread, vegetables, wine and Coca-Cola. I had thought of asking about the hard times in Argentina during dinner, but the occasion would have been extremely ill-chosen, so I refrained (wise that I am). Eating is a way of being together in a pleasant and relaxed way. One feels that very strongly in Argentina. Dragging in Scandinavian platitudes would be like the bull in a china-shop, or the undertaker at a circus. Better to let the conversation flow at will. Relate the (unimportant) events of the day. Make jokes (which I don't get). Compare Finland with Argentina, customs, good and bad, climate, geographical circumstances. Juan is apt to show off his knowledge of Spanish and Finnish, which often seems a troublesome interruption of my Spanish fluency. I must learn to think in Spanish. His eagerness about my native language stops me. Minor problems, one really has to admit.

Pancho works in a bakery. He works two shifts – always – to earn a reasonable living, which always means a sixteen-hour day, or that he leaves home at about three in the morning and gets back about seven in the evening. He is tired this evening. He is tired every evening, naturally. But pleasant, humorous in a friendly, good-natured way. Luis works in an office. Claudia took over Lilita's job as telephonist in the leather factory, when Lilita went to Finland in November last year. Norma is at home, at least for the time being. Her sight has got worse. She is somewhat younger than I am, while Pancho and I are exact contemporaries.

Yesterday was Thursday. We went to a football match. Juan and I and Luis and Daniel, who is married to Monica, Lilita's elder sister. Daniel works at the Fiat car factory. After the match, at about half-past eleven, late dinner at Monica and Daniel's place. They live in La Boca, the working-class area, originally the preserve of Italian immigrants in Buenos Aires. Like Juan, Daniel is of Italian origin. Their home consists of one room which contains no more than a bed, a table and a refrigerator. We were seven at table: Monica and Daniel, Claudia and Luis, Lilita and Juan and me. Apart from Daniel, they could all be my children. The conversation did not flow as well as I had wished. I was tired and Spanish was causing me greater difficulties than the day before. I don't understand what they say, possibly because they speak a youthful jargon alien to their parents. But on the whole, the atmosphere is very open, relaxed, inquisitively friendly. Claudia is very pretty. Seventeen years old, she has been engaged to Luis for a year. Her face lights up when she smiles and she smiles a great deal. She has a way of looking at me expectantly, curious about my reactions, openly disarming. I feel we are friends. Monica is more reserved. Claudia lives with Monica and Daniel. I can't imagine how they manage in their one tiny room. But to move in with Luis, to whom she is officially engaged, would be inconceivable in Argentina.

Saturday. 7 October. Twenty degrees, according to the television. The sun has a good chance of getting through, but the cloud-cover, although thin, is damned persistent. It is ten to twelve. A routine has begun to come into my life, which is no bad thing in this situation. I write for two, three or four hours every morning, and in the afternoon he comes – regularly – to see me and we eventually go for a stroll into the centre of town. My first week in Buenos Aires is over.

Monday. 9 October. Lovely sunny weather. It is eleven minutes to one. There is no routine in my life at all. Saturday was actually simply terrible. Late on Friday evening I paid nine hundred pesos for a bottle of wine in a bar down a side-street off Rivadavia. I drank it on my own, didn't get to bed until about two, and naturally could write no more than the seven (optimistic) lines above. Somewhat later, I was afflicted with terrible anguish and roamed around full of the most dreadful thoughts of suicide until about five o'clock on Sunday morning. What was I doing in Buenos Aires at all? Who could be interested in this banal, superficial stuff I was writing? That was the day I was to meet his mother for the first time. We were to have dinner at his sister's place. I was nervous and singularly ill-prepared.

Now I'm sitting on the bed in his and Lilita's bedroom, my typewriter placed primitively on a small stool with a mass of quilts on top. It occurs to me that, in my privileged life, I have always had a desk of some kind at my disposal. His mother, Mercedes, is here. She is washing my dirty linen on the washing-balcony alongside the kitchen. I can hear her splashing and scrubbing and carrying on, and I can see her if I bend down and peer under the venetian blind.

I am completely dependent on his intimacy, his trust, his attitude towards me. We went shopping this morning. He was to buy a refrigerator, which they really must have now for the summer. We also bought a mattress for me to sleep on in their living-room on the nights I am not in the apartment in Rivadavia. Claudio, from whom I am renting it, is a steward on Aerolinas Argentina. Consequently, he is usually away, flying all over the place. We have agreed that when he is off-duty I will live with them here in Azcuenaga. He (not Claudio, that is) whistles and sings almost ceaselessly. I sometimes feel it's aggressiveness. Aimed at me. On the other hand, I know it isn't. It is his Argentinian mentality, so unlike my own ponderous introverted Finnish melancholy.

I force him not to leave me in the lurch.

Things went wrong on Saturday when I was to write about the football match of just a few days before. One cannot describe great experiences lucidly, just as one can never relate afterwards what is funny about a funny film. I had wanted to describe the billowing sea of people, the continuous noise, singing, shouts, trumpet blasts, yells. The collective attention and the collective empathy, which is hot, swift, physical, brutal and liberating, and in a mysterious way also dangerous. It was the football team above all others in Buenos Aires, Boca Juniors, playing against a team from Brazil. Boca Juniors won three-one. Boca Juniors' colours are the same as those of the Swedish flag. Argentina's flag has the same colours as the Finnish flag. We paid no entrance fees. Juan seldom pays entrance fees. Imagine me, at the age of forty-eight, sneaking into football matches without paying! As if I were eleven! That's also an experience!

Faced with dinner at Rosa and Griseldo's, I nevertheless managed to pull myself together sufficiently so that all went well, I think. He is an afterthought. His sister Rosa is twenty years older than he is, about my age in other words, and his brother-in-law Griseldo is almost an old man, over sixty. They have a son, Gabriel, who is six, lively, intelligent, observant and not a little old for his years, as we say. Griseldo married Rosa after his first wife died. Griseldo has worked for forty years with the same firm. He has a steady job on the office side and copes quite well. He is slightly formal, slightly long-winded and solemn, and he knows a little English, which he likes to use when he talks to me. He brings out a whole battery of bottles with peculiar labels, given to him by his customers. He has gone the long road and taken a few steps into the middle classes, and it is very noticeable that he feels this entails an obligation.

Rosa radiates kindness. She is quiet, not talkative. Gabriel does all the talking for her. She has trouble sleeping. She gets up at about three or four every morning and potters about, busying herself in silence in the living-room and kitchen, reading a lot, writing when the spirit moves her. There is a core of creativity in the whole of this family, and I ask myself what would have become of them all if they had had the financial and social opportunities to exploit it. Juan's artistic talent is quite indisputable.

All my children are artistically gifted.

Mercedes has baked *empanadas*, a kind of pasty, so good they melt in the mouth. There is plenty of wine with dinner, but consumption is modest, as always in Argentina. *Bife de chorizo* and *salchichas*, a sausage, strong and tasty. I am the guest of honour, which in this slowly emerging middle-class environment is more obvious than before. Griseldo is very forthcoming, turning to me with polite attention, which is nevertheless very relaxed and without the fawning ingratiation or concealed aggression so common in corresponding situations at home in Finland.

I am shy of Mercedes. Later on, it turns out that she is equally shy of me. She is an old woman, with a bad leg, to be operated on any time now. That is why she is in Buenos Aires and not at home with her husband in Chivilcoy. Yet there is between us a wordless warmth which I feel very strongly, and also feel very strongly that it is mutual. This warmth naturally has its origins in love for her son, which we have in common. Is there anything dubious about that? I write it to prove that there is not.

She does not know me. I do not know her. And yet, I have become part of her life in the same way as she has become part of mine.

I know a great deal that she does not know. Not least about her son. She has inklings of which I have no inkling. Her life cannot have been anything like mine, in any respect. *Cannot.* Yet there must be something there, something unsayable, hidden deep down in the most secret fields of communicating humanity, a cell that has divided, a seed that has grown, sometime, somewhere. For otherwise we would not be able to share this love.

On Friday afternoon, we went on foot into the city centre. At Callao, he stops me in front of the entrance to a bar.

'*Academia,*' he says, smiling, as we go on our way. '*Academia de la vida para me.*'

Like Gorki's university, I think. With all my heart, I would wish him a future such as Gorki's.

It is six minutes past four. I am alone with Mercedes in the little apartment in Azcuenaga. We don't know what to say to each other. But she smiles. I smile back. Juan is out on business. Claudio has smuggled a gold cigarette-lighter in from the States and Juan is to sell it at a hundred per cent profit. If Claudio didn't exist, with his supreme talent for duty-free imports, Juan's situation would be considerably trickier. In Galeria del Este, the sale of seventy ivory bracelets is taking place and he reckons to make a thousand pesos out of it. Lilita comes back after six o'clock. She works at a hospital now, in the office there. Her pay is slightly lower than at the leather factory, but the hours are better and the hospital is quite close, so she saves on journeys there and back. I don't know exactly what she earns a month, but it is not likely to be more than a hundred, in pounds. At this stage, the cost of living in Argentina is approaching that of Scandinavia.

Mercedes is washing my clothes.

Half-past ten. Tuesday, 10 October. Another lovely sunny day. It's not working. It's not working.

The same atmosphere as Saturday afternoon. The impossibility, the absurdity, the insanity of this task.

Concerning him, I am sensitive to the point of insanity. His sensitivity is on the whole no less than mine, but it is on another level and, anyhow in relation to me, is not of the same calibre.

It's not really like that, either. He can't cope with my anguish. And I know it.

A small tussock tips over large loads.

Our road together – which I have long ago staked out to the end of my life . . . and in my own way – that road is mined with small tussocks, strategically placed there daily by me.

Fool!

It's not even twenty-four hours since he spoke to me above love, that enormous complication, which is a complication only for me, not for him. The Argentinian.

What if he's lying? I know he is not.

Jealousy. Those small tussocks. I must learn, not just to endure, but to accept with joy this whole huge army of friends who take up his time in Buenos Aires.

He is not mine. He is not mine. He is not mine.

A son is not the property of his father.

Yet this morning, as on Saturday, I have been almost consumed with anguish.

Then suddenly he was there. In the room. Unexpectedly. He smiled.

It is half-past eleven. She has a bed at the hospital from this afternoon. We don't yet know with any certainty when the operation will take place. Last night, all four of us slept in their apartment, Mercedes on the floor in the bedroom on four large quilts spread out alongside their bed. She always does that when she comes on a visit, he says. She likes it like that, my mother. She wants to be close to us when she sleeps. And I on the new mattress in the living-room. They regard physical proximity very differently from the way I do, i.e. from the way I was brought up. All afternoon, he petted and fondled his mother, pinching her nose, kissing and hugging her, holding her, all that. At home, it's called 'messing about'. And it's something nasty.

We sat up half the night. As usual. The television was showing the first episode of *Roots*. I hadn't seen it before. Those beautiful brave American people with their beautiful brave American morality. Only this time everything was set in Africa and the people had darker skins. Lies and damned propaganda.

What it means to me is not the same for them. What goes wrong for me, does not go wrong for them. This matter of being allowed to be alone. The matter of having a 'little corner' to oneself. This matter of not being any trouble to other people. This matter of making yourself small and preferably quite invisible, not demanding more for yourself than less than necessary. These matters that are the consequences of a bourgeois upbringing.

They have grown up in a hard world in which even children are people.

On Saturday night at about half-past twelve, as we left Griseldo's home, his restlessness. 'You're not depressed any more?' 'No.' 'Sure?' But I was. I assured him I wasn't, but in a tone of voice that would mean he knew I was lying. We were to go and listen to Edmondo Rivero, the incomparable tango singer. But there was a queue outside El Viejo Almacén, and it was clearly already full. So we went to the Laura instead, a newly opened, so less well-known place where there was singing and gambling and tango. Tango is a drama, but all music is drama in Argentina. Passion is an art form. The stormy, fiery empathy disciplined and clarified into a great modulated means of expression. Fetiche is singing there, a black woman, already forty or thereabouts, in the same class as Mercedes Sosa, a kind of magnificent combination of Gisela May and Barbara Streisand. The great tango masters are playing there on the bandonéon and the piano. A new talent is being introduced, a young tango singer, hardly more than twenty years old. The tango is going through a great renaissance at the moment in Argentina. Some people say it is manipulated from above to cool political passions and distract people's attention from repression and economic misery. I don't know whether that is so. I can well believe it. But not entirely. The tango is a part of every Argentinian in the same way as football is. It can be encouraged and supported with a definite aim in mind, but it cannot be forced, because it is already there, living, turbulent, indispensable.

While this remarkable drama was being played out up there on the stage, I was weeping inwardly all the time. A double stimulus, the artistic experience, the musical avalanche of notes mercilessly raging down on us, hour after hour, and then the knowledge of my own inadequacy, the meaninglessness of my life, the impossibility of what I had resolved to carry out. Lilita was drunk. I was thinking of suicide and did not answer when he leant across the table to explain the meaning of difficult words in the tango, the tango. At about four, we moved to the Union Bar, where everything had started two years before. The same ageing woman at the piano. The same thin brittle elderly creature with her aristocratic looks and her bandonéon. The same depraved atmosphere, the same depraved, rootless people. The same melancholy, emaciated, heart-rending Chiqueline de Bachin moving between the tables with his heart-rending flowers for sale. He doesn't recognize me. How could he? I can't even afford to buy a flower from him this time. Juan exchanges a few words with him. He disappears in his worn, ragged black jacket. *El mozo*, the waiter, fills my glass to the brim with whisky. Juan knows everyone and the price is consequently ridiculously low in comparison with that at the Laura, where we paid thirty thousand pesos for a bottle of wine. Lilita goes to the ladies. He leans forward to ask for the fifth or tenth time how I am, what's wrong with me? '*Que piensas?*' 'What are you thinking about?' I lean forward towards him so that my cheek brushes his and whisper in his ear: 'Suicide.'

To test him out. Out of malice. To neutralize my anguish, at least. He does indeed become very upset. Then it's over. I calm him down and explain. Lilita comes back. We tell each other we like each other very much. That we always will. The merry-go-round goes on.

Later in my rooms in Rivadavia, dawn over Buenos Aires. Space, the sun on the window-pane, a hundred thousand sparkling window-panes. The clean air.

I am a child. I'll soon be fifty. A nasty child.

He is my father.

Now it's Thursday. 12 October. It is eleven minutes to twelve. Cloud over Buenos Aires and an icy wind. Yesterday it was almost high summer, glorious sun and twenty-seven degrees. Lilita is ill, her legs and arms swollen and her joints aching. At first I thought she had the plague or something equally dreadful, but naturally it is no more than a severe allergy to some mysterious medicine she takes for some, to me, unidentified disease. However, yesterday evening was a dramatic evening, doctors coming and going and poor Lilita crying with pain. Juan was out on business and came home much later than he had promised, and even the doctor we'd informed was kept waiting. We sat there for hours, the two of us, waiting and worrying and talking – for the first time, for that matter – quite intimately. Then suddenly they were all there, all at once, Juan and both the doctors and all.

My work conditions are temporary, primitive and really quite unacceptable. At home, I would not even get a line written and I would be irritable to the extent of rage and go out and get drunk. The relative peace I had in their bedroom has now gone because of Lilita's illness. I sit at the table in the living-room, while she moves back and forth between the kitchen and the bathroom, occasionally glancing at what I have written. They are inquisitive about what I am doing – naturally – and I've told him that for me – although neither of them understands more than ten – fifteen words of Swedish feel roughly the same as if they were to undress completely with the blinds up. Nakedness is a curious chapter in Argentina. Though it's not all that important to him, as naturally he knows what it's about. But she doesn't. Tomorrow, I'll be back in the room at Rivadavia.

Everything coincides in a peculiar way. Even small secondary details. Not only that, but I gradually came to realize that unconsciously and for these two weeks in Buenos Aires, I had been trying to repeat much of what he on his part found difficult during those seven months in Helsinki and Stockholm. For literary empathy? No. To give something in return.

A few days ago, in my rooms in Rivadavia, I happened to have the radio on when it was announced that Singer had been awarded the Nobel Prize. I was filled with huge spontaneous delight, and later asked myself when I had last felt the same way about a Nobel Prize award. Neruda, perhaps? Azcuenaga is in the Jewish quarter of Buenos Aires. There are about four million Jews in Buenos Aires, he maintains. Yesterday it was Wednesday and nearly all the shops in that part of the city were closed, the streets empty of people as if it were Sunday. Yom Kippur! It was Yom Kippur! In my mind, these words have an almost magical content, entirely thanks to Isaac Singer's books. Orthodox Jews are naturally a very obvious element in the street life of these quarters. Elderly men in skull-caps, and younger ones with the odd little hats.

Late that evening, the second part of *Roots* was shown on television. A somewhat ageing Kunta Kinte married a woman I at first thought was the village whore. Like *Bonanza*, except with a different-coloured skin. They don't feel that way. They haven't my sophisticated intellectualism. They are captivated. They see first and foremost what is also there. A passion for freedom. An obscure, yet perfectly clear picture of class struggle, class antagonism, which they have felt all their lives beneath their skins. The ravaging painful marks of a cruel and heartless bourgeoisie.

All three of us sat curled up in the bed, the television at the foot, Lilita in the middle, occasionally whimpering with pain. How boundless (and paradoxical) is the tenderness I feel for her. We stroked the tender red lumps on her arms and legs. Half child, half father, I was at last an integrated harmonious part of their young marriage.

The godfather.

A few days ago, we were having dinner when Laura came on a visit. She is a friend of Lilita's, but she is very different from Lilita, worldly-wise, about twenty-five, her features already slightly ravaged. She sat for a while, as they do here, had some food and talked about this and that. Later, when we were alone together, he tells me about Laura, about her drink problem, about how he thinks she practises prostitution now and again to eke out her living. Yesterday evening, when we were waiting for the doctor, Lilita in her turn told me about her friend Laura. She is a prostitute. It's a hard life, and anyway has nothing whatsoever to do with her friendship. Lilita's matter-of-factness about this does not match the image her husband has of his young wife. 'Lilita is very innocent,' he says. 'She's lived a sheltered family life and has no experience of the world.' He wants it that way. It is part of the Argentinian man's ideal woman. I'll never tell him that Lilita knows Laura is a prostitute.

Laura is unhappy. She lives with a man she loves. This man is married to another woman. The Argentina of passions.

Saturday, 14 October. The time is twenty-two minutes past eleven. Sunny and eighteen degrees. Yesterday was a totally meaningless day, discounting the evening, when we had a sumptuously plentiful and delicious fish dinner at Rosa and Griseldo's. Didn't get to bed until about half-past two. I still haven't got used to Argentinian eating habits and the dislocated rhythm of the day.

On Thursday, a large and improvised family dinner at their place. Present were Mercedes, Norma, Monica and Daniel, young Gabriel, and of course Lilita, Juan and I. Pancho came later straight from work, tired but good-natured and quietly humorous. Juan and I had been out earlier to buy enough food for four people, as Mercedes still hadn't got a bed at the hospital. Then the relatives simply poured in, one after another. When people come, you go out and buy more food. It's as simple as that. If you have the money. If you haven't, which is often the case, you share what's there.

Daniel speaks indistinctly and is rather difficult to understand, but I am beginning to get used to it, and the more we get to know each other, the easier it becomes to converse. He tells one of those fantastic stories that spice Argentinian life, or which are inevitably a natural part of it. His father was a fisherman in Sicily before emigrating to Argentina forty years ago, just before the war. In a terrible storm off the Sicilian coast, the little fishing-boat sank and stayed under the surface of the water for over ten minutes. But the cabin was hermetically sealed and did not fill with water. With the power of prayer and the magical strength emanating from a church conveniently placed just opposite the shipwreck, the people on the shore managed to haul the fishing-boat back above the surface. Daniel's father was saved. As if by a miracle; or rather, by a miracle . . .

No one in the company questions the truth of such stories and they laugh delightedly when they see my doubts. As a half-grown boy, Juan once had a heart tattooed on his upper arm. A few years later he removed it. With mother's milk. Mother Mercedes confirms this. They look at me and laugh. Perhaps mother's milk in Europe is of a different and less effective composition.

We drink more wine than is usual in Argentina that evening. Pancho drinks nothing but Coca-Cola. He has to get up early as usual and wants to go home to bed. But there is nothing to stop him staying the night there, on the floor in some corner. On the other hand, Norma gulps it down, gradually becoming slightly tipsy and sentimental. She talks about the letters Lilita wrote home when she was in Finland, how fond of me Lilita is, and how she feels for me as if I were her father. I answer that the feeling is mutual, that I feel for Lilita as if she were my daughter. We hug each other, mother from Argentina and father from Finland, and I feel soft inside. Once again what we mean to each other is confirmed, what we are to each other.

That is what is inexplicable.

He has shown me a photograph from his difficult years. Buenos Aires style, jeans, mauve tee-shirt, he stands there glaring into the camera, half turned away, thin as a rake, but as beautiful as one of God's chosen. Younger than now, much younger, an expression on his face which is no longer there, challenging, insolent, at the same time inviting, gamin-like it's called. (Challenges, invitations.) That was his professional face. He doesn't need it any longer, but I have seen it in reality, once two years ago, the first time he visited me at the Hotel Eldorado.

He can fix almost anything in next to no time. He knows innumerable people in this city, from doctors and lawyers to prostitutes and petty gangsters. But on Thursday, things did not go according to plan. They never do in actual fact, but things work out. According to other plans. That day there was a hitch. After dinner, I was to move back to Claudio's apatment in Rivadavia, but the keys were in Luis' pocket and Luis was not at home. He was out somewhere. On a girl-hunt. I was very tired and irritable. Back at home, Mercedes had already gone to bed on my mattress. I didn't want to disturb Mercedes, nor sleep so primitively with the thought of the comforts of Claudio's apartment so close. And so inaccessible. A bourgeois reaction. He accepted it, but did not approve. It took him no longer than two minutes to arrange for me to stay the night in another apartment. At another friend's place. His name was Julio, a man of my own age. The apartment was not crammed, like Claudio's, but more spartan, square. He offered me a swig of whisky, which I greedily gulped down. At Juan's request, for that matter. We had a cup of coffee and sat talking about the usual things, by now rather tedious, what things were like in Argentina, what things were like in Finland, customs good and bad, but nothing important. Julio lacks the demonstrative masculinity of Juan's friends, and this sometimes makes me uncertain and uneasy. On the contrary, he is gentle, almost feminine, which makes me uncertain and uneasy to the same extent. Suddenly I am convinced that Julio is a homosexual and almost certainly an ex-client. I lie uncomfortably on the sofa in the only room, feeling the hours slowly going by without being able to sleep.

His friends. The thousand friends. The surface I can see and touch, but what lies within remains unknown. The thousand mysteries. Julio is a pensioner. At forty-eight? Cautiously, I try to find out more about him, but Juan does not respond. Luis lives with his mother. He had come home at two in the morning. His mother was waiting up for him with his dinner.

The rooms in Rivadavia also fill up with mysteries. Claudio's loneliness. His terrible, screwed-up life-rhythm. Supposing he doesn't like Lilita? Supposing he doesn't really like me? Conditions of friendship? The inevitable complication of Argentinian friendship?

Today is Monday. Sun between the clouds. Eighteen degrees. It is a quarter to three. Yesterday, Sunday, was a terrible day, icy cold and wet, only thirteen degrees, and hideous anguish. The family were celebrating Mother's Day and for some reason I was not included. Alone as a result, vulnerable, terrible thoughts of destruction crawling all around me. There are moments when I don't think I will ever leave here alive, that I won't be able to cope with parting from him yet again. Then this morning he came to see me, and I told him what things had been like for me and why. He thinks I'm insane. We discussed his – different – problems. He embraced me. 'You must be patient with me,' I said. 'I *am* patient,' he replies. 'It's *you* who must be patient.' Always so damned wise. At twenty-three he has the experience of life of an eighty-year old.

Even my dreams have reached Buenos Aires. Last night I dreamt for the first time a dream set in this city. I don't remember what it was about. I had dreamt about both Axel Grönvik (!) and Per Wästberg before. Axel was auctioning his large patrician apartment. Per was on a visit to the old house in Rulludden. Two editors-in-chief. What does it mean that I dreamt about Buenos Aires? It means that it takes at least two weeks for the whole personality, the concealed layers as well, to move from one point on the globe to another, a distant one. This naturally also explains some of the spells of anguish, the difficulties in adjustment. One is not whole; vital parts are still on their way.

Punctuality is not a virtue in Argentina.

I have at last got used to it now, but how difficult it was two years ago. The endless hours of waiting in the hotel room at the Eldorado. He hasn't come! He's abandoned me! But he always came in the end. Except for a couple of terrible times when he didn't appear until the next day, as if that were nothing; with a white lie or possibly the straight truth as an explanation. A few days ago, I decided to take my revenge, to show them what it is like. We were going to have dinner with Rosa and Griseldo, leaving at half-past seven. I was to be at their place at seven, we agreed. I arrived at eight. They hadn't even finished dressing.

Claudio's apartment, the rooms in Rivadavia. The bedroom is blue all over. Blue inside blue. Walls, lamp, rug, a blue picture, blue fitted carpet, everything blue. Arranged with taste. And all round the apartment, something mysterious in this masculine man's restless world, like a personal secret, dolls, stuffed animals. Soft toys as in a nursery. He is never completely dressed when you call on him. His girl-friend is, but he isn't. He is always just getting ready, always showering, shaving, spraying and perfuming himself, and while he is doing this, an endless stream of friends arrive on some errand, to settle some business, chattering for a few quick noisy minutes, telephone calls, telephone calls. Arranging things, fixing things, but he never gets anything done when it comes to the point, Lilita says. Talks and talks and talks. I can't make him out. He is a steward. A flight mechanic, really. He loves Verdi. His harsh voice softens when he talks about *La Traviata* and *Aida*. When we met for the first time in Copenhagen about a year ago, he bought five pornographic films which he was going to smuggle into Argentina and sell to a speculator at a hundred per cent profit. Always a hundred per cent profit. They are very close to each other. There have been moments of jealousy. I have felt jealousy, in Stockholm a year ago, when he played his cousin Claudio against me, saying Claudio was a better friend than I was, his true friend, while I . . . To annoy me, I think. To pay me back because I had put him in a position which was sometimes unendurable for him, being in Stockholm, alone with me, far from Buenos Aires, separated from everything that meant anything to him. We had triple-sex with one of my woman friends. That was the only thing that gave him a little calm and relaxation. And me. Despite everything. The moments of tenderness.

I can't make Claudio out. What he is, essentially. There have been three break-ins at his apartment. Some of the thousand friends, 'the friends', Lilita says. The third time, he wept. Everything had gone. The first time was during the worst period of police repression. The police themselves came and rang the bell, threatening to charge him if he did not give up his record-player and stereo outfit voluntarily. They knew about most of his smuggling deals, so all he could do was to submit. That wouldn't happen today. The days of repression are over.

The sun goes the wrong way. I noticed it first on Saturday. I was lying on the floor in the living-room, sunbathing in front of the open window. The sun disappeared behind the wall on my left. At home it would have been on the right. To think that it takes so long. I am not observent enough.

Griseldo showed us some home-movies of their holidays in Mar del Plata. He comes slowly walking towards the camera on the *playa*, stands for a moment and shows his handsome profile in a close-up, then walks majestically away. Then fishing-boats and lovely women in bathing suits. Then the scene is repeated, but Rosa is the actress this time. She lacks his dignified air. I felt as if I were in a Buñuel film. Yet I like them very much. Have to. Otherwise all is lost.

Tuesday, 17 October. Sun between the clouds, like yesterday. It is ten past ten. I have not checked the temperature, but when I was out at about nine for morning coffee in the bar next door, it felt fresh and pleasant in my short sleeves. About eighteen degrees, I should think. The days are rushing by. How swiftly time flies when one has got to my age. *Carpe diem*! I do my best. Drink is my worst enemy. Nothing makes one forget so definitely as alcohol. In Argentina, drink isn't a vital part of life, as it is back home. This signifies another way of living. Greater awareness, making the most of the moment, the present. *Carpe diem!*

I asked him to give me strict orders not to smoke or drink so much. He gave me strict orders. It helped. Yesterday, I drank nothing except watered wine with the meal, and I didn't smoke all evening, although we were invited to dinner with Mercedes, Rosa, Griseldo and little Gabriel. I obey him. As a child obeys his father. Or a father obeys his son. In my marriage, that has never worked. On the contrary. It's no fun obeying your wife. But obeying him is pure joy, indeed it is. Nothing has complicated our relationship so much as my drinking; and occasionally his promiscuity. The days when I came home drunk while he was living with us in Rulludden immediately caused a crisis. He was frantic. He sees drunkenness as inhuman, I think. It's difficult to behave humanly to the inhuman. I have not been drunk in Argentina. But I have drunk, largely from loneliness. That has spoilt a few days for me. I should never cope with being an alcoholic in Argentina. In Finland, on the other hand, alcoholism is part of the cultural pattern. One drinks as tradition demands. Then for Christ's sake move to Argentina while there's still time and you still have your brain intact!

Helsinki in the 'fifties. The old moustachioed commissionaire at the Kämp Hotel, whose name I can no longer remember. But his remark: 'Everything can be arranged here.' Argentina is like the Kämp.

At the entrance of the *estacione* Once, there is a doctor in a white coat and stethoscope and all the rest, taking the blood-pressure of prospective passers-by for five hundred pesos.

I had brought an ampoule of gamma-globulin with me from Finland, to be used when required. That happened yesterday for the first time. In Argentina, it is done at a chemist's. You go into a little compartment behind the counter, the chemist sticks the needle in and the whole thing is over in two minutes. I felt nothing, nothing at all. It costs four hundred pesos, less than half a dollar.

What does one talk about? One talks about what it costs. Eating and working and what everything costs. One counts in dollars as often as in pesos, in old pesos as much as in new pesos. It is confusing for the foreigner. I'm not a foreigner, am I, but all the same. Last Sunday, the Sunday issue of *La Nacion* cost three hundred pesos, this Sunday three hundred and fifty. Yesterday, matches cost fifty pesos, today sixty. At the same time the price of cigarettes went up forty pesos. A packet of

Parisienne that cost five hundred pesos when I arrived now costs five hundred and forty. An apartment can be bought with a very modest down-payment. Then eighty-seven payments have to be made in an equal number of months. But the instalments are index-linked, which means the sum is doubled in a few months' time. It doesn't work. Salary levels are fixed.

I was right about Julio. He lives with Juan Carlos, who happened to be in Cordoba the night I lodged there. Juan Carlos is a *'calculador'*, according to Juan. Exploits financially Julio's 'weakness'. Why do I put that down? Because one could imagine something corresponding in our circumstances. Because it's close to the bone, staggeringly close. It's a sensitive matter. We have talked about it. It's not true of us.

We are leaving tomorrow. At last. For Tucumán, Salta, Jujuy, Formosa. At last, together, just him and me. He says the same – 'from tomorrow onwards we have at least fifteen days to ourselves.' Perhaps he means 'from tomorrow onwards you don't have to share me with anyone else for at least fifteen days.' No. It means something to him, too, if not quite the same as it does to me.

Wednesday, departure day. What fearful complications before everything is ready. Last night, late at night, we parted in anger. This morning we met again rather stiffly. But I have the rail tickets in my pocket. And the rest? That'll work out. I know. It isn't the first time. He is offended. I become nervous at his formidable capacity for not giving me enough time to weigh things up, for lining up the alternatives like lightning, making simple things less simple by talking through them, spinning a spider's web of words. Argentinian and Finnish.

It was a day of experiences, feelings, like ground-swell.

Those moments of overwhelming happiness.

So overwhelming.

Afternoon. He comes in like a whirlwind, pleased, in one continuous movement. Was to go out again soon, but stays. We put on a record of the song he sang at sixteen during his days of glory, 'days of glory', so dubious, so degrading. I have found it – at last – in Claudio's collection of records. The voice, rather crude, almost as if just breaking, unschooled, but absolutely pure and full of expression. A popular song, done specially for him at the time he was to be launched. I have heard that voice before, seen that figure, almost the same voice and the same figure, eighteen years ago in a nightclub in Rome. Unforgettable somehow, and so . . . like a premonition. He is sitting close to me on the sofa, his arm pressed against mine. He sings. He stretches out on the floor in front of me and sings.

The Argentinian and the pompous, expressed in music. The tremendous emotional content of Argentinian music, extending tango across the whole scale of variations in the history of music. Tango like Beethoven. Tango like Chopin. Tango like Telemann. While he plays Tango on the gramophone, he expresses tango with his body, his voice, his hands, his eyes, his lips.

The borderline between happiness and pain drawn with a spiritual instrument so fine, so polished, that it is not conceivable, impossible to perceive.

Tears of joy. But internally. For they are dangerous. Like impatience, suspicion and jealousy.

Even when singing in public, he has a way of pressing his forefinger against his ear. I notice suddenly that I have unconsciously adopted the gesture. But I don't know on which occasion or for what reason I repeat it. I must be more observant.

His features. The lightning changes of expression. Continual. And his voice. The voice I know so well. The way it expresses excitement, delight. The way it expresses gravity, thoughtfulness, wisdom. The way it expresses anger and despair. His eyes, almost black, the look in those giddy moments of tenderness, affection. That dark skin. His lips.

Torn asunder by the weight of this tremendous feeling.

Football that evening. Boca Juniors versus River Plate, the eternal, excessively esteemed, class antagonists. Boca for the workers, River for the bourgeoisie. At the stadium, Boca's supporters in the southern stand, River's in the northern. Antiphon singing, enormous, leaping, yelling blocks of humanity, blocks of men trying to drown each other on either side of the field, trying to outdo each other in sheer volume of voice. The singing, born and spreading like fire through the sea of humanity, shouts, trumpet blasts, the lightning repartee, the noise that does not lessen, to be there, man amongst men. Men, men, men. Boca win two nil. River's supporters slink away. Boca's cheer like lunatics.

Anyone who has not seen a football match between Roca and River does not know Buenos Aires.

Wednesday, 8 November. It is twenty-five past one. Rain, thunder, cold for these circumstances. Lightning and thunder and downpours all night. The journey is over, the journey of strains. And the catastrophe following on our return, even that has been overcome. I couldn't get in to Rivadavia. I am living with them, sitting writing in the living-room. He has just left; we embraced. Everything is still in the spirit of reconciliation – after the catastrophe. He is very tender. I am tired.

Nothing during the journey. Two weeks, a thousand dollars, all gone up in smoke. This is all, these notes.

'He was a man in his best years and he had come to Argentina to die.'

Tucumán was like swimming in a sea of anguish. Drowning.

Salta. Saturday. He fell asleep in my arms. I could not sleep. My arm went numb.

I see nothing. I see nothing but him, and everything else I see, I see through him. 'Reflections in a Golden Eye'. Reflections in a Creole eye.

An incomprehensible reality. Yet another day lost. Reality reduced to a single person. And I. Life like a furnace. Salta. Way above thirty degrees. I'm on fire.

The black hair against the white pillow. The sleep of the beloved.

Sunday. Salta. The hotel room. Alone. Hour after hour, Catholic mass grinding out on the radio. Voices through the open window. A pink outer wall, stone. Space above. Bird-song. The future like an iron fist.

Tuesday. The moments of happiness like drops in the sea of anguish. The moments of happiness, endless drops like the sea.

The face of the loved one.

The naked body stretched out on the bed. Sleeping.

Where his nearness ends, my life ends.

Wednesday. After Humahuaca, Jujuy, the mountains like a moonscape. He is the wine the sun the canopy sky of warm nights.

The well and the water.
the vessel against my lips.

Nose tongue feet.
Eyes, lips.

'The greatest happiness is without words,
mute is the bitterest pain.'
Eyes, lips.

At the well, the thirsty.
Breathing deep,
water running from the corners of his mouth.

The well.
The cascade of water.
The taste of water.

The young skin,
And the ageing hand.
Lips pressed to the heart.

Questions and answers. No longer any business of mine. His swift smile is the questions and the answers.

Those closed eyes. That calm breathing.

The stream of tears, continuous, but within, along the blood-vessels, the cataract of the heart.

I wept in Posadas. Katarina von Kant. Night. The sky thundered, lit up by lightning. The silhouette of his face. A wretched hotel room, naked in bed during the storm and the words: 'Tears are for the dead, not for the living.'

Salta. The red trees.
and the yellow trees.
The colour of the mountains, shimmering,
like paintings.

Chaco. Night journey. Fires.
The crowded bus –
sleeping at my side.

He hears me in my sleep – my thoughts. 'I'm asleep,' he says, urgently, and then roughly the next moment: 'What did you say? Are you crying?' I haven't said anything. But my thoughts – in a language he doesn't understand – have moved across the landscape that runs straight through both of us. My anguish has brushed his concern. In his sleep.

He wakes upset. He dreamt I was dead. I spoke to him from the other side of death, saying: '*Hijo mio*, my son, it is your duty to finish our book, alone.' His anguish. How strongly he felt that duty, but that he could not do it. And the fact that he did not have a common language in which he could communicate with our publisher. I told him he had no such duty, were I to die. His relief – as if the dream had been reality. As if gratitude were needed. The tenderness. Death is a betrayal.

Whatever happens. I have no right to die.

I

From the roof of Buenos Aires to the basement of Buenos Aires.

In the basement of Buenos Aires 'the book that is writing itself' is writing itself.

An author inflated from head to foot by the most dreadful hubris: he who with his own strength wishes to reshape reality, change the course of reality.

Now on the ground floor, where one is at one's lowest. Sitting staring out at a fire-wall, only four feet away. Above me, I have seventeen floors of human dwellings, children crying, cooking smells, voices, singing women. Human life.

If I climb through the window and stand in the fire-yard, also called the patio, I can see the sky, if I bend my head right back and look upwards. It is blue. The sun sparkles against the upper part of the fire-wall in front of me. So the weather's fine. In the apartment, it is eternal dusk, the petrified unchangeable world of electric light. Daylight falls across the fire-yard, but filtered, faint and without strength. Flies move about, searching back and forth in the half-light. Not a puff of a breeze, but a slight draught upwards, taking the tobacco smoke with it. And a faint noise – as if one of crickets. Can that be possible? Down here, deep down among the stones and concrete? Not a tree as far as the eye can see, four feet. And yet.

Only two days ago, I lived in the middle, on the middle level, or slightly below, on the fourth floor. The cock crowed at dawn there. Every morning. I never understood it. In Buenos Aires? So far down among the stones and concrete? But a cock all the same. One single one.

Before that, I lived on the roof, the roof-level, the fifteenth floor, among the swallows and bats. At that time, I also entertained great hopes concerning my possibilities in the field of omnipotence. On the other hand, I learnt as a child – and what you learn as a child can never be entirely eradicated – that: 'Better to listen to the string break than never draw a bow.'

I have certainly drawn the bow – so that my sinews cracked, my hand trembling with fatigue, prepared, longing, to give up. But still not, wonderful to say, the dismal twang of the broken string.

(They weren't crickets, of course. The sound was an insignificant fault in one of the many machines that rumble and hiss down at this level. Basement level. The keep-it-going of the giant dwellings of humanity.)

Every morning I sweep up the cigarette ends, crumpled cigarette packs, crusts and other rubbish from the fire-yard, also called the patio, which is my cosy outdoor space. They all come tumbling down during the course of the evening and night from seventeen floors of noisy television evenings of seventeen floors of family circles and friends. Pop music at top volume does not disturb me. Nor do the loud boisterous conversations. But the bangs, of iron doors slamming or heavy cupboards falling over, they do. I wake at half-past one. When I peer out through the curtains to survey my indoor space, the stone ground is white with cigarette ends like newly fallen snow.

It is all about friendship, about one of the many forms of friendship. Many books have been written about friendship and this is a variation. An old theme, as old as the history of our civilization. It begins with Juan from Buenos Aires, who was a bad person. And continues with me, from Helsinki, who has never been content with less than everything I wished for.

I remember . . . I remember . . . how it began, the whole of this terrible process of writing, which is the difficult way and the only way. Two years have gone by since then. I was in Buenos Aires on other errands, with other intentions, another book in my mind. Juan afflicted me. Uninvited, he stepped into my life and at first made things quite comfortable for himself. Within a few days I realized that he had come to stay – for ever. I was staying in a hotel that time, right in the middle, in Córdoba, at the Hotel Eldorado. He started visiting me there. We could not converse. We could not exchange a single word with each other, for I knew no Spanish and he knew no English. Nor Finnish, either. One day, after he had left, one afternoon, the sun scorching, colossal heat in the room, the air-conditioning turned off, I stood in the middle of the floor, half-turned towards the window, the bed on the right, my desk on the left, stood there, shaking with weeping. Something had happened.

166

. . . stood there shaking with weeping, and repeating over and over again to myself: 'I'll write a human life . . . I'll write a human life . . .' and not only what it has been like, but also so that from that moment I would provide one of the forces that decided its future, its future direction. Write a human life.

And later, somewhat later, at home in Finland, in the harsh cold, in the lowering darkness, that mysterious feeling, that bizarre idea to be 'the book that writes itself'. At last to eliminate complete the boundary between literature and reality, at last completely fuse the human being with the writer. To be the same, wholly the same over by the typewriter, at home by the soup tureen.

> 'Be afraid, my child,
> there is more than you think
> and nothing is as you see –
> not people, nor houses, nor the flight of motor-cars.'

II

Juan: My first is my beauty. My second is my intelligence. My third is my experience of life, much greater than any of my contemporaries', much greater than yours, too.

Perhaps he is right, perhaps not. Experience depends on so many things. Age. Awareness, too. Juan calculates more in quantity. Perhaps that is so with youth. I calculate more in quality. Perhaps that is middle age.

'I know everything. *Everything*,' he says. That's an exaggeration, but I do not contradict him, for in his own area of life he is somehow right. In any case, it is not wrong. But his area of life is limited. Everyone's area of life is limited. I try to convince him of that, but he does not allow himself to be convinced.

He is beautiful. Slightly plumper today than when I met him two years ago, but still very beautiful. He stands in front of the mirror and sees his reflection in the mirror, smiling, satisfied, secure in himself. '*Lindo chico*,' he says. 'Beautiful youth.' Does it in Stockholm, while we are living there, every time we go out together. Does it here in Buenos Aires, in the lift, the mirror in the lift, every time we go down in it together, from the middle level, from slightly below the middle level, the fourth floor.

'If you're so sure you're beautiful, why do you keep having to repeat it so often?' I ask him. Slightly irritated. For I myself am not beautiful; ugly alongside him. So occasionally I experience the contradictions in our circumstances on that level, too.

'Self-irony,' he says, laughing. 'Don't you see?'

'No.'

'There are people, narcissists, who quite seriously say about themselves that they are beautiful. But I'm joking, don't you see?'

'I don't think you're joking,' I say.

I regret it at once, regret that I didn't go on agreeing with him with

my rather silly '*muy lindo, muy lindo*,' 'very beautiful, very beautiful.'
For never again after that. Never again looking in the mirror. In the
lift. Never again saying '*lindo chico*'. That lightning, definitive reaction
which I've learnt to fear. A mild correction and then never again. The
hard, definitive part of his character.

We're lying in bed chatting. In our joint home, on the fourth floor, on
the middle level, or just below. It is afternoon, the blinds down. Lilita
is at work. We have an argument about punctuality. I try to get him to
understand how unbearable it is to wait, to just sit waiting for hour
after hour. He doesn't understand.

'I have no times,' he says. 'Time means nothing to me.'

'In Europe, one sticks to one's agreements,' I say, rather pompous-
ly. 'It's a matter of consideration for other people. If you've agreed to
meet at three o'clock, you meet at three o'clock. But for you, three
might just as well be six or seven. It seems like indifference. It can be
terribly hurtful.'

He doesn't understand.

'I never wait myself,' he says. 'If I've arranged to meet someone at
three o'clock, a woman for instance, and she hasn't come by quarter
past, then I go. I don't wait, I just go and do something else. It's very
simple. And I know you're here, that you're here all the time, and that
you'll wait for me. Why should I be punctual when I know we'll meet
sooner or later anyhow?'

I am angry. He seems to care about no one but himself. I say so. He
shrugs his shoulders.

'Yesterday I was an hour late. Do you know what I was doing
during that hour? I was sitting in a bar, having a cup of coffee.'

He's not lying. It is astonishing. It is incredible. I am seized with an
irresistible desire to hurt him.

'Two years ago, when I was sitting waiting for you at the Eldorado,
there were quite definite occasions when I was absolutely sure you
would be punctual. But you mustn't be angry with me if I say so.'

'When I needed money,' he says immediately, simply, almost
without expression.

Exactly.

I am the vulnerable one. He is invulnerable.

No. It's not like that, either.

III

Language! Language!

Now I've brooded on this question of language. What we use it for and our way of using it, generally perhaps in a more destructive than constructive way. What is it for, this unique human instrument? To communicate. To dominate. To control and convince. Teach, learn, understand, create and destroy.

Juan and I communicated for five weeks almost entirely without the help of language.

Later on, in Stockholm and Helsinki, language, however elementary, imperfect and staccato, became the most important thing of all, conversations between us absolutely essential. Without conversation, we would have destroyed each other, those endless nightly conversations. (As in puberty, when you've made a friend and tell each other 'everything'.)

But sometimes we still experience, and mutually, the ambiguity of language. Silence is golden, speech only silver.

It still seems a miracle, a mystery and miracle that we got to know each other, began to like each other, liked each other, without one single word in common, in explanation, as a bridge for emotion, as a line of communication.

Summer has come at last to Buenos Aires.

Last night at about eleven, after I had returned to my basement from Juan and Lilita's apartment, where I had dinner, it was still thirty degrees outside. Through the thick veil of fumes, there was suddenly an inkling, faint but unmistakable, the scent of the tropics, tropical damp against the skin. As in Brazil, as in the Atlantic on the Equator. It is heady. The night suddenly becomes a sea of possibilities. One feels the possibilities in one's blood like suction and one wants to go out and seize them, some of them. I took a taxi. I could have got off at the corner of Charcas and my own street and gone on down towards 9 de Julio, but I didn't. Controlled myself, as I had to be up early and needed to sleep. I am no longer young.

The hot nights, the streets, meetings. For years he was as if bewitched by it. Not *only* forced into it by the iron laws of survival. Now he stays at home in the evenings with Lilita and the television. But it still happens occasionally that he has to. Go out and stay there. Twenty-three years old. It's like a drug, he says. The street is like a drug.

Their apartment consists of two rooms and a kitchen. A wide bed in the bedroom, and a stool for the television set. A light bulb in the ceiling with no shade. In the living-room, an extending dining-table with four chairs, a rattan three-piece suite, a table with a glass top, a little sofa and two armchairs. Some photographs under the glass top, Lilita in slushy snow in Paris, the Eiffel Tower in the background. Lilita on the sofa at home in Rulludden, squashed between Selinda and me, Selinda's arm round her shoulders, my cheek against her hair. And a photograph of little Gabriel in Mar del Plata and one of little Irma, a niece, in Córdoba. A refrigerator in the kitchen, a new one, bought by Juan in the second week of November. Two pictures on the living-room wall, of Paris, Cité and Place du Tertre. A wedding-present from Claudio, the flying cousin. And posters, lovely colour photographs enlarged and covered with slogans, wise thoughts, *bons mots*.

Lilita comes back from work at ten past six and immediately starts cleaning the apartment. The cleaning done in that apartment! She is very small, unusually small, but perfectly proportioned, and because of her smallness a little touching, but strong, strong-willed, strong character, clear mind. If Juan happens by some miracle ever to wipe the floor, it'll certainly not be with her.

We take the lift up to the fourth floor. Juan has left his keys at home – as usual – and I unlock the door with my key. Lilita is just finishing the cleaning. She is tired. She has a headache. The room where she works in the daytime has neither window nor ventilation and is smaller than their living-room. Five girls sit in there, typing and smoking from morning to evening.

Juan and I lie down on the bed in the bedroom. He puts the light out and we lie there staring at the television, his hand in mine, fingers playing. We can hear Lilita in the kitchen through the venetian blind. We were six at table, added to by sister and brother-in-law and little Gabriel. Once or twice, Juan gets off the bed and goes out into the

171

kitchen. 'Are you hungry?' he says when he returns. 'The food'll be ready soon.' In the end I can't stand it any longer. My upbringing screams at me to do something and I go out into the kitchen and ask if I can help. I lay the table, with a cloth and all. And table-napkins. But not like at home in my childhood, with each person having his own table-napkin and silver table-napkin ring with a monogram on it. Here a serviette is a serviette, a matter of indifference who uses which. Today I wipe my fingers and mouth on your serviette, tomorrow you'll wipe your fingers and mouth on mine. Glass plates with fish patterns on them, bought a year ago at the Kosta glass factory outside Växsjö. Knives and forks from Fiskars, a parting gift to Lilita and Juan from my mother. Wine and water and Coca-Cola.

We eat in silence. Juan has brought the television out of the bedroom and we sit watching a sensational report on the suicide sect and the thousand corpses in Jonestown, Guyana. Helicopters fly back and forth over the town and film in helicopter perspective. I tell them about the Finnish general who died up in Lapland when he forgot himself for one moment and went too close to a helicopter with its rotary blades turning. Lilita has a fit of laughter and finds it hard to stop. I laugh, too, mostly out of satisfaction at for once being able to tell a story in Spanish which has struck home. But it wasn't all that funny, was it? Juan is sulking. There is some conflict going on between them, but I have not been informed of it, presumably something she said to him during his brief visit to the kitchen. A slight reprimand. He can't stand reprimands.

Juan is difficult. There are knots inside him which only Lilita can loosen with her patience and good sense. Her femininity. 'I am not dependent on anyone, not anyone,' he often says emphatically, almost pleadingly sometimes, and sometimes with great violence. In reality he is very dependent on Lilita. And on me.

IV

When we were getting to know each other two years ago, he had nothing. No money, nowhere to live, no possessions. Absolutely nothing. In other words, he was very independent. Of everything and everyone. It was not just a distress-situation forced on him by the fierce laws of survival. He could have chosen another form of semi-starvation, the honourable, industrious kind. But there was a definite hopelessness, an unequivocal poverty in that, which neither his youth nor his imagination could accept. At the time he still lived for the day and did not give his future one single conscious thought. His sole possessions were two shirts and a pair of worn jeans.

When he tore a hole in the seat of his trousers so that his bare skin shone through, I bought him a new pair of jeans.

A week before I went back to Finland, we took the boat to Montevideo and stayed for two days in that awful, sterile, dead city, so unlike Buenos Aires. That was on the eleventh and twelfth of December. He implied that his birthday was on the thirteenth. He would be twenty-two. I decided to grasp the opportunity and buy him a new shirt for his birthday. We spent almost a whole day in the shops and boutiques of Montevideo, trying to find a shirt that was to his taste, for when it comes to clothes he is very fastidious. Finally we found what we were looking for, but it was very expensive by his standards. White, tailored, patterned on the front, the kind young people prefer today. When he saw the price, he immediately became, as they say, prey to warring emotions, and he made strenuous attempts to prevent the purchase. But I would not allow myself to be influenced. He got his shirt and was wearing it a year later when he and Lilita spent Christmas with us at home in Rulludden in Finland.

But by then I already knew that his birthday was not on the thirteenth of December, but the thirteenth of February.

Lies are a long and difficult chapter in human life and in all relationships between people. I had started out from our very first meeting know that Juan lied to me, or would lie to me. For anything else was almost inconceivable, considering the circumstances. But as I had resolved to accept him as he was, I had also decided to accept his lies, but on certain conditions. For I knew there were lies of various kinds, and that some lies can probably be quite justified.

Almost two years later, after a dismal eventless day in his and Lilita's apartment in Buenos Aires, when he had not got up until after twelve o'clock, when there was no money left and he was just roaming about achieving nothing, he suddenly says with great conviction: 'There are three things I can't cope with, three things I can't do: cheating in business, lying, being unoccupied, doing nothing.' He is very serious and completely honest.

I have never questioned his honesty, never had to, either, for that matter. For I knew from the start that nothing could spoil our friendship so easily as demonstrative distrust on my part, expressing doubts about his aims and reliability. That birthday affair, the date of his birthday, was a bagatelle, a small white lie of the kind I myself might tell at any time without giving it a thought. Yet I could not forget it. Not from any pedantic morality – I am not moralistic in that way – but because the lie was so unique, almost a one-off phenomenon in our life together. For a long time, I thought he often lied to me, but later experience always showed me that even what I had taken for the most fantastic lie was in actual fact the truth. His life had been like that.

Sometimes we have quarrelled because we have misunderstood each other, certain words having a different meaning or nuance of meaning for him than for me. For a long time the word *obligación* was one of those difficult words – obligation, duty. He maintained with great emphasis that he had no *obligación* of any kind whatsoever in relation to any person whatsoever. This upset me. I felt hurt, not only because it seemed to me a frightening lack of responsibility, but also because he had given expression to human indifference, which although it indeed concerned everything around him to the same extent, was nonetheless directed especially at me.

'No duties in relation to Lilita, either?' I said.

'No, not in relation to her, either, to no one, no one.'

It sounded like almost unbelievable insensitivity, but it wasn't, indeed it was really no less than the opposite of insensitivity. For it soon turned out that, in his mind, *obligación* was nothing but a kind of badly motivated bourgeois formality, a superficial form of superficial communication, lacking all meaning because it did not presume personal involvement. This held good for every kind of formal obligation, imposed by convention or power, in relation to people, institutions, even in relation to the nation. 'If I sacrifice my life for something, I do it because I feel it that way. Without emotional involvement, I do nothing, not for Lilita, not for you, not for anyone, not for anything.'

My upbringing had been different. Or rather, at the age of forty-eight, I had not managed to free myself so fundamentally, so evidently and pronouncedly, from the bonds of my upbringing as he had at twenty-three. According to this upbringing, which we surely had in common from the start, and which in the end was decided by society, there were obligations in border areas close to the absolute, that were beyond all personal desires, all personal emotions. One should sacrifice oneself for one's family, one's people, one's country. It was a moralistic burden which most people found almost impossible to bear, as it presumed that personal needs would count for nothing, or anyhow always come last.

He had seen enough of the dark side of bourgeois power to be able to have the right to say with a clear conscience, to hell with pompous bourgeois morality.

On my part, I had not been able to free myself as effectively as he had. But with my European cunning I had managed to circumvent the message of bourgeois morality by telling myself that, in the last analysis, it was my writing that had the right to decide over my actions, sacrifices and needs. 'My only real country is my writing. Faced with the demands of writing, everything else must give way.'

In both cases, this was a defence of the preserves of freedom. We both felt that we could not live without that freedom. Losing it meant subjection and obedience, a punishment as impossible to choose as death.

Consequently, I was sufficiently close to him in this matter to be able to understand him immediately. What I first took to be a lack of any sense of responsibility was in fact the terrible lack of any genuine human feeling for the good deeds he saw everywhere around him in the great cold world. He refused to play with the conditions of false obligation. *Obligación* – 'obligation' – was a word with negative content. His feeling was the significant, fundamental basis of all human intercourse.

We had put the pieces of the puzzle together round a word, one single word, and thus came one step closer to understanding. Yet I wonder whether the misfortunes of Argentina have not something to do with this attitude, this definition of the world *obligación*. For Juan is not alone in this. The same attitude exists – to a greater or lesser extent – in all the Argentinian men I have met. And the question is, under such circumstances, who in the last count takes charge of the affairs of state?

After this, it occurred me to that there might be a similar difference in our respective understanding of the word 'lie' – *mentira*.

I decided to ask him straight out, risking the hurt to his pride and himself, for his pride is very vulnerable and easily hurt in the most surprising contexts.

He remembers the birthday present in Montevideo very well indeed, for he never forgets anything. He started talking about easy ways out and complicated ways out, and that sometimes, in minor matters, it was morally justified to choose the easy way out. He differentiated between 'pious lies' and 'speculative lies'. Pious lies were defensible in certain situations. Speculative lies, on the other hand, could never be defended. When he resisted the purchase of the shirt in Montevideo, it was because in his view the price was so high, the pious lie bordering on a speculative lie. I maintained I would have bought him the shirt under any circumstances, regardless of how much he had lied to me, even if he had tried to cheat me in some other way, as I knew he needed the shirt, indeed that he needed several, quite apart from how he behaved to acquire them.

At first, he found this view difficult to take. He thought it sounded like credulity to the point of stupidity. He thought I was lying.

He produced another couple of examples of pious lies, for the sake of an easy way out, which he later quite voluntarily put right again.

'But lies, all the same, that is, something dubious in the moral sense?' I said.

'Naturally.'

I then maintained that in Argentinian national literature there were elements which made me think that the pious lie, according to genuine Argentinian understanding, was not to be taken as a lie in the moral sense, but rather as a kind of simple and practical verbal tool, possibly a kind of usable emergency way out, among people from whom some advantage could be extracted. He denied it.

A lie is a lie. Always.

Yet this conversation left me with some doubts. But I lie myself, don't I? Everyone tells lies. In that case, is my demand for absolute truthfulness on his part simply a consequence of my feelings for him being so boundless?

V

One Sunday, we go out into the country. We are eleven adults, four children and six dogs in a delivery van and a station wagon. Don Pedro is host. He owns a little piece of land just outside Buenos Aires, out on La Pampa.

Don Pedro is really a Spaniard, but he has lived in Argentina for many years. He speaks Spanish in the Spanish way, not like the others. Not like me, either, as I have made it a point of honour to confine myself to the finesses and idiosyncracies of Argentinian Spanish. That makes it easier to communicate, to say, for instance, *dos palos* instead of *veinte mil pesos* – twenty thousand pesos. Don Pedro also owns a house outside Madrid, where he goes sometimes when he considers he can afford to take a holiday. He still calls it 'going home'.

Don Pedro owns a little bakery in Buenos Aires and does good business. He is a clever business man, but at the same time a great friend of humanity, with a warm heart. His employees consist partly of a colourful array of originals and mental-deficients on whom he has taken pity as no one else wished to employ them. Lilita's father is not one of them; in fact it is he who takes the responsibility for the bakery in Rosario, and another in Mar del Plata. Now he has invited his right-hand man and confidant and his family and friends to a Sunday outing.

The weather is not of the best. The air is rather chilly for the time of year, the sky covered with rain-laden clouds. It takes an inconceivably long time before we are ready to leave, running in and out with baskets, bottles, things, crying, laughing, questioning and explaining, as in Chekhov or a Fellini film. Juan looks at me and laughs. We stand on the street outside the bakery like idle spectators. Once again he has instinctively understood how I see it all – as theatre. 'This is Argentina,' he says. At last everything is ready. The children and the dogs make themselves comfortable in the back of the delivery van. Don

Pedro and his *patrona* and Lilita's parents go in the station-wagon. Also included is one of the oddities Don Pedro has taken on, a thin, dry, leathery little man, who is very ill today, complaining about pains all over his body. No one takes him seriously.

I join the young people, although as I am old enough to belong in the station-wagon. It is Lilita's father's birthday today. He is forty-eight. So we're contemporaries. Don Pedro himself is well over fifty.

There are six of us in the front seat. I am sitting squashed between Juan and Claudia. Lilita is sitting on Juan's lap. Then there is Monica, and her husband Daniel at the wheel. Pop music from the car-radio at top volume, so we have to yell to make ourselves heard. The conversation does not cease for one single moment. The noise is deafening, but I am used to it. Almost. They talk quickly and indistinctly, using words and expressions I don't know. I find it difficult to keep up. They also talk about things which have nothing to do with me, mutual friends, what has happened among their friends. Claudia tells us that one of her friends got her head caught between the heavy steel swing-doors at the Banco Nacional de Argentina the other day, and died within fifteen minutes. It is very tragic, but the atmosphere does not accept the tragedy.

VI

I break off here.

I can't possibly go on. Not like this.

The mission is fulfilled.

It has been completed.

We write today, Saturday, 23 December, 1978. Tomorrow is Christmas Eve. We shall celebrate it in the family circle, Lilita's family. Selinda arrived in Buenos Aires the day before yesterday, the twenty-first. Yesterday, Friday the twenty-second, Juan signed the contract to purchase a small apartment, a two-roomer in the La Boca district. The building is brand new. The apartment will be finished within thirty days.

Their present tenancy runs out on the first of February. So it fits exactly. Everything.

I have done my bit. I can return, I can disappear out of their lives. I can die if I want to.

It is a relief. It is a vacuum, too. And bitterness. For I have got used to it. Like Professor Higgins, 'I've grown accustomed to his face . . .' Although he was no Pygmalion in relation to me, would not want to be, was not allowed to be. But like it, very like it sometimes.

'And haven't I dragged you up out of the gutter . . .' Not like that, either. Only one human being and another human being. Two people, any two people. To think that it was possible. The impossible became possible. I made the impossible possible. Together we made the impossible possible.

The last few weeks have been a merry-go-round, Juan hunting for an apartment, on top of troubles over his sick mother, and I incapable of writing a line. Too late, I realized his anguish. In my self-absorption. Despite everything, the money was not going to be enough. It was too expensive and, despite everything, we had too little. The terrible inflation of Argentina.

We quarrelled. Days went by without us speaking to each other. He was shameless, I pathetically reproving, like the obviously stronger party in a marriage. Yet marriage is most of all exactly what we least wished our relationship to resemble.

We have our marriages. Friendship is not marriage.

Everything repeats itself with a consistency that is sometimes so obvious I feel like screaming. With astonishment. Or horror. Everything repeats itself with a logic, the innermost principle of which I still do not understand.

Juan's behaviour in Stockholm and Helsinki, his infantile protests against a way of life he neither could nor would adjust to. All this, almost as if sleepwalking and with my own form of infantilism, I have repeated here in Buenos Aires, over three months in Buenos Aires which have been like nothing I have ever experienced before in my whole life.

Yet my starting-points were quite different from his, my intentions. *He* couldn't adjust, of course not, for he had his roots in Buenos Aires, and he had never known anything else except Buenos Aires. While I, with my Finland-Swedish rootlessness, my education, my inborn curiosity, good heavens, I ought to have been able to. But I wasn't. For that was not meant.

Selinda's arrival, summoned almost in panic, just as Lilita was summoned to Stockholm in November last year. Yesterday, Sergio dropped in to meet Selinda. He had a Christmas present with him, a bottle of wine wrapped in fine Christmas paper. We sat chatting for a while about this and that. He said roughly the same things Juan would have said in a corresponding situation two years ago. That he not only liked me, for instance, but Selinda too, that he appreciated us both a great deal. He was very polite. Sergio is repeating Juan. I could repeat Juan with Sergio. But I don't, no, never.

Sergio is not Juan.

What I denied Juan in Stockholm and Helsinki, he has denied me here in Buenos Aires. He wanted to sleep with Selinda, but was Argentinian enough to ask my permission first. I forbade him to, referring to the unsuspected complications that it might lead to. I don't even dream of sleeping with Lilita, but there are other comparisons. And just as violently as he always and everywhere defended his right to social and human contacts apart from me, have I, over three months here in Buenos Aires and sometimes with the same bitterness as a result, defended my right to be alone.

When I met him two years ago, he was a child who had long before learnt the art of playing at being an adult. Now he is adult, with a violent longing to be a child at last. I stopped being a child when I was twelve. I have never got over it. We are two children meeting under the pretext of adult friendship. We're playing with each other. We're curious about each other like children, without inhibitions, like children. Then he takes my ball away from me and throws it in the sea and it floats away with the offshore wind. I hit him on the head with my tin soldier. But at night we still lie in the same bed and talk until dawn. Juan and I. The young and the old. Saul and David. The boy from the back alley and the fine gentleman.

I'm showing off. I'm flirting with a class-difference, a social inequality neither of us has ever taken much into consideration and which has usually never been of anything but secondary importance. There have been innumerable occasions when Juan, with a kind of triumphant but unaggressive delight, has cried '*burgués, burgués*' at me, the rare times, for instance, when I wore a tie, or when I knocked on the door before going into a room. In a similar way, there have been innumerable occasions when I have noted his lack of 'education', that he doesn't read newspapers, or read at all, really, that his handwriting is clumsy and he makes spelling mistakes in his letters which even I with my limited Spanish notice; and that at the beginning of our acquaintance, he was clearly faced with a dictionary for the first time in his life and didn't know how to use it. But on the level which we usually frequent, all that is unimportant.

A few days ago, over a cup of coffee in a bar down in the Underground, *subte*, during a conversation in which we were able to control our aggressiveness only with difficulty, when only with an effort Juan held back his – unjustified – jealousy in relation to Sergio, and only with an effort I held back my bitterness over his absence, his silence, his obvious desire to avoid me, during this conversation, with an equally obvious desire to catch me unawares and render me defenceless, he fired off a question about whether I really believed he didn't 'speculate in me' during our early time in Buenos Aires two years ago. I replied that I am convinced that he did, that I know he did, and even counted on him doing so, for anything else would have been inconceivable. He doesn't believe me, because he doesn't want to. This is to defend the only weapon he has at present. Against me.

We cannot communicate. We don't understand one another. I don't add that the one who really speculated was not him. But me.

For he speculated, with his Argentinian modesty, in small things, in shirts and imaginable possibilities in life on the level of chance. While I was already speculating in his person, speculating in his life. That is the difference between Argentina and Europe. Speculation in the small things, honour in larger issues on the side of the Creoles. While on the part of Europe, honour to inessentials, to conceal the studied speculation on the level of enormity.

'Whatever you do, they always cheat you in the end.' That is not so. On the contrary. Whatever they do, *we'll* always cheat them in the end.

An Argentinian can never cheat a European.

He thought he was clever. I was bloody cleverer.

Because he lives, as Argentinians live, for the day.

But I live, as speculating European Protestants live, for eternity.

His aim in life: to be happy.

My aim in life: to build a cathedral.

But when it comes to the point, it is not really like that, either. For neither of us really wants to cheat the other. On the contrary. 'Cheating' is nothing but a trump-card in a game which is really about something else, about the opposite: trusting each other, wanting to trust each other. On his part, being as trustworthy in the small things as he is naturally in the big things. And on my part, being as trustworthy in the big things as I am naturally in the small. He is not typical. Neither am I. That was where the basis of our friendship lay.

It would be a lie to maintain that I have always been as clear-sighted as I am now, or that I am as clear-sighted today as I will be in a year or five years' time. In moments of bitterness, he sometimes accuses me of being a great egoist. I protest then – 'sensitively' – and say it's absurd to call me an egoist, considering all I have done for him over the last two years. He has nothing to say to that, but persists all the same in saying I am an egoist. Of course he is right. There are moments when I've been so overwhelmed by my personal sense of happiness that I've neither seen nor wanted to admit that I've been alone in it.

Has he ever been happy with me at all? Yes, he probably has, but to be perfectly honest, it has never been the same total, absolute happiness as I have felt. Naturally not. I've never been quite so innocent that I would have expected or even asked for such total unanimity between us when it came to happiness. On the other hand, I have all too often been sufficiently innocent not to see, or to be able to see, that my happiness in him has on the contrary been indifference or, even worse, suffering, produced directly by my own need for happiness.

An outsider could maintain with good reason that, consciously and in cold blood, I have placed not only him, but four or five other people in a situation which has caused complications and unnecessary suffering for everyone involved except myself, and that I am invulnerable, because as a writer I can find a use for everything that happens, everything that arises, in the last count even my own mortal anguish.

Our friendship, 'our friendship', is it even real? Yes, it is real. It is real now, but in reality became real far later than I at first imagined, because I was so blinded by my feelings, so led astray by his uninhibited Latin way of being.

In actual fact, it is rather ironic to think that everything began with mutual misunderstanding. He saw in me a stupid tourist, who could be exploited. He thought I was stupid. I saw in him a young man, who, contrary to what I expected, spontaneously inspired trust. He thought I was stupid. Thus we created an 'as if' situation, as if it had been friendship. We acted the parts of friendship, naturally he more than I. In the end we acted them with such empathy, we could no longer sense where the border between acting and reality came. In the end, neither of us could resist the pressure of reality, the real feeling, the need for true friendship. We were two actors finally realizing we were playing a game with desires that could equally well be fulfilled in reality with honesty, as in the game with cunning.

But a long time had passed by then; he was in Stockholm, in Helsinki and in fact we found ourselves faced with a situation which brought with it added difficulties, added complications.

VII

Not a line written yesterday. I was once again prepared to give up. Selinda was intractable about everything, negative about everything. Buenos Aires was rotten, everything was rotten all round. I thought she was impossible and told her so, laying it on thick by saying that in my view all our twenty-four years of marriage had been nothing but a gigantic mistake. She agreed. It was a scorching hot day in Buenos Aires, thirty-five degrees. Furious and wounded, she went off on a four-hour-long walk on her own so that I should have peace and quiet to write in. That was what we had agreed on.

After she had gone, I felt very tired and could write nothing at all for four hours. I considered divorce. According to her, my self-absorption was monumental. I was utterly ruthless in relation to everyone around me, and for that reason destructive. She is right. It's true. I cannot deny it. I'm a swine, a blood-sucker, a monster. Yet I wish everyone so well.

'He wished everyone well.'

'When the child is given what it wants, it doesn't cry.'

'When I get what I want, I don't suffer.'

'When I get what I want, everyone else should also be content.'

'When I get what I want, everything is arranged for the best and anyone who maintains anything different can go to hell.'

So this is a drama. My drama, supremely mine. Not Selinda's drama, not even Juan's drama or Lilita's drama. But mine, staged by me, produced by me, directed by me. I am the demon producer and if the actors in anyway deviate from the scenario I have given them, attempting a personal interpretation, I am furious.

Selinda cannot tolerate it. Neither can Juan. In the long run, no one can tolerate it. So they are in agreement, forming a united front against me, all of them convinced of my egoism, my arrogant desire to dominate and rule over others.

I have become so tired of all this, because I wish everyone so well. That is when I consider leaving it all, leaving Selinda, leaving Juan, leaving Buenos Aires, the whole bloody lot, and going off to some other distant latitude to put an end, slowly, to my life, in my own way, without involving any of those whom in reality I love, those who I know, ultimately, love me. Sergio would come with me, I know. Some of the way, at least. And if he were sure I had enough money to be able to guarantee the good life for some time. But I have no money. Juan has devoured my money. Nevertheless, Sergio would come with me for a while. Out of curiosity. Because at the moment he has no better alternative, and finally also because of the peculiar Argentinian mixture of affection and calculation that is so seductive, so promising and so irresistible.

But it won't happen. I won't leave. Things happen all the time to make me think otherwise. Last night, when I got to Juan's and Lilita's apartment for dinner as usual, Selinda was already there. I was sour. She wasn't at all sour. She had already been venturing out in Buenos Aires, alone, and she wanted to talk about it. She told me, almost eagerly, and I listened, sourly at first, intractable, superior. Then I couldn't keep it up any longer. She had begun to adapt and that was what I wanted. The thought of divorce, the dream of divorce, dissolved as a cloud in summer sometimes mysteriously dissolves against the blue summer sky.

The family gathered. Lilita came back from work, gasping with exhaustion in the suffocating heat. Not a breath of air in the apartment. She had beads of sweat on her forehead and the bridge of her nose. I was soaked with sweat and did what Juan usually did, pulled off my shirt. Shortly after that Juan appeared, cheerful, talkative, filling the apartment with life.

The message of death came shortly afterwards, suddenly and unexpectedly, as that kind of message nearly always comes. His godfather, one of the real ones, one of the proper ones, no colleague of mine in other words, an uncle, had died of a heart attack that day, on the steps of his father's house in Chivilcoy. Juan made brave attempts to appear unmoved. Argentinian manliness does not like to allow emotionalism, even in the shadow of death. But he was moved, upset. It was 'Bombillo'. And now Bombillo was suddenly dead, gone.

'Why was he called Bombillo?'

'Well, he looked like an electric light bulb, small and fat. But always cheerful, always full of stories, always keen on food and wine.'

Bombillo had died at the age of seventy-two, Juan's father's brother and best friend, only a year younger. He was a widower and his brothers and cousins were all he had in life. But the family is large in Argentina, a cousin is like a brother, a brother like a father – there is no difference; one loves one's relatives as one loves oneself. When Juan spoke to his father on the telephone, his father had wept, almost.

We are standing talking in the kitchen. Suddenly he can't go on any longer. 'I can't talk about it. I'll start crying,' says Juan. He goes out on to the little kitchen balcony and stands there with his back to us, leaning on the balcony rail, staring out into the summer dusk settling of Buenos Aires' jumble of buildings, trying to control the tears, his back tense, inaccessible.

Can I say it? At that moment, I am jealous even of death, that something else apart from me, something else in general, ever takes up his attention and feelings.

Then I am a man again, adult, forcing myself to be so. I try to reach him with compassion. I touch his arm with my hand. He looks at me. We look into each other's eyes. He smiles. I smile back. We pretend it is nothing.

'I can't believe Bombillo is dead, I just can't believe it,' Juan keeps repeating. Late that night, at about half-past eleven, he sets off to Chivilcoy. He hitches. At that time of night there are no more buses or trains.

Today, Lilita, Selinda and I are going to Chivilcoy to celebrate the New Year in the house of mourning.

Juan has already said goodbye to us all and closed the front door behind him. In the lift, he remembers something and goes back. We hear the key in the lock as he opens the door again. He is standing in the doorway, saying gravely:

'The Christmas tree, it was the Christmas tree. I knew it. I said so.'

'No, Juan, it wasn't the Christmas tree, it couldn't be, I'm sure,' I try to convince him, with my dry Scandinavian realism. But he is not convinced.

On Christmas Eve, the Christmas tree had caught fire. A horrible event in itself, as none of those present had ever before been involved in a fire in a city apartment. But it was all right, and in fact was all over in a few minutes. Lilita wept a little in my arms, as the Christmas tree had long been a favourite treasure. Selinda and I found this rather difficult to understand. We didn't think it even looked like a Christmas tree, a strange object made of plastic, which to us looked more like a bunch of drooping green donkey's ears fastened to a stick. Anyhow we agreed that the object was beautiful, even regarded as a Christmas tree, when decorated with the usual arsenal of bright glass balls and God knows what else. Juan burnt his hands trying to put out the fire. I remember very clearly him saying, after it was all over, that it was a bad omen and one of us could now expect some bad news in the near future.

So Bombillo's death was presaged in this way. Juan knew it to be so. He is convinced of his telepathic resources.

Sometimes I almost think he is right in his convictions. Argentina is not Sweden. The spirits live in Argentina. I have felt their presence myself, so strongly, so clearly, that cold shivers have gone down my spine and the hairs on the back of my head have stood on end.

New Year in Chivilcoy. In his childhood home. On his childhood street, an ordinary street, a quiet side-street off an almost deserted main road, not even made up; brown earth, which in summer threw up huge clouds of dust and in winter was a sea of loose mud. The jacaranda trees offered little shade. An unpainted wooden fence separated Marcelo's yard from the street. The door was nearly always open. In the yard and along the low façade of the house were flowers, weeds, vegetables, a long-neglected garden. The gable of the house faced the street. The door from the yard was so low you had to bend down to step into the porch, which also served as a storeroom. The food was prepared there, the meat cut, the vegetables washed and sliced. The kitchen and toilet on the left, the kitchen bathed in perpetual green light, as a sheet of green plastic had replaced the piece of corrugated iron that had rusted away on the roof above the stove. The living-room on the right of the porch was almost entirely filled with the enormous dining-table, and beyond that, in constant half-light, the bedroom with its great double-bed, and the window facing the street shuttered day and night. In addition, a tiny cubby-hole where, in his old age, Marcelo usually slept nowadays, Juan's old room, the nursery.

A grape-vine grew up the house wall. The eaves of the roof were so near the ground you could grasp them if you stretched up your hand. Between the eaves and the fencing separating Marcelo's yard from his neighbour's was a trellis over which the vine spread out its thick network of branches, bunches of half-ripe grapes hanging from it. You could sit and chat and rest in the shade of the vine, in the midday heat, and late in the evening you could take out tables and chairs and have dinner by candlelight, crickets chattering and nocturnal insects swarming round the flames.

From the kitchen gable, Marcelo's yard extended a little further towards a back-yard world of neighbouring plots, derelict houses and overgrown vegetations. In a little yard-house, almost like a small tumbledown gingerbread house, lived Elena, Juan's aunt, his father's sister, now that she was a widow. The peach tree with ripe peaches on it, fig trees and lemon trees, grew so close here that they formed an almost impenetrable little wood. We picked sun-warmed peaches and let the juice dribble out of the corners of our mouths. On the far corner were the ruins of Marcelo's hen-house, where five hens still clucked round, scratching at the earth. Elena looked after them, mostly for something to do.

We arrived in Chivilcoy in the middle of the night, the last but one night of the year, Lilita, Selinda and I. Juan was already there, owing to this unexpected death. Mother Mercedes was waiting up for us, her leg in plaster up on a stool. We kissed her on both cheeks and on her mouth, and she held us and smiled her warm smile. A week before, Pancho had driven her back home from Buenos Aires in the borrowed bakery delivery van. She had lain stretched out on a mattress in the back, the heat growing more and more suffocating as the sun blazed down on the metal, like a huge precious loaf of bread left to rise in the Argentinian summer.

Marcelo put out food, bread and wine and cheese and sausage. We exchanged timid, simple, hesitant words, laughing in between, often. If felt almost like childhood, safe and expectant, like in childhood when you suddenly come to a new house with new people and feel welcome. That kind of warmth, human warmth. And fatigue. We slept on the floor in one of the small rooms in Elena's house, Selinda and I.

The following day, the main body of the family made their entrance. Brothers and sisters and cousins and their wives and husbands and children, and their wives and husbands and children in an endless stream of people, in the end utterly confusing. A stream of friendly people, smiling and talking and laughing, coming and going and then coming back again. Over the holiday we visited those who didn't come, for what is more important than meeting the family, exchanging a few words, breaking bread and drinking wine together? We were very tired at the end. So many people!

New Year dinner with the brothers diagonally across the street,

José and Ernesto, the latter also called El Niño, the child. They were both bakers, owning and running a small bakery supplying Chivilcoy with its bread. José was married to La Negra and had only one daughter, Graziela, now in her early twenties and engaged for the last five years to the slightly older and blasé man-of-the-world, Gustavo. José was in his sixties, Ernesto a few years older than me, between fifty and sixty, but as he was the youngest of the tribe of brothers he had to remain the child, *niño*, all his life. He was indeed unmarried.

Nothing was really real in this house, almost like visiting another century, yet it was quite real, just that Europe was so far away. The bakery's huge oven was fired with wood, giant logs which lay there glowing all night and had to be attended every two or three hours; the wooden table for the freshly baked bread, wooden loaf-spades heavy and long like lances from a medieval jousting tournament. Marcelo mocks his brothers, saying they are lazy, baking only three nights a week, when the money runs out. But José is not lazy. He is restlessly active and never sleeps, or sleeps for an hour now and again, mostly in the midday heat when the whole world is sleeping. El Niño is a passionate poker-player, and cannot resist the cards, a cause of some worry to his brothers. He gambles away everything he owns, once even José's new bread-van as well.

El Niño was an old bachelor and slightly odd. He was still good-looking and had certainly been very handsome in his youth. Nowadays his figure was slightly bowed and his face showed signs of melancholy, of worries, and imperceptible nuances of bitterness. He smoked a great deal. Twenty years ago, he had felt a twinge in his heart and had thought the end was near. He still thought so, every hour, every minute of the day. The fingers of his right hand moved constantly across his chest round his heart. This had gone on for twenty years. The result was that he had long had an inflamed furrow in his skin, about an inch or so wide, which year by year penetrated deeper and deeper between his ribs, in the place where his sick heart was. In summer, when it was hot, he massaged his skin directly, but in winter, when it was chilly, he let his shirt and jersey remain between. José maintained he had worn out several dozen shirts and jerseys in this way over the years. But no one teased him, or interfered with this unusually insistent expression of extreme hypochondria.

At home, we would have called it a neurosis and made El Niño go to a psychiatrist. Here it was just one of innumerable expressions of human behaviour, accepted without objection, because everyone was the same deep down inside, but looked different and behaved differently and had a right to do so. That was the difference. The European idea of human tolerance, so impossible to realize in practice, and the Argentinian practice of human variety, so natural and spontaneous, so humane and liberating.

New Year in Chivilcoy. We ate, then slept after dinner in order to be able to eat again. It was nearly high summer, windless, the heat oppressive. On New Year's Day, dinner again for over ten people, this time in Marcelo's house. He had prepared all the food himself. He loved cooking and sang as the food bubbled and hissed in the red-hot kitchen, and he stood there, stripped to the waist, singing an old tango by Gardel, his white hair on end, his black eyes sparkling with pleasure. Boiled pork. Marcelo searches in the pan for a delicious morsel and puts it on my plate. It is the scalp with parts of the brain, eye-sockets and the snout with teeth still in the upper jaw. Everyone looks at me and laughs. I realize it is to test me. I try to put a good face on it, abandon knife and fork, pick it up with both hands and start gnawing at the pork fat and brain. I don't know what it tastes like and have to make a great effort not to be sick. Approving comments. Marcelo nods with approval and smiles shrewdly. I have passed the test.

Much later, Juan tells me that his father has ruined himself to celebrate this New Year, spending almost two months' pension to make it a success. For Selinda and me? Because of the European trip? Because of the new apartment waiting for Lilita and Juan in La Boca? No, for the pleasure of it. For the great joy of it all.

We leave Chivilcoy. A few weeks later, we leave Argentina. When we say goodbye, Marcelo embraces me, kissing me lightly on the mouth. That is friendship. He could be my father. His eldest son is the same age as I am. But it is not that. His youngest son could be my son. Juan stands beside us, looking on as we say goodbye. A few days later he confided in me that a shiver had gone through him when he saw his physical father embrace me, a shiver down his spine, just as when the inexplicable beauty of music pours through one's consciousness. He felt very strongly, very clearly, he says, that at that moment Marcelo transferred his fatherhood to me. It was mystical. It was the untouchable mysterious bond of humanity uniting us all, its origins in what Juan meant to me and I to him, the shimmering overwhelming feeling surrounding us, where we would be together for ever, two human creatures or two human emotions, unexplained, transformed into

191

secret flowers as in a kaleidoscope, and because of that visible in what is invisible in God's purpose with human beings; I mean, God's purpose, if it exists, must be what we did, Juan and I, made human bonds, made bonds of friendship, across the oceans, developing and enhancing life on a foundation of love.

Buenos Aires in November 1979.

It is the sea and I am on the sea and the sea is calm. Like the old Cuban, I am in the boat and the boy is with me and I do not feel it as he does.

The sun.

Far below us are the sharks and we sense their movements as almost imperceptible nudges against the hull.

The boy dives. Again and again, he dives and stirs up flames in the roadway of the sun, his body glittering with drops of water. I look at his body and feel the wheel of the world slowly turning through us both. It is ageing, and he is where he is and I am where I am, and there is an infinite distance between us, yet I can stretch out my hand and touch his hand as it grasps the rail.

He is in the water. I am in the boat. He smiles. I am the old Cuban and the boy is not the fish. The boat drifts on the current. We are no longer fishing. The horizon is like a mouth smiling. The lips of the sea. And of the sky.

No land in sight as far as the eye can see. We have come into harbour, for the sea is the harbour and the safest thing in the world, for there is nothing but the sea. In the mild night, the moon and the roadway of the moon carrying our dreams away, leaving behind what is real and what burns.

I am the old Cuban and I knew it already in Iguazú, but the waterfall and the Devil's Throat are not the sea. There the water is like blood in the veins of mankind as it boils with rage or anguish. The sea is calm. The sea is the harbour.

Death is in the waterfall, but it is far away. The sharks deep down below the hull are not concerned with us. So long as we don't fish. We have stopped fishing. We drift on the current.

The boy heaves himself up into the boat. Supple as a puma. He laughs. It is because he is alive. He sits naked beside me and says he is hungry. I go to the galley and get bread, cheese and wine.

In the evening he will leave me, as he does every evening, taking the route across the roadway of the moon and disappearing into the light that shimmers like silver. And I will think, as I think every evening, that it is dreams that destroy life. I will lie down alone in the cabin and feel the bitter grief that ageing nourishes.

In the morning he will return, as he does every morning, so that I shall at last see it is not dreams that destroy life, but life that takes to itself even the most wonderful, even the cruellest dream and transforms it into reality. Without asking. Without responding.

While we were still fishing.

While we were still fishing, we fell out, because the boy's fish were not where mine were. He thought he knew, but I was the one who knew, in the strength of my age and experience. He was envious of my equipment. I was so dependent on his strength and dexterity that the very thought that he might leave made me whimper with anxiety. Because of that, he wanted to leave. We fished in silence. I hated his youth because I loved it. He hated my dependency because he shared it.

The boy was the fish. At times, the fish was me. Fishing is the profession of the fisherman, but in a different sense it is a bad occupation. Fishing for people. The sea is freedom. Fishing is robbing someone of freedom. Wriggling in the net, or with a hook in its throat and its throat torn and bleeding from the barbs of the hook, the pain throbbing. The soundless scream when fish scream with pain. Tying the fish to the rail and slowly approaching land, only to see it hour by hour devoured by the greedy sharks. The boy was not waiting on the shore. He was with me. He was the fish. At times, the fish was me. We no longer fish.

Let the fisherman fish.

We made our way upriver and came to the waterfall and we anchored in the whirlpool near to Garganta del Diablo. We had reached Iguazú. The sun.

The heat numbing and the roar of the waterfall unceasing but drowning both anguish of heart and calculations of brain with its merciless roaring. Inland, the jungle with its fat lizards, like small alligators lying in wait for their prey. The silent pumas. Swallows darting across the hurtling waters and vanishing into the foam. The mouth of death, sucking and sucking at all living things.

He leaves me there. He was so cruel. How could he be so cruel, his gentle face turned to stone, leaving me with a shrug, because I was fishing, because he was the fish, and I, the irresistible desire to steer the boat towards the devil's mouth, straight into the swirling waters, the speaking, calling, roaring waters, at last solving the mystery of life and death, the water hurtling down and the foam, like words of death, calling and calling to me, a curtain of whirlpools, behind it the dwelling-house of death and a resting-place for the despairing, and I, so as not to despair, so as still not to despair, seeking in the rivulets of life, now but a tiny trickling rivulet, his hand, and then it occurs to me, clutching at a straw, that I am the old Cuban and he is the boy, that my only home is writing and that I ought to write about it for that reason, a book on destruction, in order to save myself once again from destruction.

He returned. His hand on the rail. It was the boy.

While we were still fishing.

Millions of butterflies in clusters like scavengers and fat lizards and death's curtain of crying water. Foaming. Not like the sea, calm. Like the blood in the veins of the despairing, bound by its fall, bound by its own invincible movement.

The waterfall at Iguazú.

It was to be on destruction and that the boy was my destruction, and that I left everything for his sake, my family, my work, everything. My whole past. And that we floated round on a sea which no longer bore us, and anchored in harbours which no longer wished to know us, on islands which seemed to turn their backs on us in mute hostility. Impregnable islands in a blue sea which hated us. And that I slowly sank into another sea, a sea of alcohol, shattering body and mind, guarding the boy with corrosive craving, avarice, watching his looks, his lips, every movement he made, to find a sign. Forced by this tremendous feeling, rent by this tremendous feeling. And that he could not endure it, for why should he be able to endure it, so left, but returned, and I was already irretrievably in the grasp of death.

Write about destruction to save yourself from destruction.

But I wasn't the old Cuban, I was the old European.

The boy was the boy. He was Juan. A year went by and we were on the sea and the sea was calm and the sea was the harbour.

We no longer fish.

It is freedom.

There is nothing else but the sea.

In the middle of Argentina. The town is called Chivilcoy. We were here a year ago, at New Year, Selinda and I, and now I have come back. It is Europe and it is Argentina and east is east and west is west and that's how it is.

The end is not in Iguazú, because it could not end there. The end is not here, either. There is no end. We are a beginning of something without end and if it ever is ended, it will be others who do it, by what means we do not know.

We went through the eye of the needle. Now we are at sea and the sea is the harbour.

It is afternoon. I woke at dawn as the cock crowed, then the chorus of small birds and the dim light slowly filled the room, giving the meagre furniture contours. I was surrounded by Juan, his family, his parents sleeping on one side, Lilita and himself on the other. I was alone, but didn't mind, for I was at sea and the sea was the harbour. They had taken me to them and I had taken them to me, all of them, and it was not like overcoming oneself, it was like fulfilling a thought that was once born as a spark from the fire of love.

The wind in the fig tree.

Marcelo's yard. He is an old man and tells me that he has signed a contract with death that says he may live until he is a hundred. But the years already weigh heavily. The wheel of the world creaks.

Mealtimes. Mercedes limping between the stove and the table. This simple chipped world of security, to which Juan constantly and always returns, from a universe of insanity where something is constantly collapsing. A molecule of security. Bread and wine.

The starry sky in the mild night, with neither questions nor answers.

Argentina is a shimmer of the sun which at times blinded me completely. I am Europe and Europe is the owner, but I do not own. Not Juan. Not the earth I tread on. I own nothing.

We have relinquished nothing except ownership. Thus the sea. Thus freedom. Thus this indescribable happiness, constantly pierced with burning shivers of despair.

My eyes that were dazzled have become seeing.

Wholly submerged in the fluid that is love.

Wholly filled with that fluid which is love.

Like existing in the element of love, as in fire or the depths, as in alien elements, and yet being able to breathe, live.

In the element of love.

With both feet on the ground.

The first time I went to Argentina, I was looking for the past and found Juan.

The second time I went to Argentina, I returned to Juan and came to Iguazú and Argentina was reduced so that it corresponded entirely to the figure of Juan. The black youth representing a whole continent. And I. Dazzled by the shimmer of the sun. Dazzled by my own origin. Dazzled by Juan.

The third time in Argentina and my eyes are once again seeing, my perspective widened, the continent regaining its true extent. Juan no longer covers it all, but it is oozing out through his limbs, leaving his body, so that now it is he who is reduced, transformed from myth and continent to a human being, becoming a part of the whole, so that I see him as part of the whole, and my despair, the burning shudders of despair are not because of this, for we are completely immersed in the element of love, but because of what my seeing eyes see, the pain, the wretchedness of stunted human conditions, and the terrible sacrifices people have to make simply to survive.

In the morning, in the dim light of the room, on the stone floor, under a roof of corrugated iron, so close that I can touch it if I stretch up my hand, while the others are still asleep, in the morning, as Mercedes hands me the hot bowl of maté, her dark wrinkled hand and the silent smile on her old Indian face, as I take the spout between my lips and the scalding drink runs down my throat, oxygenating my blood, penetrating my brain, life-giving, in the morning this swiftly departing moment of confidence, her hand on my hand and the hot bowl of maté, as she hands me the hot bowl of maté, the sensation of wonder, all this preserved, kept together and real, and that I am here on their conditions, but am not one of them.

The food, the rhythm of life, feeling of life.

And never to be alone.

I am not one of them.

What is devouring them is fire; what is devouring me is ice. That was why I came, in the end that is why I came here, to be part of the fire.

It is the fire, now it is the fire that is devouring me and it is pain.

For I am not one of them.

In the endless nights of poker games with the old master, now angry, sometimes *distrait,* his cunning preserved, superior. The poker game with life as the stake, because lesser stakes do not exist in this world of fire and poverty. I tremble with fatigue, empty, he gambling my very life away, unmoved, chuckling with satisfaction.

The joy of poverty. The memories of food. People coming and going. Fragments of conversation. In the middle of the flood of words, hands fumbling in the language, as if in water, to grasp it, grasp fragments of it, holding up the fragments before you, like mirrors, to see more clearly what devours man and what preserves his life.

Language flowing past like the waters of the river.

I dreamt that an eagle came down in my yard and I took the eagle and broke off its wings, and I hated myself for breaking its wings and I told my dream to my son, the second one, the real one, and he asked if he were the eagle and I said I didn't know, because I felt guilty and kept saying that I didn't really want to, had never wanted to, never, for the only thing I really wanted was to see the eagle fly.

Juan. The wings as Achilles tendons. To keep him.

That evil dream. That evil temptation.

It is not calm, now it is no longer calm. The waves. It is windy. It is the *passada*. Is it the *passada*? It is the *passada*.

The eagles fly away. It is my pain, sealed, forbidden. At the same time happiness, the unspeakable, for the eagle that flies returns, but the eagle with broken wings is lost.

The only thing I really want is to see eagles fly.

Pouring rain in the siesta hours, rattling against the corrugated iron roof. Marcelo snoring, so close I can stretch out my hand and feel his ageing body, slack in sleep. Mercedes at his side. On the other side, Juan and Lilita. I am alone. I mind. I want to go out into the rain and let it dissolve me, press me down into the earth where all the wealth of nature lies in inexhaustible quantities and man is transformed to nothing.

We are in the boat in the pouring rain and it is not calm and does not feel like a harbour.

The earth that reeks of fertility and the same earth when it reeks of blood. The sun and the rain and the earth constantly boiling, for it is all in the element of fire and I alone transferred from frozen water. But seeing, seeing at last. Cruelty charged beneath the soft surface of warmth, violence charged beneath the tense surface of patience. The earth when it reeks of blood. Poverty, and when the membrane of patience bursts, again and again, century after century. Because of human insanity. Finally seeing and with a branch of despair pressing against my eyeballs.

The wheel of the world, which in its indifference slowly turns on its axle, invisible to my seeing eye. The sand in the hour-glass.

His moment on earth.

My moment on earth.

He is a tree growing inside me. He is everything that signifies something else. The fish, the eagle, the tree.

We are no longer fishing. The fish does not worry me. I do not want it. I do not want to catch it. No fish, ever again, nor the boy, nor the huge formation of scales which in the myth are tied to the rail by the old master. It doesn't matter.

And the eagle that flies away.

For he is a tree growing inside me, its branches slowly penetrating into my brain.

Split like the skin when the fruit ripens, emerging from my eyes, ears, slowly turning me completely into a tree. Into a tree that is him.

Split like the mountain when the tree becomes a tree in its crevice.

I gave him a handful of earth to strike root in, and I forgot myself and left the earth on my own soil. He struck root and he is a tree and growing inside me.

I split. Now I am splitting, absorbed in the tree that is him, disappearing, continuing to exist in him, the tree. For he is the son. And I am the father.

Fastening on to his youth, like splitting bark, my own roots torn up, sprawling in all directions, no . . .

We are on the sea. He is the boy and I am the old man; without the boy I am worthless.

I gave him a handful of earth and he struck root.

We are on the sea and the sea is the sea and the sea is the harbour.

The sea is the harbour.

Buenos Aires – Helsinki – Stockholm – Buenos Aires, 1976–79.